**Publishing history**

First Edition January 2014
Email: petelevene@hotmail.co.uk

ISBN 978-1-291-73341-9

Cover designed by Simon Levene,
Astorias, Oregon, USA

Best wishes to
Andrew + Jude
2 fellow nutters!
Pete

# FOREWORD

This book is dedicated to my long-suffering wife Susan. She has been forced to spend almost 50 years listening to snatches of Chuck Berry, Johnny Cash, Jerry Lee and nearly all the other Rock 'n' Roll artists in my vast collection.
This wouldn't be so bad, but she doesn't like Rock 'n' Roll much! She is a fan of the Musicals of Andrew Lloyd-Webber or the Operettas of Gilbert and Sullivan.

The book does not pretend to include every Rock 'n' Roller, that would be nigh on impossible. I just wanted to give the reader a pen-picture of the artists I thought had most impression on me during the 50s and 60s', and would give a brief outline of their careers without having to purchase a large number biographies or autobiographies.

I would like to thank Paul James, a volunteer like myself at Pure Fm Stockport, for his programme 'Rock 'n' Roll legends' which stimulates me and

encourages me to listen to some of my least played records.
My favourites? Chuck Berry, Jerry Lee Lewis, 'Fats' Domino', Buddy Holly and the Crickets, Charlie Rich, Johnny Cash and Don Gibson. The best label? Sun Records, by a long way. I would also like to thank Lisa Warburton and Derek Morgan from Isis Stockport for their help in publishing this book.

It will be noticed that there are no British artists included; this is because when my interest in Rock 'n' Roll music began there were no British artists that I would listen to.

## ABOUT THE AUTHOR

**Peter Lawrence Levene was born in Edgeley, Stockport on the 18$^{th}$ June 1941 to Norah and Leslie. Leslie was a Bespoke tailor with his own business on (at that time) King Street, virtually under the town's famous viaduct. (He later moved to various premises, the most prestigious (perhaps not quite the right word) was to a shop in the Market Place. I am married to Susan, and have two sons, Simon, who resides in Denver, Colorado, and Stuart who lives in Grange Park, North London.**

**I worked my way through two Junior Schools, (Adswood and Banks Lane, Offerton) and then attended Dialstone Lane Secondary Modern School. It was here that music came into my life. A great friend of mine, David Wild and myself were appointed disk-jockeys at the Friday night Youth Club. We were given some money to buy records (initially 78 rpm records and later 7" 45 rpm discs from White and Swales record shop in Underbank, Stockport.**

**I remember that among the first records we bought were Chuck Berry's 'Schoolday', Jerry Lee Lewis's 'Whole Lotta Shakin', Fats Domino's 'Blueberry Hill' and a few others.**

**I have always collected records/CDs, and have a collection of over 1000.**
**In 1985 I decided I would try to collect every record an artist had released. The choice of artist was very difficult – Jerry Lee Lewis was too large – it was unlikely that the target would be attained. Chuck Berry was more realistic, but in the end I settled on Waylon Jennings.**
**I think I am nearly there, but one can never be certain. Do you class two records with the same content, but in different sleeves as different records? I currently have 218 Waylon Jennings albums/CDs/DVDs/ Videos/Books.**

**I have a two-hour radio show 'Play Something Country' on Stockport's Pure 107.8Fm Community radio station.**

# A BRIEF HISTORY OF ROCK 'N' ROLL

by Pete Levene

***'Rock and Roll' (Rock 'n' Roll).***
A style of popular dance music originating in the 1950s with a strong beat and elements of the blues' - The Oxford Dictionary

When did Rock 'n' Roll start? Who invented it? Who were the first Rock 'n' Roll singers and who were the first record companies?

All the above questions are virtually impossible to answer. Music historians with a far greater knowledge than I, cannot agree. They can only arrive at answers that some agree with, and others disagree. Even talking to some of the old singers and musicians doesn't bring concrete answers as most of them that are still alive are in their 80s and have forgotten what happened in the 'old days'. For example, when Chuck Berry was asked, 'Who was the pianist on 'Wee Wee Hours'. Was it Otis Spahn or Johnny Johnson? Berry could not remember who was in the studio that day. Nor could Chess Records answer the question as their studio records had long since been lost.

There has always been Rock 'n' Roll, but that wasn't the name the music at the time was given, and it wasn't played with the same instruments that were used after the 50s. It was called 'The Blues'. Played mainly by workers on the cotton plantations of the Deep South. At that time most of the music was made purely by the voice – singing. Most were too poor to own an instrument, and if someone did, it was usually a battered old acoustic guitar, banjo or an harmonica or 'harp' as the instrument was known in that part of the world.

As in all walks of life this music didn't stand still. It moved on and it moved because its exponents got better at it. Their instruments improved. A fiddle

(violin) would appear, then maybe a sparse drum kit was included.
People formed groups or choirs, singing mainly gospel songs. Their technique improved and people composed songs especially for this type of music. Stephen Foster and W.C. Handy were famous for their songs. Famous, yes, but rich from it, no. Despite writing dozens of very popular songs Foster died a pauper from pneumonia and alcohol in 1864.
A link between the country and the city was formed by the black vaudeville entertainers who played in minstrel shows and on riverboats. W.C. Handy was possibly the top artist in this field. He eventually became one of the States' top music publishers and record producers.
New Orleans and Memphis were a hotbed of this music which in the early 1900s became known as jazz. Jazz bands played day and night.

Sheet music was the big money spinner. Song pluggers would slip a pianist a piece of sheet music with a few 'bits' (cents) to play and /or sing the piece.

In homes around the U.S. the music was taking on. The man in the street wanted to play as well as listen. A mail order company called Sears & Roebuck sold instruments to the public. Guitars, violins and banjos could be bought from anything from $2.50 to $25.00: a piano was $98.00.

In 1946 a young guy named Riley B King (later to become B.B.King) drifted into Memphis. In attempting to play Blues like his cousin 'Booker' White and failing to master the 'bottleneck' style of playing, King developed his own style by using his powerful fingers to bend the strings to produce so far unheard of notes, and not too far from his original intention.
McKinley Morganfield, a fine guitar picker, traveled up to Chicago from Mississippi to try his luck, but the Blues was losing popularity by now and Morganfield struggled. Someone suggested he change his name, which was too much of a mouthful. McKinley Morganfield became 'Muddy' Waters and the bookings just kept coming in.

By 1947 the sales of records (12" 78rpm shellac discs) were picking up. Radio airplay was promoting artists like a young Alabaman called Hank Williams. Western Swing as played by Bob Wills and his Texas Playboys was extremely popular. A guitar player called Chester 'Chet' Atkins had a hit with 'Guitar Blues'. Other bands and artists like Wynonie Harris and The Blue Sky Boys became very popular. Eddy Arnold was big as were ladies like The Andrew Sisters and Dinah Shore.

The large labels like Decca, RCA and Columbia were intent on producing records by single vocalists with lush string backings. They lumbered on. Most of their output sold well enough, it was nice music, but there was little excitement in the music. The small independent labels that were springing up knew where the action was, and boy did they find it.

A guy called Samuel Cornelius Phillips from Florence, Alabama was a musician and radio engineer who wanted to better himself, so he moved to Memphis,

Tennessee. He took a job as an announcer at radio station WREC. In January 1950 he opened the Memphis Recording Service at 706 Union Avenue using the bye-line 'We Record Anything, Anywhere, Anytime'. Most of the recordings were of weddings, bar mitzvahs, civic meetings or spoken programmes for radio stations.

In 1952 Phillips started to record amateur musicians like Riley (B.B.) King, Howlin' Wolf and Junior Parker. He knew the records were good and could sell but he didn't have the wherewithal to complete the job. No disc pressing plant, no admin people. Phillips hit on a way of getting the records to the public. He would sell them to the bigger independent labels that did have the necessary backing like Leonard and Phil Chess in Chicago. The records were then released on the Chess (or subsidiary Checker) labels. Chess Records was formed in 1950. It was termed "The Greatest Blues Label" and probably was. Its first release was a 78 rpm record called "My Foolish Heart" by Gene Ammons. The Chess's struck up a relationship with Sam Phillips and in 1951 released the Sun

recorded "Rocket 88" by Jackie Brenston. The record that became called 'The first ever Rock 'n' Roll Record'.
Chess had had many records in the charts, particularly great songs by Charles Anderson Berryn, better known as Chuck Berry. Songs like 'Maybelline' 'Sweet Little Sixteen', 'Rock 'n' Roll Music', 'Roll Over Beethoven' and 'Johnny B Goode'. Berry couldn't miss, but Chess had to wait many years for its first record to top the 'Billboard Hot 100', it was a Chuck Berry song recorded live in Coventry England called 'My Ding-A-Ling'. Chess also had a few hits by a guy called Elias McDaniel – he changed that name to Bo Diddley.

Whilst Chess was scoring big in Chicago, Sam Phillips in Memphis opened out his recording service with some financial aid from a man called Jim Bulliet. He decided to release his own records rather than sell his recordings on. He chose the name 'Sun Records'. That name possibly became the greatest name in Rock 'n' Roll recording history. Phillips's Sun Studio

was what was termed an 'Open' studio. He would record black or white artists.
His first release was by Johnny London called 'Drivin' Slow/Flat Tire. in April 1952. (There was an earlier record by 'Little Walter' called 'Blues In My Condition' but negative reactions caused Phillips not to release the record.) Records by Walter Bradford, Gay Garth, Rufus Thomas and Big Memphis Rainey followed. The Prisonaires were a group that had been formed by inmates at Tennessee State Penitentiary. They were really great, but Phillips had to take his equipment to the prison to record them for obvious reasons. Their record 'Just Walking in the Rain' hit the charts in July '53.

As well as recording bar mitzvahs and all the other stuff, Phillips also recorded the man in the street, who could, for four dollars could record two songs. A young truck driver who hailed from Tupelo, Mississippi, but worked in Memphis, stopped by one day to record a song for his mother's birthday present. Phillips was not there that day, so his office manager, a lady called Marion Keisker, did the recording and kept a copy. Some months later Phillips needed a singer for a song called 'Without You'. Keisker badgered Phillips into sending for the young truck driver who worked close by at an Electrical plant. His name was Elvis Presley. He came over and recorded the song. It was terrible, so Phillips asked Presley what else he could do. He returned later with two workmates, Scotty Moore, a guitarist and Bill Black who played slap bass. Whilst waiting for Phillips to set the studio up they warmed up by singing an Arthur 'Big Boy' Crudup song called 'That's All Right Mama'. Elvis made five singles for Sun Records, each was a rocker coupled with a Country song on the 'b' side. All made the charts. Phillips was forced to sell Presley's contract for $35,000 to RCA Victor Records. People said that Phillips was crazy to sell his top-selling artist, but it was either that or go under.

Anyway, by this time Presley wasn't the only artist selling large amounts of records for Sun. Carl Perkins had good sellers with 'Movie Mag', 'Matchbox' and a song called 'Blue Suede Shoes' which did extremely well but was denied the No.1 slot by the Elvis Presley version. A recently de-mobbed airman called in at Sun with his two friends, a guitar picker called Luther Perkins (no relation to Carl), and a bass player named Marshall Grant. His name? J.R.Cash (known as Johnny although he was never christened that name). Sun had numerous hits with Johnny Cash and the Tennessee Two (later to become Tennessee Three with the addition of W.S.'Flook' Holland on drums). The first in June '55 was 'Cry! Cry! Cry! Eighteen more were to follow before Cash 'defected' to Columbia Records.

A young man traveled over from Wink, Texas for an audition, made several records that didn't do too well and was told by Phillips to 'try elsewhere son, you'll get nowhere singing like that'. The voice in question belonged to Roy Orbison, and the statement by Phillips was perhaps one of his few mistakes.

Most of the artists that came to Sun were guitarists, but one day a young blonde-haired pianist from Ferriday, Louisiana called in for a chance to demonstrate his talent to Mr Phillips. He sat down at the tired old studio piano and proceeded to knock old Sam cork-legged. The dollar signs were flashing before Sam's eyes. He envisaged (and received) millions of record sales from the 21 year old who called himself 'The Ferriday Fireball' – real name Jerry Lee Lewis. Lewis did indeed sell millions of records in a short time. He was a failed trainee minister, expelled from the Waxahachie Bible institute in Texas for 'playing the hymns with a boogie-woogie beat'.

He was soon headlining package tours with Chuck Berry, The Everlys and 'Fats' Domino, but a tour to London proved disastrous for Lewis when it was leaked to the Press that he had married his 13 year old cousin Myra, and it was fairly certain that he wasn't divorced from his first wife. The tour was soon abandoned and for two years Lewis was back to playing Honky-tonks in saloons in Natchez. Eventually

Lewis resurrected his career to become probably the greatest country singer ever.

## The Labels

Chicago and Memphis weren't the only places where Rock 'n' Roll was big, and getting bigger. Chess and Sun were not the only recording companies finding talent and selling it to the man in the street.
The larger companies were Dot, Specialty, Imperial, Cadence, Atlantic and Top Rank, but there were thousands of smaller recording studios dotted about all over the states. The size of the company certainly didn't dictate whether you produced a hit record or not. Many tiny companies had No.1 hit records although they may not have had a second hit during their existence.

Some of the biggest hits came from ***Imperial Records*** based in Hollywood. Formed in 1947 it focused mainly on R&B, Country and Mexican music. Their big hitters were Antoine 'Fats' Domino, Ricky (Rick) Nelson, Frankie Ford and Slim Whitman.

***Specialty Records*** was based in Los Angeles. It was noted for R&B, blues and gospel. They started out in 1946 and had huge sellers from Little Richard (Penniman), Larry Williams, Sam Cooke and John Lee Hooker.

***Atlantic Records*** had it's studios in Manhattan and was founded in 1944 by two Turkish brothers Neshui and Ehmet Ertegun. Specializing in R&B and jazz. They had a distribution deal with Stax records that greatly enhanced their sales potential. Big names to record at Atlantic include Big Joe Turner, Sonny Terry and Brownie McGee, Sara Vaughan and Django Reinhardt on the jazz front, whilst Clyde McPhatter, Ray Charles, The Coasters, The Drifters and Bobby Darin were top sellers of R&B and R 'n' R.

***Cadence Records*** were situated in New York City, founded by Archie Bleyer. Their big hitters were Andy Williams, The Everly Brothers, Johnny Tillotson and a close harmony group called The Chordettes

***Dot Records*** moved from Tennessee to Hollywood in 1956. Pat Boone was their big name. He topped the charts several times with a variety of songs from ballads to Rock 'n' Roll covers.

***Coral Records*** was a subsidiary of Decca. They started life in 1949 issuing a variety of records including jazz, swing, pop and r 'n' r. Its notable artists were the McGuire Sisters, Teresa Brewer, The Johnny Burnette Trio and Buddy Holly and the Crickets. Holly's recordings were done by NorvaJak in Clovis, New Mexico but distributed by Coral.

***Liberty Records'*** early releases focused on film and orchestral music. Its first big vocal hit was 'Cry Me A River' by Julie London. Other top sellers were Eddie Cochran, Billy Ward and his Dominoes, Del Shannon and Bobby Vee. A man called Ross Bagdasarian sold millions of records on the Liberty label, but he is better known as The Chipmunks!

There were also hundreds of other small labels, some of which distributed their own products and others which passcd their records on to companies with bigger facilities whilst an agreement would keep their label on the record. The list is endless but some of the more successful smaller labels were, **Jamie** (Pennsylvania), **Big Top** (New York), **Anna** (Detroit), **A&M** (Phoenix) and **Amy** (also New York).

## The Instruments

The majority of the early records were by solo artists as very few had money to pay backing musicians, they usually accompanied themselves on an acoustic guitar or 'harp' (harmonica).
A man called ***Leo Fender*** had a radio and amplifier repair shop in California, he also tinkered around with guitars, designing and making pick-ups to amplify the sound. In 1951 he came up with the first solid-bodied electric guitar which he called the 'Esquire' or 'Broadcaster. After some modifications it was renamed the 'Telecaster'. A couple of years later he designed a guitar with three pickups which he called the 'Stratocaster'. Both became iconic instruments and it was a rare band that didn't use one or the other. The **Les Paul** models, **Gretsch, Guild, Washburn** and **Ernie Ball 'Minuteman'** were also very popular guitars.

Some of the bigger bands that backed singers like Little Richard, 'Fats' Domino and Larry Williams employed a couple of saxophone players to produce a 'fuller' 'rounder' sound.

The 'slap' bass or give it its real name double bass as used by Bill Black (Elvis Presley) and Joe B Mauldin (The Crickets) was difficult to transport because of its sheer size. It was a blessing to bands when it was superseded by the electric solid bass. Again Fender was the instrument to possess.

The most popular line-up for 4-piece bands was vocalist/ rhythm guitar, lead guitar, bass and drums. J. I. Alison, drummer with Buddy Holly and The Crickets is renowned for substituting his drums for a cardboard box or slapping his thighs to produce unusual sounds.

# THE BIG HITTERS

## Index

## The Artists

Rock 'n' Roll artists came from all walks of life. Originally the majority were the black blues singers. Most were self-taught musicians or received basic tuition from fathers or friends, very few received proper music lessons. One of the few examples of professional training was Neil Sedaka who was a very competent classical pianist.

It would require a very large tome indeed to list all the Rock 'n' Rollers, even just from the ten years from 1955 to 1965. With this in mind I shall write pen pictures of only the more famous or popular artists, ninety-five per cent of which are included in my collection of vinyl records and CD's.

## Chuck BERRY

Charles Edward Anderson Berry (real name Berryn) (born 18/9/26 in St. Louis Missouri) is a figure of immense influence and one of the pioneers of Rock ‘n’ Roll music.

He is a fine guitarist and possibly the best lyric writer in the genre ever.

He was one of the first musicians to be inducted into the Rock ‘n’ Roll Hall of Fame.

In 1955 Berry went to Chicago to see Leonard Chess of Chess Records. He made a demo called ‘Ida Red’ which he

renamed *'Maybellene'* using Johnny Johnson (piano), Jasper Thomas (drums), Jerome Green ( from Bo Diddley's band) on maracas and blues legend Willie Dixon on the bass. *' Maybellene'* was a pop hit and also reached No.1 on the R & B charts. Many other hits followed. *'Roll Over Beethoven', Johnny B Goode, 'Sweet Little Sixteen', 'Rock and Roll Music', 'The Promised Land'* and many, many others.
Whilst Berry scored a string of hits, he couldn't avoid scandal. In December 1959 he was found guilty of enticing a minor (a 14 year old Apache girl) across the State line and was arrested under the Mann Act. He was fined $5000 and sentenced to 5 years in Lompoc County Prison. After his release in 1964 he continued to score hits with *'No Particular Place To Go', 'You Never Can Tell', 'Nadine' and 'My Ding-a-Ling'.*

Chuck Berry has never been the easiest person to deal with. When on tour he insists on his money up front ("No cash, no show"). There are no rehearsals. A local band is hired and given Berry's records to learn. He never takes his musicians, Johnson, Spahn or Thomas with him.

A live version of *'My Ding-a-Ling'* was his only ever No.1 hit.

At 85 years of age he continues to perform both in the USA and Europe.

## Pat BOONE

Charles Eugene 'Pat' Boone was born in Jacksonville , Florida on June 1st 1934. He was not a rock 'n' roller in the moulds of Berry, Lewis, Domino and Perkins, but more of a crooner who would make cover versions of the others hits and have just as big hits with them. He sold over 48 million albums and had 38 Top 40 hits. He also appeared in 12 Hollywood films. The only artist to sell more records in the late 50s was Elvis Presley. He was played

by radio stations where black artists would not be played.
Boone has a deep religious faith, and has recorded many top selling Gospel albums. He has been inducted into the Gospel Music Hall of Fame. He is also involved in politics having campaigned for Ronald Reagan.  He supported the Viet Nam War, writing numerous newspaper and magazine articles on the subject.

Pat Boone's biggest hits

*'Aint That A Shame' (1): 'I'll Be Home' (4); 'I Almost Lost My Mind' (1); 'Don't Forbid Me' (1);  'Love Letters In the Sand' (1); 'April Love' (1) 'A Wonderful Time Up There' (4) 'Moody River' (1); 'Speedy Gonzalez' (6).*

**Johnny BURNETTE**
**(and the Rock 'n'Roll Trio)**

John Joseph Burnette was born on March 25th 1934 In Memphis, Tennessee.
He was a very keen sportsman being a linebacker in the school football team, and later (along with his brother Dorsey) became a Golden Gloves boxing champion. His early life was spent working on the Mississippi river barges as a deckhand.
He learned to play acoustic guitar, and with Dorsey on Bass, and friend Paul Burlison (lead guitar) they formed the 'Rock and Roll Trio'.

They won a talent contest (three times in a row). The prize was a contract with Coral Records, but the three records released failed to make the charts, although 'Train Kept 'a Rollin' became a much sought after collectors item.

In 1959 Johnny went solo and got a contract with Freedom Records. They released three singles which sold well but didn't quite make the charts. Freedom folded and in 1960 he was moved over to Freedom's parent company Liberty Records. He recorded a song called 'Dreamin' which rose to No.11 on the Hot 100 charts and followed that with 'Your Sixteen' which did slightly better going to No.8. 'Little Boy Sad' made No. 17.

In early 1961 he was hospitalized with a ruptured appendix and was unable to promote his next single which just failed to make the Hot 100.

He did, however, manage to make successful tours of Australia and the United Kingdom.

On August 14th 1964 his fishing boat was struck by a by a cabin cruiser on Clear Lake, California. Burnette was knocked overboard and drowned.

Johnny Burnette's biggest hits

*'Dreamin' (11); 'You're Sixteen' (8); 'Little Boy Sad' (17)*

## Dorsey BURNETTE

Brother Dorsey's (born December 28th 1932) solo career also started with a couple of unsuccessful single releases, Then 'Tall Oak Tree' reached No 23 and its follow up 'Hey Little One' got to No. 48. He had several hits on the U.S. Country charts.
Dorsey succumbed to a massive coronary at his home in Conoga Park, California on August 19th 1979.

Dorsey Burnette's biggest hits

*'Tall Oak Tree' (23) ; 'Hey Little One'(48);*

**Freddy CANNON**

Freddy Cannon was born Frederick Anthony Picarello Jnr on 4/12/39 in Swampscott, Massachusetts, and was to become known as Freddy 'Boom Boom' Cannon.
Inspired by Chuck Berry and 'Big' Joe Turner, he learned to play guitar and formed a group called Freddy Karmon and the Hurricanes [no connexion with Johnny and the Hurricanes]. They were very popular in the Boston area.
His first release which was on Swan Records was a song called 'Tallahassee Lassie, which, after several re-records and overdubs rose to No.6 on the Billboard

'Hot 100'. Cannon had 22 other songs on the Billboard 'Hot 100'.
His up tempo version of 'Way Down Yonder In New Orleans', an early 1920's song made No.3 on the charts and earned Cannon a Gold Disc.
Freddy Cannon lives in California and occasionally takes part in Rock 'n' Roll revival shows.

Freddy Cannon's biggest hits

*'Tallahassee Lassie' (6); 'Way Down Yonder in New Orleans' (3); 'Palisades Park' (3).*

**Eddie COCHRAN**

Eddie Cochran (3/10/38 – 17/4/60) was born and raised in Minnesota. In a brief career he made a lasting influence with hit records *'C'mon Everybody'; 'Three Steps To Heaven', 'Summertime Blues' and 'Something Else'.* He was a good guitarist, bass player, pianist and drummer. He was one of the earliest singers to experiment with multi-tracking and overdubbing. He lost his life in a car accident in Chippenham, Wiltshire,

England. His biggest hits were released during his lifetime but many other recordings were released posthumously. Cochran's songs can be heard in the films '*The Girl Can't Help It' and 'Twenty Flight Rock'*. He was inducted into the Rock 'n' Roll Hall of Fame in 1980.

## Bo DIDDLEY

Bo Diddley was born Ellas Otha Bates on December 30th 1928 he was also known as Ellas McDaniel, the name coming from an aunt who took him in, and was one of the great singers, songwriters and guitarists of the 50s and 60s. He was nicknamed 'The Originator' because of his major part in the transition from blues to rock 'n' roll.
He was a great influence on a host of artists among whom were Buddy Holly, The Beatles, The Rolling Stones and numerous others.
He became proficient on the violin and was good enough to play in the local orchestra, but he preferred the pulsating beat that could be produced by the guitar.

The reason for the name Bo Diddley is unclear. Several theories have been put forward. Diddley himself originally thought he was called it as an insult. Leonard Chess of Chess Records for whom Bo Diddley recorded, thought it was the name of a onetime local comedian. It was also the name used by a local boxer.

Diddley produced his own guitars, usually rectangular instruments. He was also renowned for the 'Bo Diddley Beat', a chord sequence that was used or imitated by others. He had numerous hit records with his band that included 'The Duchess' (Norma Jean Wooford), 'Lady Bo' (Peggy Jone) and Jerome Green, his famous maracas player. Roosevelt Jackson, Jody Williams, Billy Boy Arnold, Lester Davenport and Otis Spann formed the backbone of Diddley's recording musicians.

In later life Diddley moved to Valencia County, New Mexico where he became Deputy Sheriff. So keen was he on the post that he even bought three new police cars out of his own money.

He was inducted into the Rock 'n' Roll and Rockabilly Halls of Fame in 1989, plus numerous other awards.
He died of heart failure on June 2nd 2008

Bo Diddley's biggest hits
*'Bo Diddley'; 'Diddley Daddy'; 'Pretty Thing'; 'Who Do You Love'; 'Cops and Robbers'; 'You Can't Judge A Book By It's Cover'.*
*'Have Guitar Will Travel' LP; 'Bo Diddley Is A Gunslinger' LP.*

**Bobby DARIN**

Bobby Darin's real name was Waldon Robert Cassotto. He was born on May 14th 1936 in the Bronx, New York. He started his musical career as a songwriter (mainly for Connie Francis) before starting his own recording career. His first hit was 'Splish Splash' in 1958, which he followed up with 'Dream Lover', 'Things' and 'Early In The Morning' (a song also recorded by Buddy Holly).
He forsook rock 'n' roll songs, and took to recording standards. His album 'Bobby

Darin sings Johnny Mercer' is a much sought after collectors item.
He had huge success with 'Mack the Knife' from Kurt Weill's 'The Threepenny Opera. And Charles Trenet's French song 'La Mer' which Darin recorded as 'Beyond the Sea'.
Darin starred in film and t.v. roles and had his own series for CBS and a detective series on NBC. He won a Golden Globe award for acting and a French Film award at the Cannes Film Festival.
In the mid to late 60s he turned more towards folk and country music having success in both genres.
Bobby Darin had a great interest in politics and worked with Robert Kennedy during his Presidential campaign. He was present when J.F.Kennedy was assassinated.
There is little doubt that Bobby Darin would have been a very great showman along with the likes of Dean Martin, Sammy Davis Jnr and Frank Sinatra, but he was a sickly person having suffered from rheumatic fever as a child. He had had heart valves replaced and these also malfunctioned necessitating replacement.

Darin never regained consciousness and died on December 20th 1973 at only 37 years of age.

Bobby Darin's biggest hits

*'Splish Splash'(3); 'Early In the Morning'(24); 'Queen of the Hop'(9) 'Dream Lover'(2); 'Mack The Knife'(1); 'La Mer' (6) 'Clementine' (21); 'Lazy River' (14); 'Things'(3); 'If I Were A Carpenter' (8).*

## Antoine 'Fats' DOMINO

Antoine 'Fats' Dominique Domino was born 26th February 1928, and is one of the classic R&B and rock 'n' roll singers, songwriters and pianists. In the 1950's and 60's he was the best-selling afro-American singer. His personality and rich accent have made him one of the most sought after stage shows ever.

Born in New Orleans he had his first record in the charts as far back as 1949. It was on Imperial Records and was called 'The Fat Man'. It peaked at No.2 in the charts. Domino is calculated as having sold in excess of 110 million records.

He hit the charts with *'Ain't That A Shame'* in 1955 although Pat Boone's milder version sold more. This was said to

be due to racially segregated radio airplay. 'Fats' would eventually release 37 Top 40 singles. These include *'Blueberry Hill' 'Walking To New Orleans'* , *'Red Sails In The Sunset', The Big Beat',* and *'Hello Josephine'.* His last Top 100 hit was in 1968 and was a version of the Beatles *'Lady Madonna'.*
He appeared in two films '*Shake, Rattle and Roll'* and *'The Girl Can't Help It'.*

He quit touring in the 1980's claiming the only food he liked was in New Orleans'. He elected to stay at home during Hurricane Katrina as his wife was not well enough to move. A news report said he was thought to be dead and fans painted 'RIP Fats' messages on the wall of his home, but he had been rescued by a US Coast Guard helicopter.

## EVERLY BROTHERS

The Everly Brothers (Don 1/2/37) and Phil (19/1/39) are Rock 'n' Roll and Country performers. They are probably the best close-harmony duo ever to hit the charts. The duo were elected to the Rock 'n' Roll Hall of Fame in 1986. Both are excellent guitarists. Don sings baritone whilst Phil sings the tenor part. They toured throughout the late 50's and early 60's on package shows with Chuck Berry, Jerry Lee Lewis, Little Richard and Buddy Holly and the Crickets.

Signed to Columbia Records in the early 50s, their first single was a flop and they were swiftly dropped by the label. RCA's Chet Atkins thought they were pretty good and got them a contract with Cadence Records. Their first Cadence single ('Bye Bye Love') had been rejected by numerous other artists including Elvis Presley – the Everly's version shot to No.2 in the charts.

Many other hits followed – most written by Felice and Budleoux Bryant –

'Bird Dog', 'All I Have To Is Dream', 'Problems', 'Wake Up Little Susie', 'Till I Kissed You' and 'Cathy's Clown' all made the charts. Towards the end of the 60s their popularity began to wane and in 1973 there occurred an acrimonious break up. It is reported that Don and Phil only spoke to each once in ten years and that was at their father's funeral.

There was a reunion in 1983 and a few recordings made. They had a final Country chart hit with 'Born Yesterday' in 1986.

Everly Brothers biggest hits

*'Bye Bye Love' (1); 'Wake Up Little Susie' (1); 'Bird Dog' (1);'Problems' (17); 'Till I Kissed You' (8); 'Cathy's Clown' (1); 'Walk Right Back' (7).*

**Connie FRANCIS**

This lady, with the real name of Concetta Rosa Maria Franconero, was the top selling female pop artist of the 50s and 60s. Despite several interruptions to her career she is still in great demand. She came from Newark, New Jersey and was born 12/12/38.

Her career didn't get off to a great start. Dozens of record companies turned her down until a demo disc called 'Freddy' was accepted by MGM (It is said the demo was only accepted because one of

the company executives at the session was called Freddy!)
Her breakthrough came when she recorded 'Who's Sorry Now' which went to No.1 in the UK and No.4 in the U.S. Being part Italian she recorded a quantity of albums in that language which sold extremely well to the large amount of Italians living in the States.
Two tragedies blighted her years between 1974 and 1981. She was brutally raped in a Motel and almost suffocated to death, and in 1981 her close brother George was murdered by Mafia hit men. She also completely lost her voice and suffered from manic depression.
She has recovered to a great extent and still appears on stage regularly.

Connie Francis's biggest hits

*'Who's Sorry Now' (4); 'Stupid Cupid' (14); My Happiness' (2); 'Among My Souvenirs' (7). 'Don't Break The Heart That Loves You' (1).*

## Bobby FREEMAN

Bobby Freeman was born on 13/6/40 in San Francisco, California.
He recorded for Josie Records and had two top-selling records 'Do You Wanna Dance' in 1958 then in 1964 he scored again with 'Come and Swim'. Freeman had several minor hits between his two top selling efforts and is still a big draw in night clubs in and around the Bay area.

Bobby Freeman's biggest hits

*'Do You Wanna Dance' (5) 'Mary Ann Thomas' 'Betty Lou Got A New Pair of Shoes'; 'Come and Swim' (5)*

## Don GIBSON

Don Gibson in 1970

Donald Eugene Gibson was born on 3/4/28 in Shelby, North Carolina.
He formed a band called 'Sons of the Soil' and made a few records for local sales. In 1957 he traveled to Nashville to work with Chet Atkins at RCA Records. With Chet Atkins playing lead guitar, Floyd Cramer on piano and D.J. Fontana on drums plus several other top Nashville session players and singers backing him it seemed difficult for Gibson to miss – and

he didn't. He soon became one of the biggest selling artists. Not really country and not really pop. Don Gibson became known as a crossover artist. One who could hit it big in both fields.
He was also a very talented songwriter becoming known as 'The Sad Poet' because many of his songs were about lost love and loneliness. Over 700 other artists recorded, and had big hits with Don Gibson songs such as Patsy Cline, Roy Orbison, Ray Charles. Orbison even devoted a whole album to him called simply 'Roy Orbison Sings Don Gibson'.
He was inducted into the Songwriters Hall of Fame in 1973 and the Country Music Hall of Fame in 2001.
Don Gibson died from natural causes on 17/11/2003. There is now a Don Gibson Theatre in uptown Shelby.

Don Gibson's biggest hits

*'Sweet Dreams' (9); 'Oh Lonesome Me' (1); I Can't Stop Loving You' (7); Blue Blue Day (1); 'Give Myself A Party' (5); 'Look Who's Blue' (8); 'Who Cares' (3);*

*'Don't Tell Me Your Troubles' (5); 'Just One Time' (2); 'Sweet Dreams'[re-issue] (6); 'Sea of Heartbreak' (2); 'Lonesome Number One' (2); 'Yes, I'm Hurting' (6); 'Funny, Forgotten Feelings' (8); 'There's A Story' (7); 'Country Green' (5); 'Woman (Sensuous Woman)' (1); 'I Can Mend Your Broken Heart' (5).*

## Charlie GRACIE

Charles Anthony Gracie was born in Philadelphia, Pennsylvania on May 14th 1936. He s a rock 'n' roll pioneer. He learned to play guitar when he was 14 years of age. Like many others, his first attempts at a hit record failed. Cameo Records started up in Philadelphia and Gracie was signed by them. His first record for them 'Butterfly'/'Ninety Nine Ways' shot to No.1 on the Billboard jukebox plays chart. 'Butterfly' was followed up by 'Fabulous', which was

also a substantial seller for Cameo as were 'Wandering Eyes' and 'Cool Ways'.
Gracie appeared on 'American Bandstand, and the 'Ed Sullivan Show' and toured extensively with Chuck Berry, Bo Diddley and the Everley's.
He has been recognized by the Rockabilly Hall of Fame and still makes personal appearances to this day.

Charlie Gracie's biggest hits
*'Butterfly'(1); 'Wandering Eyes'(71/ 6 UK); 'Fabulous' 'Cool Ways'.*

**Bill HALEY and the Comets**

William John Clifton Haley (6/7/25 – 9/2/81) was one of the first American Rock 'n' Rollers. Many state that it was Haley's music which he performed with his band The Comets that first popularized this genre of music. He had million selling records with *'Rock Around The Clock'; 'See You Later, Alligator'; 'Shake, Rattle and Roll and 'Razzle Dazzle'*. He sold over 25 million records. He was the band's vocalist, could play guitar and slap bass.

**Buddy HOLLY and the Crickets**

Born in Lubbock, Texas (7/9/36) Charles Hardin Holl**e**y had possibly more influence on other up and coming singers than any other artist at that time.

He had two older brothers Larry and Travis who taught their younger brother (who was always called 'Buddy') to play guitar, banjo and lap steel guitar. He was so good he was winning talent contest from the age of five.

In 1952 Holley teamed up with a friend called Bob Montgomery to form a duo called "Buddy and Bob". They recruited Larry Welborn as bass player and played at local shows, and also had a show on local radio station KDAV. They opened for Elvis Presley who was doing a gig in Lubbock. It was as a result of this that they were offered a recording contract with Decca Records.

Decca released two records ‘Blue Days, Black Nights’ and ‘Modern Don Juan’. The labels misspelled Holley’s name as Holly, omitting the ‘e’. Holly was to keep this spelling of his name for the remainder of his career.

The records didn’t sell so the disillusioned Montgomery and Welborn continued with their careers leaving Holly to soldier on alone.

Holly was convinced he could make it as a musician so he formed another band with his friends Niki Sullivan (guitar), J.I.[Jerry] Allison (drums) and Joe B. Mauldin (bass). They hired Norman Petty’s studio in Clovis, New Mexico to cut some demo discs. Whilst listening to the playbacks Petty noticed a quaint sound. One of the party discovered a large cricket near to a microphone. The boys adopted the insects name as the name for the group.

Petty recorded several demos and took them to Coral Records who were quite impressed and released 'That'll Be The Day' which topped the US Best Sellers Charts on September 23rd 1957. Several other singles were released, most of which climbed into the charts, particularly in Britain and mainland Europe where Holly and the Crickets seemed to be more popular than in the US.

After several tours, Holly wanted to take time out to decide his career path. He moved to New York. He wanted to try recording with large orchestras. He also married a lady called Maria Elena Santiago in Lubbock on August 15th 1958. Holly was having problems with his manager Norman Petty, who was slow to release any royalties due to the boys. Holly found himself with a cash flow problem that needed correcting. He had been offered a tour of the Mid-West states by a company called GAC. He baulked at it at first. He had contacted the Crickets who had returned to Lubbock. He told them of the tour but they declined. They didn't want to tour the Mid-West in mid-winter. Holly was tasked with finding a new band. He recruited Tommy Allsup (guitar), Carl Bunch (drums) and a singer he was nurturing called Waylon Jennings as a bass player. Jennings didn't possess a bass and couldn't play it anyway. Holly bought him an instrument and Allsup showed Jennings how to play the necessary chords to get by.

The tour was a disaster in more ways than one. The itinerary was horrendous with sometimes three to four hundred miles to be covered between each concert in sub-zero temperatures. The buses had no heaters and were constantly breaking down. Bunch was sent home suffering from frostbite in his toes. Dion DeMucci of Dion and the Belmonts who were also on the bill was drafted in as emergency drummer.

After a performance at the Surf Ballroom in Clear Lake, Iowa on February 2$^{nd}$ 1959 Holly declared that he needed to get to the next venue (Moorhead, Minnesota) quicker than the buses could get there so he could get the band's laundry done before the next show. A local air charter company was contacted and manager Jerry Dwyer allocated Roger Peterson to fly Holly, J.P. Richardson (The Big Bopper) and Richie Valens, both supporting acts, to Moorhead. Richardson had talked Jennings into giving him his seat on the plane as he [Richardson] was suffering with a cold. Allsup gave his seat to Valens to ride in the bus with Waylon and play cards.

The night was pitch black with snow flurries. Peterson was not qualified to fly on instruments and was soon disorientated. He thought he was flying up – he wasn't. He was flying down. A farmer, Reeve Eldridge was woken by a 'bang' at 1 am. The Bonanza had smashed into the frozen ground. Holly, Richardson, Valens and Peterson were killed instantly.

GAC wouldn't even cancel the rest of the tour which had 13 more nights to run. Jennings and Allsup weren't allowed time off to attend Holly's funeral.

The Crickets continued to record and tour after Holly's death with various line-ups. Carl Bunch became a preacher, Allsup a record producer, and Jennings became one of the most successful country singers ever.

Buddy Holly (BH) and Buddy Holly & the Crickets (BHC) biggest hits.
Holly had an unusual contract with Coral. He could record as a solo artist or as The Crickets.
*'That'll Be The Day (1)BHC; 'Peggy Sue' (3) BH; 'Oh Boy' (10)BHC;*
*'I'm Gonna Love You To' (BH); 'Maybe Baby' (17) BHC; 'Rave On' (37) BH;*
*'Think It Over' (27) BHC; 'Early In The Morning' (32) BH; 'It's So Easy' (BHC);*
*'Heartbeat' BH; 'Brown Eyed Handsome Man' BH; ' Reminiscing' BH;*
*'Bo Diddley' BH; 'True Love Ways' BH.*

**Wanda JACKSON**

Wanda Lavonne Jackson, one of the most versatile Country, Rockabilly and Rock 'n' Roll singers, was born on October 20th 1937 in Maud, Oklahoma.

She was a superb songwriter, pianist, guitarist and singer. She was extremely popular from the mid 50s to the end of the 60s and gained the soubriquet 'The Queen [or First Lady] of Rockabilly. In her early days of touring she was often paired on the bill with Elvis Presley. Presley would coach her in how to sing rock 'n' roll and they dated for a short time.

She still performs and records to this day and was a guest on Jools Holland's Hootenanny Show at the end of 2010

Wanda Jackson's biggest hits

*'You Can't Have My Love' (8); 'Right or Wrong' (6); 'In The Middle of a Heartache' (6); 'Let's Have A Party' (10).*

## Marv JOHNSON

Born Marvin Earl Johnson in Detroit, Michigan 15/10/38. Johnson ran the gamut of Doo-Wop groups until he was discovered by Berry Gordy. He recorded his first single called 'Come to Me' in May 1959. The record made No.30 on the Hot 100 chart. Between 1959 and 1961 he issued nine singles all of which climbed into the Hot 100. He has two Gold Records for 'You Got What It Takes' and his last release '(You've Got To) Move Two Mountains'. He was also very popular in Australia, and also had two top ten hits in the UK. Johnson died of a stroke in Columbia, South Carolina on 16th May 1993.

Marv Johnson's biggest hits

*'You Got What It Takes (10)'; '(You've Got To) Move Two Mountains' (20); 'I'll Pick A Rose For My Rose'; 'I Love The Way You Love (9)'.*

**Jimmy JONES**

James 'Jimmy' Jones (2/6/37 – 2/8/2012) hailed from Birmingham, Alabama. He had two monster smash hits 'Handy Man' #2 and 'Good Timin' #3, both in 1960. The intro to 'Handy Man' is unusual in that writer and arranger Otis Blackwell had to whistle the opening bars because the flute player failed to turn up for the recording session. Jones was famous for his falsetto voice. Del Shannon said he was influenced by Jones' sound.

Subsequent attempts by Jones failed to make the charts but he kept active in the industry as a writer and producer.

## Brenda LEE

Brenda Lee was born Brenda Mae Tarpley on December 11th 1944 in Atlanta, Georgia. She earned the soubriquet of 'Little Miss Dynamite' not only because she only stood 4 feet 9 inches tall, but because she could belt out rock 'n' roll songs with them the best of 'em. Lee was primarily a country singer, merging into rockabilly, then to rock 'n' roll, returning to her roots in country when her popularity faded in the late 60s. She has been inducted into the Rock 'n' Roll, the Rockabilly and the Country Music Halls of Fame. She charted 37 times in the 60s.

A figure only surpassed by Presley, Ray Charles, Connie Francis and the Beatles. She has released over 80 singles, many of which entered the charts, and upwards of 40 studio and compilation albums.
She got her first recording contract with Decca Records in 1959 and is currently with MCA Nashville where she resides. She is also the subject of the Chuck Berry record 'St Louis to Liverpool'. She married Ronnie Shacklett in 1963. Unlike many showbiz marriages this one has stayed intact. The couple have two daughters and three granddaughters.

Brenda Lee's biggest hits

*'Rockin' Around The Christmas Tree'; 'Let's Jump The Broomstick'; 'Sweet Nothin's'(4); 'Speak To Me Pretty'; 'All Alone Am I' (3); 'I Want To Be Wanted' (1).*

**Jerry Lee LEWIS**

Jerry Lee Lewis was born September 29$^{th}$ 1935 in Ferriday, Louisiana. He is known as 'The Wild Man of Rock 'n' Roll'. He is currently known as 'The Killer', but early in his career was called 'The Ferriday Fireball' and 'The Great Ball of Fire'. In recent years he has been known as 'The Killer'.

Lewis started playing piano in his youth. His big influences were his cousin Carl McVoy (later to join Bill Black's Combo), and the established country-boogie star Moon Mullican. He was enrolled at the

Southwestern Assemblies of God University in Waxahachie, Texas but was expelled after only a short time for 'playing hymns with a boogie-woogie beat'.
Like many others Lewis took himself along to Sun Studios where he was auditioned by producer Jack Clement. Lewis and his band, which consisted of Roland Janes (guitar) and James Van Eaton (drums) [and occasionally his uncle Jim Brown on bass].Clement recorded '*Crazy Arms/ End Of The Road'*. The record sold well, but not well enough to make the charts. Sam Phillips and Clement were confident that future offerings from Lewis would do the trick, and they weren't wrong. '*Whole Lotta Shakin Goin On'/It'll Be Me'* (released 15/3/57) climbed to No.3 whilst *'Great Balls of Fire'/'You Win Again'* (3/11/57) fell just one position short of the top spot.

The 22 year old Lewis was hot, very hot. Not only in the US but British fans were very keen to see the 'Ferriday Fireball'. So a short concert trip was organized for May 1958. Lewis hadn't been in Britain for more than hour or so (at Heathrow Airport) when his world imploded. A [the only] reporter called Ray Berry discovered that Jerry Lee's wife, Myra, who was with him, was his third wife and she was only 13 years old! Lewis insisted she was 15.

It was even suspected that Lewis wasn't divorced from his other wives.

Britain didn't like Jerry Lee and his entourage, and the three concerts that were staged were a disaster. The Lewis clan left for home with their tails between their legs.

The News followed them, and Lewis was blacklisted from TV and radio shows.

His earnings collapsed from $10,000 a night to $250 a night in pokey honky-tonks.

Lewis was still under contract to Sun Records and continued to release some very good singles but never broke into the higher echelons of the charts. His Sun contract ended in the mid 60's. He went to Smash Records but it was not a successful venture. Another move, this time to Mercury Records was more successful

and Lewis turned himself into 'possibly the best Country singer ever'. Selling millions of records and being virtually a permanent member of the Country charts.
Lewis' popularity in Europe and the UK has recovered and recent concerts have been a huge success. His live album *'Jerry Lee Lewis at The Star Club Hamburg'* with the Nashville Teens has been considered as the finest live rock 'n' roll album ever. He continues to record excellent albums at 78 years of age.
He has been inducted into the Rock 'n' Roll Hall of Fame, The Rockabilly Hall of Fame, and the Country Music Hall of Fame.

Jerry Lee's biggest hits
*'Whole Lotta Shakin', 'Great Balls of Fire', 'Break Up', 'You Win Again'*
*'What'd I Say', 'Good Golly Miss Molly', 'High School Confidential', 'Breathless'.*
*Recent CD's 'Last Man Standing', 'Mean Old Man'.*

## Carl MANN

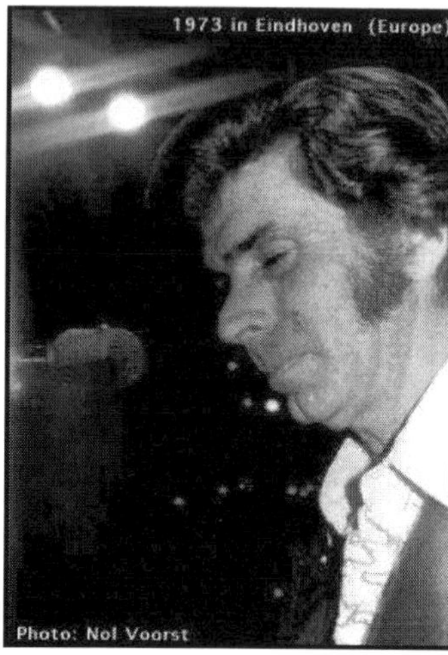


Carl Mann was born near Jackson, Tennessee. His parents owned a timber business (Carl Mann still runs the company today). Mann had a couple of records out on the Jaxon label that sold quite well locally. W.S. Holland (Carl Perkins and later Johnny Cash's drummer) managed Mann and took him to Sun Records in Memphis. Sun released several singles by Mann (on their subsidiary label Phillips International) mainly up-tempo versions of standards. 'Mona Lisa' and 'Pretend' both charted.

An L.P. called 'Like Mann was issued (also on Sun's subsidiary label Phillips International), but it failed to sell well [It is now a collectors item], and Mann went back to the logging company and a battle with alcoholism which he eventually won. He came out of music retirement in 2005 to make some country records with Sun friends Holland and Rayburn Anthony. A book on his life called 'The Last Son of Sun' has recently been released.

Carl Mann's biggest hits

*'Pretend'; ' Mona Lisa'; 'Rockin' Love' 'South of the Border'.*

## Clyde McPHATTER

Clyde Lensley McPhatter was born on November 15th 1932 in Durham, North Carolina. He was to become one of the most imitated singers of his era. In 1950 he won an 'Amateur Night' talent contest and was recruited by the group Billy Ward and the Dominoes as a tenor. It is widely regarded that the group would not have been as successful as it was if it hadn't been for McPhatter.

McPhatter left the group in 1953, and was persuaded by Ehmet Ertegun, head of Atlantic Records to form a group of his own. The original group was not what

Atlantic had in mind, and Clyde was asked to reform the group. This time Ertegun was pleased with the results. McPhatter called his group 'The Drifters'. The group had numerous changes of personnel (See separate entry: The Drifters) although McPhatter stayed at the helm until he was inducted in the Army. On his release from the Forces he pursued a solo career.

He went through several labels having hits but never quite managing a No.1.

Through the 60s tastes changed and McPhatter's popularity waned. As more of his recordings failed to chart so he turned to alcohol, stating that "All my fans have left me".

At the age of only 39, heart, kidney and liver complications brought on by alcohol abuse caused his untimely death.

Clyde McPhatter's biggest hits

*'Money Honey' [with The Drifters] (1); 'Honey Love' [With The Drifters] (1) ; 'A Lovers Question' (1); 'Lover Please' (7).*

**Ricky (or Rick) NELSON**

Rick (or Ricky as he was sometimes known) was born Eric Hilliard Nelson on 8/5/40. He was a child star in his parents (Ozzie and Harriet Nelson) t.v. show 'The Adventures of Ozzie and Harriet'. The show ran from 1952-66).

Ricky (as he was known at the time) recorded his first hit in 1957. The record 'Poor Little Fool' went to No.1 on the Billboard hit lists. He received the 'Most

Promising Newcomer' award for his part in the John Wayne and Dean Martin film 'Rio Bravo' in which he played the part of a young gunslinger called 'Colorado'.
On May 12th 1961 [his 21st birthday] he officially changed his name to Rick.
In the mid 60s Nelson started to move away from Rock 'n' roll music into the field of Country. Nelson's last hit came in 1972 with the song 'Garden Party', a song he wrote after being booed off stage during a concert at Madison Square Garden because he did not include any of his old hits on the show. Nelson had a fear of flying, but did so because of the distances involved between shows. He had bought a DC-3 aircraft that once belonged to Jerry Lee Lewis but it was plagued with mechanical defects. After a show in Guntersville, Alabama, Nelson and his band and entourage boarded the 'plane for a flight to Dallas, Texas. The aircraft crash-landed close to the runway at Dallas. All were killed except the pilots, one of which was badly burned.
Rick Nelson was inducted into the Rock 'n' Roll Hall of Fame in 1987

Rick Nelson's biggest hits

*'A Teenager's Romance' (2); 'I'm Walkin'' (4); 'Stood Up' (2); 'Poor Little Fool' (1); 'Lonesome Town' (7); 'Travellin' Man (1); 'Believe What You Say' (4); 'Never Be Anyone Else But You' (6);'Hello Mary Lou' (9); 'Young World' (5); 'Garden Party' (6).*

## Roy ORBISON

Roy Kelton Orbison was born 23/4/1936 and passed away on 6/12/88.

He was known as 'The Big O'. He grew up in Texas and sang country and rockabilly music with his band 'The Wink Westerners'. When he was in his late teens he changed the band's name to 'The Teen Kings'. The band was signed by Sam Phillips at Sun Records in Memphis, Tennessee. Sam Phillips released four

singles by Roy Orbison and the Teen Kings only 'Ooby Dooby' having a modicum of success by reaching No.59 in the Hot 100. Producer Jack Clement is reported as saying to Orbison, "You'll get nowhere with a voice like that son!"
After a short stay and little success at RCA, Orbison signed with Joe Melson at Monument Records. Orbison and Melson co-wrote a song called 'Only the Lonely', and as they say, the rest was history. The soaring falsettos and superb songwriting did the trick. Hit followed hit for years to come. Orbison toured the world headlining the biggest shows.
Tragedy was no stranger to Orbison. In June 1966 Roy and his wife Claudette, who were motorcycle fanatics, were riding home from Bristol, Tennessee when she was struck by a huge semi truck and killed instantly. Whilst on a tour of the Midlands in England he received word that his home in Hendersonville, Tenn. had burned down and his two eldest sons had perished.
In 1987 Orbison was working on a project with Jeff Lynne (of ELO fame). They decided to contact George Harrison and

Tom Petty who agreed to form a 'supergroup' which they called The Traveling Wilburys', named after an imaginary character. Orbison sometimes used to be called Lefty Wilbury after one of his heroes Lefty Frizzel.
Orbison spent December 6th 1988 flying model aeroplanes at Hendersonville. After dinner that evening he complained of tiredness and died of a heart attack. He was only 52 years of age.

Roy Orbison's biggest hits

*'Ooby Dooby' (59); 'Only The Lonely' (2); 'Running Scared' (1);*
*'Crying' (2); 'Dream Baby' (4); 'In Dreams' (7); 'Mean Woman Blues' (5); 'Oh Pretty Woman' (1); 'It's Over' (9); 'You Got It' (9).*

## Carl PERKINS

Carl Lee Perkins was born in Tiptonville, Tennessee on 9th April 1932. He learned the rudiments of the guitar on an instrument his father made for him out of a cigar box, stick and some wire. (a diddly-bow?) When he was 13 years of age he won a talent contest with a song he had written called 'Movie Magg'. A song he later recorded for Sam Phillips at Sun Records.

In late 1955, Perkins wrote a song called 'Blue Suede Shoes' which he recorded at Sun Records. It became his first and only No.1 chart hit (that is Country charts, it was No.2 on the Pop music charts) and the first record by the Sun label to sell a million copies. Perkins, however, could not reap the rewards due to him for the hit as he had been involved in a near-fatal car accident and therefore missed out on countless personal appearances due to his hospitalization. Elvis Presley had also covered the song which, although not as successful chartwise as Perkins version tended to steal some of the limelight from Perkins.

Perkins never had another top 40 hit and left Sun to record for Columbia Records. In 1968 a Perkins composition 'Daddy Sang Bass' was recorded by Johnny Cash and shot to No.1 on the Country charts. As a result Cash took Perkins in to his entourage to be part of the Johnny Cash Roadshow along with June Carter and the Statler Brothers.

The Rockabilly revival of the 80's, particularly in Europe brought Perkins back into the public eye. Perkins starred in live shows and many television shows along with likes of George Harrison, Eric Clapton and Ringo Starr.
Perkins had the sobriquet 'The King of Rockabilly' and was inducted into both the Rock 'n' Roll and Rockabilly Halls of Fame in 1989.
He was a quarter of the famous 'Million Dollar Quartet' the iconic Sun album that was 'accidentally' recorded at Sun Studio.
Carl Lee Perkins died from throat cancer in Jackson, Tennessee on January 19th 1998.

Carl Perkins' biggest hits
*'Blue Suede Shoes' (1); ' Movie Magg'; ' Matchbox'; 'Turn Around'; 'Honey Don't'. 'Dixie Fried'; 'Class Of '55'.*

## Elvis PRESLEY

Elvis Aaron Presley (8/1/35 – 16/8/77) was born in Tupelo, Mississippi. He was one of a pair of identical twins, his brother Jesse Garon was stillborn.

He is probably the most famous and popular singer of all time.

At school Presley was teased because he was 'different'. He was quiet and known as a mama's boy. The Presley's moved to Memphis so that his father Vernon could find work and escape the law for transporting 'bootleg' liquor.

On July 18th 1953 Presley went to (what is now known as) Sun Sudio at 706 Union and paid $3.98 to record a double – sided demo. The songs recorded were '*My Happiness and That's When Your Heartaches Begin'*. He gave them to his mother as a belated birthday gift even though the Presley's didn't own a record player. A second demo '*I'll Never Stand In Your Way'* and '*It Wouldn't Be The Same'* was recorded on 4th January 1954.

Sam Phillips (Sun's owner) needed a singer to record a song he had acquired, he could not identify the singer on the demo so, at his secretary Marion Keisker's insistence he sent for Presley. The song was recorded, but Phillips deemed it to be poor and unusable. Phillips asked Presley what else he could do, so Presley teamed up with friends Winfield 'Scotty' Moore, a guitarist and Bill Black, a slap bass player. The trio started 'acting the fool' with Arthur 'Bib Boy' Crudup's 'That's All Right Mama'. Phillips was knocked out by what he heard and decided to release the song with a Bill Monroe composition 'Blue Moon of

Kentucky' a Country blues on the 'B' side (Sun 209). It was released on July 19 1954 with advance sales of 6000. Four more Presley, Scotty and Bill singles followed from Sun Records, 'Good Rockin' Tonight'/ 'I Don't Care If The Sun Don't Shine' (Sun 210 22/9/54). 'Milkcow Blues Boogie'/'You're A Heartbreaker' (Sun 215 8/1/55). 'I'm Left, You're Right, She's Gone'/'Baby Let's Play House' (Sun 217 25/4/550 and finally 'Mystery Train'/'I Forgot To Remember To Forget' (Sun 223 1/8/55).
On November 21st 1955 Sam Phillips dropped a bombshell on the music world – he sold Presley's contract to Bob Neal and Col. Tom Parker of RCA Victor Records (Parker was never a Colonel it was merely a sobriquet).
The recording fraternity were saying that that was the end for Sun Records, but it wasn't – it was just what Sun needed. Without the $35,000 dollars that RCA paid Sun they would have had to go into liquidation. But Sun found a new life. OK, Presley's sales were gone but other artists were selling by the million for Phillips. Johnny Cash, Jerry Lee Lewis,

Carl Perkins were topping the charts and selling millions of records.

Elvis Presley's No.1 hits
*'Heartbreak Hotel'; 'I Want You, I Need You, I Love You'; 'Don't Be Cruel'; 'Hound Dog'; 'Love Me Tender'; 'Too Much'; 'All Shook Up'; 'Teddy Bear'; 'Jailhouse Rock'; 'Don't'; 'Hard Headed Woman'; 'A Big Hunk Of Love'; 'Stuck On You'; 'It's Now or Never'; 'Are You Lonesome Tonight'; 'Surrender'; 'Good Luck Charm'; ' Suspicious Minds'.*

## Little RICHARD (Penniman)

Richard Wayne Penniman born 5/12/32 in Macon, Georgia was better known as Little Richard. He started out in the mid 50s. His dynamic showmanship has lasted six decades. He has been honoured by many associations including the Rock 'n' Roll Hall of Fame and the Songwriters Hall of Fame. Most of Little Richards successful recordings were on the Speciality label. He had 28 hit records but never a #1 on the Billboard Hot 100 charts, but he did make the #1 spot 3 times on the R&B charts.
He appeared in several films including 'The Girl Can't Help It', 'Don't Knock The Rock', 'Hail, Hail Rock 'n' Roll' and some twenty others.
His sexual orientation has long been a topic of debate. He was jailed for three days for 'lewd

conduct'. He attended theological college and i ordained minister and has officiated at cele weddings. He is ranked 8th on Rolling S magazine list of Greatest Artists Of All Time.

Little Richard's biggest hits

*'Tutti Fruiti' (17); 'Long Tally Sally' (6); 'Rip Up' (17); 'Lucille' 21;*
*'Keep-a-knockin' (8); 'Good Golly Miss Molly' (10); 'Jenny Jenny' (10).*

** 'Long Tall Sally', 'Rip It Up' and 'Lucille' wen #1 on the US R&B charts*

**Tommy ROE**

Thomas David Roe (b 9/5/42 in Atlanta, Georgia) had three big hits 'Sheila' #1 in 1962, 'Everybody' #3 in 1963, and 'Dizzy' #1 in 1969. His song 'The Folk Singer' went to #4 in the U.K.in 1963. He occasionally performs in revival concerts with 60s stars Freddy Cannon, Bobby Vee and the like.

**Jack SCOTT**

With a real name of Giovanni Dominico Scafone something had to change. For a start all that name wouldn't fit on a record label. So the young singer from Detroit, Michigan changed it to Jack Scott. He was actually Canadian by birth born in Windsor, Ontario on 24/1/1936. He grew up listening to Hillbilly music on the radio. His father taught him to play guitar.

When he was 18 years of age he formed a group called the 'Southern Drifters' but after three years he left for a solo career. Scott had two good-selling records on the

ABC-Paramount label, but switched to the Carlton label where, in 1958, he had a double-sided national hit with 'Leroy'/'My True Love'. The record selling more than 1million copies thus earning him a Gold Disc. Scott had more hits (19) in a shorter period of time than any other artist with the exception of the Beatles. He also wrote all his hit songs except one 'Burning Bridges'.

It is said that along with Orbison and Presley he had the finest voice in Rock 'n' Roll.

He still sings and tours today and still resides in a suburb of Detroit.

Jack Scott's biggest hits

*'Leroy' (11); 'My True Love' (3); 'Goodbye Baby' (8); 'The Way I Walk' (35); 'What In The World's Come Over you' (5); 'Burning Bridges (3)*

## Neil SEDAKA

Neil Sedaka was born 13/4/39 in Brooklyn, York. Sedaka showed musical ability from an age, and was bought a piano by his mother who him trained to become a concert pianist, but Se was more interested in popular music and event teamed up with Howard Greenfield to for songwriting team.
After being in a band with his classmates Se branched out as a solo artist in 1957

His first single 'The Diary' got into the top 15 but his next two efforts fared less well although 'I Go Ape' just made the top 40 in the U.S. it do go to #9 in the U.K. It took a couple more failures before 'Oh Carol' hit #9 and 'One Way Ticket To The Blues' topped the charts. Several hits followed including 'Calendar Girl' 'Next Door To An Angel' and 'Happy Birthday Sweet Sixteen'. Sedaka's popularity started to wane in the late 60s. He lost his recording contract at RCA, but was picked up by Elton John's Rocket label. This lasted a few years but with minimum success John lost interest in Sedaka who went back to the U.S. and was offered a contract with Electra Records.

In 1971 Sedaka had written and recorded 'Is This The Way To Amarillo', but it lay dormant until 2007 when British comedian Peter Kay used it in a video, and Tony Christies 1971 cover version was re-released and went to No.1 on the U.K. charts for seven weeks. Sedaka's recent concerts in London and the Provinces have played to packed houses.

Neil Sedaka's biggest hits

*'Oh Carol', 'One Way Ticker To The Bl*
*'Calendar Girl', ' Next Door To An An*
*'Breaking Up Is hard To Do', 'Laughter In the R*
*'I Go Ape', 'Stairway To Heaven', 'Happy Birt*
*Sweet Sixteen', 'Laughter In The Rain'.*

# Del SHANNON

Del Shannon's real name was Charles Weedon Westover. He was born on 30/12/34 in Grand Rapids, Michigan. He became a ukulele and guitar player and was a great fan of country singers Hank Williams, Hank Snow and Lefty Frizzell. He worked part-time in a band called the Moonlight Ramblers.

On leaving the band (because the leader Doug DeMott had been fired) he travelled to New York City where he and a friend signed for the Big Top label as singers and composers. It was here that the name change to Del Shannon took place. Early recordings were not successful but on the 21st January 1961 they recorded a song called 'Runaway' which reached the top spot on the Billboard Hot 100. (It is said, but not proven that that the piping organ on this recording is played by Paul Tezluk of Johnny and the Hurricanes), 'Hats Off To Larry' and 'Little Town Flirt' were good but not quite so successful.

Shannon suffered from depression and took his own life with a rifle on February 8th 1990.

Del Shannon's biggest hits

*'Runaway' (1); 'Hats Off To Larry' (5); 'Little Town Flirt' (5); 'Keep Searchin'' (9).*

**Bobby VEE**

Robert Thomas Veline was born 30/4/43 in Fargo N.Dakota. He has had 10 Billboard Top 20 hits plus a further 28 records which have entered the Top 100. Bobby Vee (as he was known) received a kick-start to his career with the death of Buddy Holly at the Winter Dance Party tour. Holly's next show was to have been at Moorhead, Minnesota and Vee was hastily drafted in to fill the spot tragically vacated by Holly. Vee was a success, sounding not unlike Holly (possibly by design), and had a very successful career for many years and still records to this day.

Bobby Vee's biggest hits

*'Rubber Ball' (4UK); 'More Than I Can Say' (4UK); 'Take Good Care Of My Baby' (3UK); 'The Night Has A Thousand Eyes' (3UK)*

## Gene VINCENT

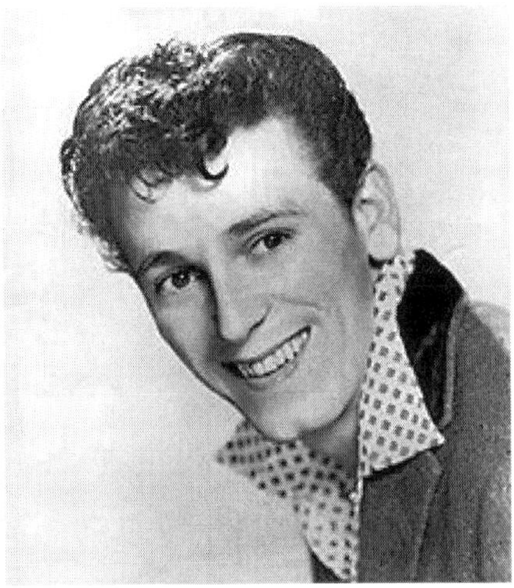

Gene Vincent was born Vincent Eugene Craddock (11/2/35 – 12/9/71). (He was a Rock 'n' Roll and rockabilly pioneer). He was leader of the Blue Caps, and had a top 10 hit with *'Be-Bop-A-Lula'*. Vincent moved to Britain to work on Jack Good's t.v. show 'Boy Meets Girl'. He wore black leather clothes, gloves and a gold medallion. On 15th December 1959 he was in a car with Eddie Cochran and Cochran's girl friend Sharon Sheeley when they were involved in a high speed

crash. Sheeley and Vincent were injured, but Cochran suffered brain damage and died the next day.
Vincent attempted to revive his career in the U.S. in 1963 but despite making some well-received recordings none sold particularly well.
Gene Vincent died from a ruptured stomach ulcer on 12th October 1971.
He was the first inductee in the Rockabilly Hall of Fame, and is a member of the Rock 'n' Roll Hall of Fame.

Gene Vincent's biggest hits

*'Be Bop-a-Lula' #5; 'Wear My Ring' #13; 'Dance To The Bop' #23;*

# Larry WILLIAMS

(May 10, 1935 – January 7, 1980) was an American rhythm and blues and rock and roll singer, songwriter, producer, and pianist from New Orleans, Louisiana. Williams is best known for writing and recording some rock and roll classics from 1957 to 1959 for Specialty Records, including "Bony Moronie", "Short Fat Fannie", "High School Dance" (1957),

"Slow Down", "Dizzy Miss Lizzy" (1958), "Bad Boy" and "She Said Yeah" (1959). John Lennon was a fan, and the Beatles and several other British Invasion groups covered several of his songs.

Williams' life mixed tremendous success with violence and drug addiction. He was a long-time friend of Little Richard.

Williams was found dead from a gunshot wound at his home in Los Angeles, California. His death was reported as suicide but there was much speculation as to the cause. No person or persons were ever charge with his death.

**Jackie WILSON**

Jack Leroy Wilson was born 9/6/34 in Detroit, Michigan. He was known as 'Mr Excitement'. His early years were spent as a member of Billy Ward and the Dominoes, a hugely successful group,before going solo. He was considered to be a master showman and one of the most dynamic R & B performers ever. Most of Wilson's hits were on the Brunswick (Coral) label. He was inducted into the Rock 'n' Roll Hall of Fame in 1987 and was ranked No.69 on the 'Rolling Stone' magazine all time 100 Greatest Artist list.

On September 29th 1975 Wilson was performing at Dick Clark's 'Rock 'n' Roll Revue in New Jersey when he collapsed during the song 'My Heart Is Crying'. The audience thought this was part of the act, but Wilson had suffered a heart attack. Carl Gunter (lead singer of The Coasters) rushed on stage to give artificial respiration, and Wilson, to some extent, recovered. He was admitted to a nursing home where he slipped into a comatose state. He died on January 21st 1984.

Jackie Wilson's biggest hits

*'Reet Petite (1UK)'; 'Lonely Teardrops(7)'; 'To Be Loved (22)'; 'I'll Be Satisfied'(20); 'Night'(4); 'Baby Workout'(5); 'Higher and Higher'(6).*

## The Groups

## The BEACH BOYS

The supergroup The Beach Boys were formed in 1961. The original group consisted of brothers Carl, Brian and Dennis Wilson, cousin Mike Love and Al Jardine. Their close harmony singing lent itself to the 'Surf Sound' that they popularized in Southern California. They have sold in excess of 100 million records, are listed at No.12 in the Rolling Stone magazine '100 Greatest Artists of all Time' and were inducted into the Rock 'n' Roll Hall of Fame in 1988

Beach Boys biggest hits

*'Surfin Safari' #14; 'Surfin USA' #3 'Surfer Girl' #7; 'Be True To Your School' #6; 'Fun, Fun, Fun' #5; 'I Get Around' #1; 'Help Me Rhondda' #1; 'Good Vibrations' #1;*

**The Cadillacs**

The Cadillacs were a rock 'n' roll /doo-wop group. They originated from Harlem, New York in 1953 and were active until around 1965. They started life as The Carnations with lead singer Earl 'Speedoo' Carroll plus, Bobby Phillips, Lavern Drake, and Gus Willingham, but when James 'Poppa' Clark was added to the group their name was changed to the Cadillacs.

From 1957 the group experienced several splits, re-formations and new members – 21 in all during the 'life' of the group. They had four Billboard Hot 100 hits, *'Peek-a-Boo' # 28; 'Speedoo' #17; 'What You Bet' #30 and 'Rudolph' # 11.*

## The COASTERS

The Coasters had a string of hits in the late 1950s. The first was 'Searchin'/'Young Blood' which was followed by 'Yakety Yak', (their only No.1), 'Along Came Jones'; 'Charlie Brown'; 'Poison Ivy' and 'Little Egypt'. The original members of the group were Carl Gardner, Billy Guy, Billy Nunn and Leon Hughes who alternated with Young Jessie in the studio. They recorded for Atlantic Records on its subsidiary label Atco. Their producers and songwriters were Jerry Leiber and Mike Stoller.

The group had several changes of personnel and still perform today at Rock 'n' Roll Revival shows. There have been several other groups performing under the name The Coasters but Carl Gardner held the legal rights to the name. Two of their member's saxophonist King Curtis and Nate Wilson were murdered. Former manager Patrick Cavanagh being found guilty of Wilson's murder. Cavanagh was sentenced to death but the sentence was commuted to Life Imprisonment.

The Coasters biggest hits

*'Young Blood' (8); 'Searchin' (3); 'Yakety Yak' (1); 'Charlie Brown' (2) 'Along Came Jones' (9); 'Poison Ivy' (7).*

**The CRICKETS (see Buddy Holly)**

**The CRYSTALS**

The Crystals all-girl group were not unlike The Ronettes except there were four Crystals (occasionally five). They were also based in New York. The original group consisted of Barbara Alston, Mary Thomas, Dolores "Dee Dee" Kenniebrew, Myrna Girard and "Patsy" Wright. As with The Ronettes they signed to Phil Spector's Philles label records. Their hit records featured different lead singers, 'There's No Other (Like my Baby)' featured Wright. Later, a pregnant Girard was replaced by Dolores "LaLa" Brooks. Other members included Francis

Collins, Pat Pritchett-Lewis, Darlene Love and Melissa "SoulTree" Grant.

The Crystals biggest hits

*'There's No Other' (2); 'Uptown' (2); - with Barbara Alston as lead.*
*'He's A Rebel' (19), He's Sure The Boy I Love' (11) – with Darlene Love as lead.*
*'Da Doo Ron Ron' (3); 'Then He Kissed Me' (6), - with "LaLa" Brooks as lead.*

# DANNY and the JUNIORS

Danny and the Juniors were a doo-wop quartet from Philadelphia. The group consisted of Danny Rapp (lead tenor) [9/5/41 - 5/4/83]; Joe Terranova (baritone) [b 30/1/41]; Dave White tenor) [b 1/9/39]; Frank Maffei (second tenor) [b 15/12/39]; Bobby Maffei (tenor).

They hailed from Philadelphia and scored big hits with 'Twisting USA', 'At The Hop' and 'Rock and Roll Is Here To Stay'. 'At The Hop' (#1 1957) was re-released in 1976 where it entered the Top 40 for a second time.

Danny Rapp apparently committed suicide in a hotel in Arizona on 5/4/83.

The group, now featuring Joe Terry still performs concert tours.

## The DIAMONDS

The Diamonds were a group from Canada. In the 50s and early 60s they accumulated sixteen Billboard Hot 100 hit records. The original Diamonds were Dave Somerville (lead), Ted Kowalski (tenor), Phil Levitt (baritone) and Bill Reed (bass). All except Dave Somerville have passed on and been replaced. The replacement Diamonds are still active in concert to this day.
They were inducted into the vocal Group Hall of Fame in 2004.

The Diamonds biggest hits

*'Why Do Fools Fall In Love' (12); 'Silhouettes' (4); 'Little Darlin' (2); 'The Stroll' (4).*

## The DEL-VIKINGS

The Del (or Dell) Vikings were a doo-wop group formed in the 1950s, and made up from members of the USAF who were stationed in Pittsburg. It was one of the first racially integrated groups on the 50s. Over the years the band has had 21 members. Some of the founder members were Clarence Quick, Kripp Johnson, Don Jackson, Samuel Patterson and Bernard Robertson. The origin of the band's name is unknown, but it may come from a local football team called the Vikings. The group and/or their music have appeared in such films as 'American Graffiti', 'American Hot Wax', and 'Stand By Me'.

The Del Vikings biggest hits

*'Come and Go With Me', 'They Sing They Swing', 'A Singing, Swinging Session'.*

## DICK and DEEDEE

This duo were very popular in the early to mid 60s. They consisted of Dick St John and DeeDee Sperling. Their biggest hit was ‘The Mountains High’ which went to #2 on the Billboard Hot 100, it was originally released on the small Lama label later to be leased to Liberty Records for better promotion and distribution when it began to sell in large quantities. They had eight other hit records with five reaching the Top 30. Other big hits were

‘Young and in Love’ #6, ‘Thou Shall Not Steal’ #22. ‘The Mountains High’ sold over 1 million copies.

## DION and the BELMONTS

Dion DeMucci and his group The Belmonts were from The Bronx area of New York City, the other members were Carlo Mastrangelo (bass-baritone), Fred Milano (2nd Tenor), and Angelo D'Aleo (1st Tenor).

The group name was derived from the fact that two of the group lived on Belmont Avenue, The Bronx and the other two lived nearby.

As with most acts of the time their first single release was a failure. It was on Mohawk Records. The group moved to Laurie Records for their next attempt and recorded 'I Wonder Why'. It went to

No.22 on the Hot 100. The group appeared on 'American Bandstand' hosted by Dick Clark. Their next single 'A Teenager In Love' reached No.5 in the chats. Their biggest hit 'Where or When' hit No.3 in November 1959.

That was the peak of their success. Dion was hospitalized for a heroin addiction problem and further releases failed to chart. In 1960 Dion decided on a solo career and had hits with 'Runaround Sue' and a few other songs although the labels were sometimes incorrectly annotated 'Dion and the Belmonts' when the backing group was actually the Del-Satins who never received label accreditation.

Dion and the Belmonts were inducted into the Vocal Group Hall of Fame in 2000.

Dion and the Belmonts (and Dion) biggest hits.

*'I Wonder Why' (22); 'A Teenager In Love' (5); 'Where or When' (3)*

*Dion only – 'Runaround Sue' (1); 'The Wanderer' (2); 'Ruby Baby' (2)*

## The DRIFTERS

The Drifters are possibly the most long-lived of the doo-wop/R&B groups.
They began life as a backing group to Clyde McPhatter. Whilst The Drifters have had dozens of charting singles, they have also had numerous (almost 60) different members, the most famous being Clyde McPhatter, Bill Pinkney, Ben E King and Johnny Moore.
They were formed in 1953 and are still going strong today. There have been several splinter groups called 'The Drifters', some consisting of ex-members and others with completely new line –ups.

This state of affairs has led to legal action taken by the original owners of the name. The 'Original Drifters' and 'Ben E King and the Drifters' have been inducted into the Vocal Group Hall of Fame. Ben E King also had a #1 hit with 'Stand By Me' as a solo artist.

The Drifters biggest hits

*'There Goes My Baby' (2); 'Save The Last Dance For Me' (1); 'Up On The Roof' (5); 'On Broadway' (9) 'Under The Boardwalk' (4).*

**The FIESTAS**

The Fiestas were an American Rhythm and Blues musical group from Newark, New Jersey. Formed in 1958, The Fiestas contracted with Old Town Records company in 1959 after the company's owner, Hymie Weiss, overheard the group singing in a bathroom adjacent to his office in Harlem. Their debut single was 1959's "So Fine", written by Johnny Otis; the song was a hit in the U.S., reaching #3 on the Black Singles chart and #11 on the Billboard Hot 100 with a hidden gem, "Last Night I Dreamed", on the flip side. A series of soul singles followed from the group, among them "You Could Be My Girlfriend", "Anna", and "Think Smart", but only 1962's "Broken Heart" managed to chart, scoring #18 on the Black Singles chart.

## The FLEETWOODS

The Fleetwoods were a singing trio who hailed from Olympia in Washington State. They were formed in the late 50s and their original members were Gary Troxel, Gretchen Christopher and Barbara Ellis. They had 11 hit records, their biggest hits being ‘Come Softly To Me’ and ‘Mr Blue’ both of which went to #1 on the Billboard Hot 100.

## The FOUR SEASONS

The Four Seasons in 1960

Valli and the Four Seasons in 2012

The Four Seasons were formed in Newark, New Jersey. Their first record was released in 1961. It was generally agreed that The Four Seasons were the most popular vocal group before The Beatles. Since 1970 the group has been known as Frankie Valli and the Four Seasons. The original group consisted of Frankie Valli (lead), Bob Guadio (keyboards & tenor), Tommy DeVito (lead guitar & baritone), and Nick Massi (bass guitar and bass vocals). Over the years there have been 35 other members. They are still very active and very popular in 2013.

They have recorded for several labels including Gone, Vee-Jay, Mowest, Warner Bros, MCA & Curb.

## The Four Seasons biggest hits

1962: "Sherry"#1

1962: "Big Girls Don't Cry", #1

1963: "Walk Like a Man, #1

1963: "Ain't That a Shame", #22

1963: "Candy Girl", #3/"Marlena", #36

1964: "Dawn (Go Away)", #3

1964: "Stay", #16

1964: "Ronnie", #6

1964: "Alone", #28

1964: "Rag Doll", #1

1964: "Save It for Me", #10

1965: "Let's Hang On!", #3

1965: "Don't Think Twice", #12

1966: "Working My Way Back to You", #9

1966: "Opus 17 (Don't You Worry 'bout Me)", #13

1966: "I've Got You Under My Skin", #9

1966: "Tell It to the Rain", #10

1967: "Beggin'", #16

1967: "C'mon Marianne", #9

1967: "Watch the Flowers Grow", #30

1964: "Big Man in Town", #20

1965: "Bye, Bye, Baby (Baby Goodbye)", #12 ("Bye Bye Baby" on initial release)

1965: "Girl Come Running", #30

1968: "Will You Love Me Tomorrow", #24

1975: "Who Loves You", #3

1975: "December, 1963 (Oh, What a Night)", #1

1994: "December, 1963 (Oh, What a Night)", #14 (remixed dance version)

## The ISLEY BROTHERS

The Isley brothers were a trio from Cincinatti, Ohio. They originally consisted of O'Kelly, Rudolph and Ronald Isley. There was a fourth brother Vernon, but he died two years after the group was formed. They started out performing gospel music, but after moving to New York they jumped on the rock 'n' roll and R&B scene. They released three records with little success until the fourth release 'Shout' initially stuttered but eventually sold over a million copies. The inclusion of younger brothers Ernie (lead guitar, drums) and Marvin (bass guitar) and Rudolph's brother-in-law Chris Jasper

(keyboards) turned the trio into a fully-fledged self contained band.
The six-member lineup of the band splintered in 1983, with Ernie, Marvin and Chris Jasper forming the short-lived spinoff group Isley-Jasper-Isley. Eldest member O'Kelly died in 1986 and Rudolph and Ronald released a pair of albums as a duo before Rudolph retired for life in the Christian ministry in 1989. Ronald reformed the group two years later with Ernie and Marvin in 1991; five years later in 1996, Marvin Isley left the group due to complications with diabetes. The remaining duo of Ronald and Ernie would accomplish mainstream success with the albums *Eternal* (2001) and *Body Kiss* (2003), with the former album spanning the top twenty hit, "Contagious". As of 2013, the Isley Brothers continue to perform under the lineup of Ronald and Ernie.

## The KALIN TWINS

The Kalin Twins, Hal and Herbie (b.16/2/34 Hal died 24/9/2005 and Herbie 21/7/2006) were born in Port Jervis, New York). They were the archetypical one hit wonders, that one hit being 'When'. The song was written by Paul Evans and reached #5 on the Billboard charts but reached #1 in the U.K.

They made one tour of the U.K. supported by Cliff Richard. They retired from the music business sometime in the 60s after failing to reproduce another hit record.

## LYNRYD SKYNRYD

Formed originally in 1964 as The Noble Five in Jacksonville, Florida, the band didn't really come to the forefront until the 70s when they became known as Lynryd Skynryd and produced the driving southern rock sound that is synonymous with their hits such as 'Sweet Home Alabama' and 'Freebird'. They lost three members in an air crash in 1978. The band, which consisted of Ronnie Van Zandt, Steve Gaines, Cassie Gaines, Allen Collins, Gary Rossington, Leon Wikieson, Billy Powell, Artimus Pyle and Leslie Hawkins. Van Zandt, and both Gaines plus road manager Dean Kilpatrick, and both pilots were killed as the plane ran out of fuel and crash landed en route to Baton Rouge, Louisiana. A Lynryd Skynrd band still performs to this day – and very successfully too, but only Gary Rossington of the original line-up remains.

They were inducted into the Rock ‘n’ roll Hall of Fame in 2005.

## The MARCELS

A doo-wop group formed in 1961. They had a #1 hit with a most unusual version of the old standard 'Blue Moon'. The Marcels were Cornelius Harp (lead), Fred Johnson (bass), Gene Bricker, Ron Mundy and Richard Knauss. Whilst touring in 1961 they encountered racial problems (the group was bi-racial), and the white members, Knauss and Bricker left the group. They were replaced by Allen Johnson and Walt Maddox. The group dissolved around 1995. Bricker died in 1983 and Johnson in 1995, and Harp in 2013. New members were recruited. They were inducted into the Vocal Group Hall of Fame in 2002.

'Blue Moon' was their only #1 hit, but they did have several other songs in the lower echelons of the charts.

**The MAR-KEYS**

The Mar-Keys were formed in 1958 as a session backing band at Stax studios in Memphis, Tenn. There were 13 members including such names as Booker T, Donald 'Duck' Dunn, Steve Cropper and Isaac Hayes.

They made six albums and 13 singles in their own name although none made the top twenty in the charts.

## MARTHA and the VANDELLS

Martha and the Vandellas (or known as Martha Reeves and the Vandellas from 1967 to 1972) made their claim to fame with a series of hit singles on the Motown label. They started 'life' in 1960 with a group that consisted of Annette Beard, Rosalind Ashford and Gloria Williams. In 1962 Williams departed the group to be replaced by Martha Reeves who took over as lead singer. In the nine years from 1963 to 1972 the group had 26 hit records, ten of which made the Top 10 and two reached the top spot.

They are still performing today on a part-time basis, the present line-up being Martha, Lois and Delphine Reeves. Until recently Martha Reeves held a seat on Detroit City Council.
'Rolling Stone' magazine ranks them 96 out of 100 Greatest Artists of All Time.

Martha and the Vandellas biggest hits

*'Heatwave' (4); Quicksand' (8); 'Dancing In The Street' (2); 'Nowhere To Run' (8); 'Jimmy Mack' (10).*

## The PLATTERS

Whilst strictly not a rock 'n' roll group, The Platters were one of the most successful groups ever. They had a most distinctive sound and recorded mainly ballads and standards. Like most groups, the Platters went through several changes of personnel, but their most successful line-up comprised lead tenor Tony Williams, David Lynch, Paul Robi, Herb Reed and Zola Taylor. Between 1955 and 1967 they had 40 hit singles on the Hot 100 charts and four #1 hits.

The Platters started their career in Los Angeles with Ralph Bass as manager.
The original group which comprised Alex Hodge, Cornel Gunter, David Lynch, Joe Jefferson, Gaynel Hodge and Herb Reed recorded several sides on the Federal label, but met with little success [an early version on 'Only You' can still be found on Federal, and if in good condition could be worth a small fortune] until songwriter Buck Ram 'adjusted' the line-up bringing in the dulcet tones of Zola Taylor.
Not unlike The Drifters, The Platters were subjected to impersonation by other groups purporting to be The Platters and many legal battles followed.
Currently there are four acts using the name 'The Platters'. The only original Platter to appear on all Platters recordings was Herb Reed who died in June 2012 at the age of 83.

The Platters biggest hits
*'Only You' (5); 'The Great Pretender' (1); 'My Prayer' (1) 'You'll Never, Never Know' (11); 'Twilight Time' (1); 'Smoke Gets In Your Eyes' (1); H*
*'Harbour Lights' (8).*

## The RONETTES

The Ronettes were possibly the most popular girl group of the 60s. They came from Manhattan, New York City and consisted of lead singer Veronica Bennett, older sister Estelle and cousin Nadia Talley. They had eight songs on the Hot 100, five of which entered the top 40.

In 1963 the then unsuccessful trio moved from Colpix Records to be with producer

Phil Spector at Philles Records and the hits began to flow. After a tour of Europe opening for the Beatles, and another unsuccessful record release, the group decided to go their own way. Each member deciding that marriage was the way to go. Veronica actually marrying Phil Spector and becoming [according to her accounts] a 'prisoner' in a twenty-three roomed mansion, only being 'released' in 1969 to make another unsuccessful record for the A&M label.

The Ronnettes biggest hits
*'Be My Baby' (1); 'Baby I Love You' (24); 'Walking In The Rain' (23)*

# The SILHOUETTES

The Silhouettes were a doo-wop group from Philadelphia, Pennsylvania. They were formed in 1961. The group members were Rick Lewis (tenor) [2/9/33-22/3/2001]; Bill Horton (lead)[25/12/29-23/1/95]; Earl T Ball (baritone) [18/7/24-22/4/2001] and Ray Edwards (bass) [22/9/22-1997].

Their biggest hit 'Get A Job' was originally intended to be the 'B' side to 'I Am Lonely' In 1957 it reached #1 on both the Billboard Hot 100 and the R&B charts. The group never reached the charts again, but did work together until the 80s.

## The SUPREMES

Between 1957 and 1976 The Supremes have consisted of seven different line-ups. The original quartet consisted of Florence Ballard, Diana Ross, Mary Wilson and Betty McGlown, but were primarily known as The Primettes. In 1960 McGlown was replaced by Barbara Martin and the group was renamed The Supremes. In the years to 1967 they became a trio losing Martin, and in 1967

Florence Ballard left to be replaced by the aptly named Cindy Birdsong. Between 1970 and 1977 there were several personnel changes with Jean Terrell, Linda Laurence, Sherri Payne and Susayne Greene coming into the group. Only Mary Wilson has been a member from start to the last concert by the group in 1977.

The Supremes were formed in Detroit in 1957 and worked for the Holland-Dozier-Holland production and songwriting team at Motown Records.

They were inducted into the Rock ‘n’ Roll Hall of Fame in 1988 and have a Star on the Hollywood Walk of Fame (1994). They also entered The Vocal Group Hall of Fame in 1998.

The Supremes biggest hits

*'Where Did Our Love Go' (1); 'Baby Love' (1); 'Come See About Me' (1); 'Stop In The Name of Love' (1); 'Back In my Arms Again' (1); 'I Hear A Symphony' (1) 'You Can't Hurry Love' (1); 'You Keep me Hanging On'' (1); 'Love Is Here' (1); 'The Happening' (1); 'Love Child' (1); Someday We'll Be Together' (1).*

## MAURICE WILLIAMS and the ZODIACS

Maurice Williams and the Zodiacs were one of the top doo-wop groups of the mid 50s and early 60s. The group had several names (Royal Charms, Gladiolas, Excellos) before deciding to stick with the Zodiacs in 1959.
Williams (b 26/4/38) came from Lancaster, South Carolina.
The group consisted of Williams (lead), Henry Gatson, Wiley Bennet, Charles Thomas, Little Willie Morrow and Albert Hill. Their recording of 'Stay' is reckoned

to be the shortest song ever to reach #1 on the hot 100 chart. They released several other good records but never made the higher echelons of the charts again, although a 1965 recording of 'May I' sold over a million copies but over a long period of time.

Maurice Williams is still active in the music industry today mainly in his town of Charlotte, North Carolina.

## The Instrumental Groups

## Bill BLACK'S COMBO
## (see Scotty Moore and Bill Black)

## B. BUMBLE and the STINGERS

B.Bumble and the Stingers were not really a Rock 'n' Roll band in the normal sense. They were just a bunch of session musicians that worked for Rendezvous Records in Los Angeles. Earl Palmer, Plas Johnson and Rene Hall, all from Louisiana worked for Rendezvous as part of the 'house' band that backed the majority of artists that recorded at Rendezvous. In early 1960 they were a little short of cash and decided to make a record and see if it sold. They chose the Glenn Miller tune 'In The Mood' and used the name 'The Ernie Fields Orchestra'. The record reached No.4 on the U.S. Hit Parade.

## Booker T and the MG's

Booker T Jones and the MG's were a 60's instrumental/funk band. (MGs stood for Memphis Group). They consisted of Booker T Jones (organ, piano); Steve Cropper (guitar); Lewis Steinberg (bass) and Al Jackson Jnr (drums). They made up the majority of the house band at Stax Records and played on hundreds of recordings by Wilson Pickett, Sam and Dave, Carla and Rufus Thomas. In 1965 Steinberg was replaced by Donald 'Duck' Dunn.

They were inducted into the Rock 'n' Roll Hall of Fame in 1992 and the Musicians Hall of Fame in 2008.

Booker T and the MG's biggest hits

*'Green Onions' (3)[#1 US R&B]; 'Hang 'Em High' (9); 'Time Is Tight' (6)*

## The CHAMPS

The Champs were one of the original American Rock 'n' Roll instrumental bands. Their music had a Latin influence hence the titles of some of the tunes, 'Tequila', 'Chariot Rock' and 'El Rancho Rock'.

Originally formed by Executives at Challenge Records in Santa Paula, California the original members were Dave (Dupree) Burgess (Guitar), Chuck Rio (Sax), Dale Norris (Guitar & keyboards), Bobby Morris (Bass) and

Gene Alden (Drums), Paul Senz (Guitar), Benjamin Van Norman (Bass), Glen Campbell, Seals and Crofts also played on some sessions.
In their big hit 'Tequila' the shout of 'Tequila' is credited to Chuck Rio but it is actually Danny Flores who says the words, this is because Rio was contracted to a different record company at the time and so could not be named.
The Champs biggest hits

*'Tequila' (1); 'Chariot Rock' (59); 'El Rancho Rock' (30); 'Too Much Tequila' (30); 'Limbo Rock' (40).*

## CORNBREAD and JERRY

Cornbread and Jerry were an instrumental duo better known as Bill Justis and Jerry Smith. Justis worked at Sun Records. Little is documented about Smith although he did have minor hits with a group called The Dixiebells in 1963. The songs were '(Down at) Papa Joe's' and 'Southtown USA'.

The hit for the duo was Loco Moto/ Lil' Ole Me' in 1961.

## Duane EDDY and the REBELS

Duane Eddy was born April 26th 1938 in the town of Corning, New York and began playing guitar at the tender age of five. When he was 16 he obtained a 'Chet Atkins' model by Gretsch. Eddy devised a method for playing the lead parts of a tune on the bass strings thereby producing a low, twangy sound. He journeyed to Phoenix, Arizona to team up with producer Lee Hazelwood. In order to record a tune called 'Movin' 'n' Groovin' they needed an echo chamber. The studio didn't have one so Hazelwood bought a 2,000 gallon water tank, and used that to accentuate the 'twangy' sound. The record made No. 72 on the charts. The follow-up, ‘Rebel Rouser’ with squawking sax by Steve Douglas made the Top 10. Eddy’s band The Rebel Rouser’s had several members including brothers Al and Corky Casey and Jim Horn.

Eddy also appeared in several films including ‘A Thunder of Drums’ and the t.v. series ‘Have Gun, Will Travel’. He also produced numerous albums including those for Phil Everly and Waylon Jennings. In 1994 he was inducted into the Rock ‘n’ Roll Hall of Fame and was presented with ‘Guitar Player’ Magazine ‘Legend Award’.

Duane Eddy’s biggest hits

*‘Movin’ and Groovin’ (72); ‘Rebel Rouser’ (6); ‘ Ramrod’ (27); ‘Cannonball’ (15); ‘Peter Gunn’ (6); ‘Forty Miles Of Bad Road’ (9); ‘Because They’re Young’ (4)*

## JOHNNY and the HURRICANES

Johnny & The Hurricanes Prior To The Beatles' Impact

Johnny and the Hurricanes started life as The Orbits in Toledo, Ohio in 1957.
The leader was saxophonist Johnny Paris (died 1/5/2006). Their first release 'Crossfire' made No. 23 in the charts in 1959. Their follow-up 'Red River Rock' (an upbeat version of Red River Valley) became a top 10 hit both in the U.S and the U.K. and sold over 1 million copies. At that time the band consisted of Paris, Paul Tesluk (organ). Dave Yorko (guitar), Lionel 'Butch' Matiss (bass) and Bill 'Little Bo' Savich on drums'

Most of their recordings were up tempo versions of old tunes. 'Blue Tailed Fly' became 'Beatnik Fly' and the army 'Wake Up' call became 'Revellie Rock' and dozens more. Many entered the charts. Paris continued to front the band until 2005. He claimed more than 300 different musicians had played in his band in its 50 year existence. Johnny Paris died in hospital in Ann Arbor, Michigan after contacting infections after an operation.

Johnny and the Hurricanes biggest hits

*'Crossfire'; 'Red River Rock'; 'Reveille Rock'; 'Beatnick Fly'; 'Ja Da';*
*'Buckeye'; 'Rocking Goose'.*

## The KINGSMEN

The Kingsmen were a five-piece instrumental band from Portland, Oregon. Their best known hit record was 'Louie Louie' which was a #2 hit in 1963.
The original members were Don Gallucci, Joe Ely, Lynn Easton, Mike Mitchell and Bob Nordby. Since their formation they have had in the region of twenty different band members. In 1958 there was another group operating with the same name, they were ex-members of Bill Haley's Comets.

**The PHILLIP UPCHURCH COMBO**

Phillip Upchurch (b 19/7/41) came from Chicago, Illinois. He was a fine musician and an excellent guitarist and bassist. His band, the Phil Upchurch Combo had a million selling hit with 'You Can't Sit Down Pts I & II' in 1961. He has worked with several larger bands including Quincy Jones, Ramsey Lewis and George Benson's band.

**The RAMRODS**

The Ramrods were an instrumental group from Connecticut. They were active from the late 50s to mid 60s. In 1961 they had a #1 hit with '(Ghost) Riders In The Sky'. The band consisted of Claire Lane (drums), her brother Rich (sax), Vinny Lee (lead guitar), and Gene Moore (rhythm guitar).

The follow up record, 'Loch Lomond Rock' which featured a bagpipe solo was not successful, neither were any subsequent recordings. The group became changed its name to the Russ Cook Combo before disbanding in the early 1970s.

## The VENTURES

Classic lineup of the Ventures

The Ventures are a Rock ‘n’ Roll instrumental group that was ‘born’ in Tacoma, Washington. The group was formed by Bob Bogle and Don Wilson, and in its time has had various incarnations. The Ventures have sold over 100 million records and is the best selling instrumental group of all time. They started out in 1958, and still record and tour to this day, where they are still extremely popular, particularly in Japan. The photograph shows the original quartet of Don Wilson, Mel Taylor, Nokie

Edwards and Bob Bogle. (Bogle and Taylor are now deceased).
Other members of the group over the years include Bob Spalding, Leon Taylor, Howie Johnson (dec), John Durrill and Dave Carr (dec). There are several others who found short term employment with the band.
They were inducted into The Rock 'n' Roll Hall of Fame in 2008.

The Ventures biggest hits

*'Walk Don't Run' (2); 'Perfidia' (15);*

**The WRECKING CREW**

The Wrecking crew was a name invented by drummer Hal Blaine for a group of session musicians that played anonymously on hundreds of records in Los Angeles in the 60s. The played on almost every genre of music and backed such acts as The Monkees, Bing Crosby, Nancy Sinatra, Bobby Vee. The Mamas and Papas, The Beach Boys, Simon and Garfunkel and Nat 'King' Cole.

Some of the members included – Guitars Glen Campbell, Al Casey and James Burton. Saxes – Jim Horn, Nino Tempo. Keyboards – Leon Russell, Larry Knetchel. Drums – Hal Blaine, Earl Palmer. Bass – Carol Kaye.

Harmonica – Tommy Morgan. Arranger – Jack Nitzsche. Backing vocals were by The Ron Hicklin singers.

They were inducted into the Musicians Hall of Fame in 2007

## The One-Hit Wonders

The term 'one – hit wonders' can seem to be a derogatory remark. Of course it implies the artist(s) had just one hit record. This may not be the case. A hit record usually refers to an entry into the Billboard (or other Sponsor) Top 100 record sales, but some record companies, particularly in the early days of rock 'n' roll did not intend some of their releases to be national hit records. Sun Records, Chess, Big Top, Stax and many others did not have the finances or personnel to promote records that would receive national radio airplay, and were only intended for local or regional sales. So whilst the following artists did have at least one national hit record, they probably had several regional or local hits. There are many cases where records that 'missed' could have been 'hits' if the chance had been taken on the promotion of the record.

## Sonny ANDERSON

Walter 'Sonny 'Anderson (14/8/23 – 3/8/2010) had one great hit record in 1959 called 'Yes I'm Gonna Love You / Lonely, Lonely Train'. Both songs were written by Johnny and Dorsey Burnette, and were recorded on the Imperial label. Anderson became Director of Talent and Casting for Disneyland, Disney World and Epcot.. He died in Orange, California in August 2010

# The BIG BOPPER (J.P.RICHARDSON)

'The Big Bopper's real name was Jiles Perry Richardson. He was born in Sabine Pass, Texas on October 24th 1930, and he died along with Buddy Holly, Richie Valens and Roger Peterson at Clear Lake, Iowa on February 3rd 1959.
Primarily a disc jockey and song writer (Richardson wrote 'White Lighnin' for George Jones and 'Running Bear', the Johnny Preston hit). Richardson joined

'The Winter Dance Party' tour as part MC, part comedian and part singer (to promote his record 'Chantilly Lace').
J.P. Richardson is a member of the Rockabilly Hall of Fame.

The Big Bopper's biggest hits

*'Chantilly Lace' (6).*

## The FENDERMEN

The story of **the Fendermen** is one of those too good to be true stories of the business, but true nonetheless it's one of two guitarists, Jim Sundquist and Phil Humphries, born on the same day and month in two different towns who didn't meet until they were teenagers. Mutually infused with the rock 'n' roll bug, they started playing as a duo, naming themselves after the Fender guitars both of them plugged into a single amplifier. One of the songs that always received the biggest response when the duo played live the local bars was a hopped up, rockabilly rendition of Jimmie Rodgers' "Mule Skinner Blues," complete with goofball yodels and hot guitar licks. A local entrepreneur convinced the boys to record it sans drummer or bassist and had it pressed up on the local Cuca label in Wisconsin, then it was re-recorded for a Minnesota label, Soma. Inexplicably, the record caught on nationally, zooming up to the Top Ten in 1960. Humphries and Sundquist grabbed a local drummer and hit the road, touring behind their massive hit and eventually recording an entire album before the duo went their separate ways two years later. A one hit wonder group, the Fendermen nonetheless made full blooded, energetic rock 'n' roll and provided one of the last gasps of rockabilly in a teen idol infested era.

The Fendermen's biggest hits

*'Mule Skinner Blues' (5).*

## Eddie FONTAINE

Eddie Fontaine was born Edward Reardon in 1927 in Massachusetts. He was primarily an actor appearing in 'The Gallant Men', '77, Sunset Strip', 'Quincy', 'Ironside', 'Starskey and Hutch', 'The Rockford Files', and many other tv series. He also had a part in the Rock 'n' Roll film 'The Girl Can't Help It' with Jayne Mansfield in which he also sang.

In 1958 his single 'Nothin' Shakin' (But the Leaves on the Trees) was his only chart entry. It was a highly thought of rocker, so much so that The Beatles did a cover version some time later.
Fontaine died from cancer in April 1992.

Eddy Fontaine's biggest hits

*'Nothin' Shakin' {No chart position recorded}*

**Frankie FORD**

Frankie Ford was born 4/8/1939 as Francis Guzzo in the small town of Gretna, Louisiana. He has a Gold Record for his mega hit 'Sea-Cruise' which made the Top 20. He still tours for upwards of 200 days a year.

Frankie Ford's biggest hits

*'Sea Cruise'*

## Bill JUSTIS

William Everett 'Bill' Justis (14/10/26 – 15/7/82) was born in Birmingham, Alabama but spent the majority of his life in Memphis, Tennessee.

He was employed by Sam Phillips at Sun Records mainly as a composer, and arranger, but occasionally recorded with the house musicians. His recording of the tune 'Raunchy' climbed to No.2 on the Hot 100 charts in 1957. His only other release of note was 'College Man' which made it to No.42.

He arranged and recorded music for Johnny Cash, Jerry Lee Lewis, Charlie Rich, Roy Orbison and several other Sun

artists. Bill Justis also composed music for films including 'Smokey and the Bandit and 'Hooper.
He died from cancer in Nashville in 1982.

Bill Justis's biggest hits

'Raunchy' (2).

**Buddy KNOX**

Buddy Wayne Knox was born 20/7/33 and died on 14/2/99. His one big chart hit was 'Party Doll' which climbed to No.2 on the U.S. charts and No.29 in the UK. After performing on the same radio show as Roy Orbison he was advised to go to Clovis, New Mexico to audition for Norman Petty (the man who recorded Buddy Holly and the Crickets). Petty cut three records with Knox which were released on the Roulette label. The most notable was 'Party Doll' which went to No.2 [No.1 on the Cash Box charts].
Knox had two more minor hits but never managed to repeat the success of 'Party Doll'. He was elected to the Rockabilly Hall of Fame.

Buddy Knox's biggest hits

*'Party Doll' (2)*

## Jody REYNOLDS

Jody Reynolds (born Ralph Joseph Reynolds on 3/12/32, Denver, Colorado, died 7/11/2008 in Palm Desert, California, aged 75) was an American singer and guitarist. His biggest hit single was "Endless Sleep", which reached #5 in the U.S. Billboard Hot 100 chart on July 7, 1958. The song was later one of Hank Williams Jr.'s first singles, hitting #46 on the country charts in 1964.

Reynolds' follow-up song, "Fire of Love", managed only #66 on the charts in August 1958; it was Reynolds' last charting hit.

In 1999, a Golden Palm Star on the Palm Springs, California, Walk of Stars was dedicated to him.

Reynolds grew up in Shady Grove, Oklahoma. He died on November 7, 2008 of liver cancer at 75.

**Richie VALENS**

Born Richard Valenzuela on 13/5/41 in the San Fernando valley near to Los Angeles. He was keen on music from the tender age of five and with some coaching from his father became fairly proficient on the guitar, drums and trumpet. His early lessons on the guitar were easy as the old instrument only had two strings! At 16 he joined a band called 'The Silhouettes' to play at local parties and social events.

Valens made a few records for local sales, and was contracted to play support for Chuck Berry, Duane Eddy and Jackie Wilson on Dick Clarke's 'American Bandstand' tv. programme. As a result of his popularity on this show he was chosen to support Buddy Holly and the Crickets on the 'Winter Dance Party', a tour of towns in the mid-west states. On February 3rd 1959 at Clear Lake, Iowa, Holly hired an aeroplane to take him, Waylon Jennings and Tommy Allsup to Fargo, North Dakota. Jennings and Allsup were persuaded to swap with J.P.Richardson and Valens. In the early hours of February 2rd 1959 the 'plane crashed into a farmers field killing all three singers and pilot Roger Peterson instantly. It became known as 'The Day The Music Died' and is immortalized in song by Don McLean's 'American Pie'.

Richie Valens biggest hits

*'Donna' (2); 'La Bamba' (22).*

## Thomas WAYNE

Thomas Wayne Perkins was born on 22nd July 1940, in Battsville, Mississippi, USA. He died in a car crash on 15th August 1971, Tennessee, USA. Wayne was a classic one-hit artist, the younger brother of Luther Perkins, the guitarist who developed and first played the trademark two-string guitar style behind Johnny Cash. Wayne attended Humes High School in Memphis, where a few years earlier the young Elvis Presley had come and gone with little fanfare. There Wayne formed a group called the De-Lons, which was recorded by Scotty Moore, guitarist for Presley, for the Fernwood Records label, which Moore co-owned. That first single did nothing, but Wayne's second single for Fernwood, a weepy ballad titled 'Tragedy', made it to number 5 in the US national chart. The song had renewed life in 1961 as a hit for the Fleetwoods. Wayne recorded for other labels but was unable to follow that hit, although Presley recorded a song he had written, 'The Girl Next Door Went A Walking', in 1960. Wayne eventually moved into production work, but his life was tragically cut short when he was killed in a car collision near Memphis in 1971.

Thomas Wayne's biggest hits

*'Tragedy' (5).*

## Link WRAY

Frederick Lincoln 'Link' Wray was one of the first guitarists to use heavy distortion on his recordings. His hit recoding was called 'Rumble' which he recorded with his band the Ray Men (some labels say Wray Men). Rolling stone placed Wray at No.45 in their 100 greatest guitarists of all time. Wray was born in Dunn, North Carolina on 2/5/29 and passed away on 5/11/2005. Wray served with the Army in Korea where he contracted tuberculosis which necessitated the removal of a lung and twelve months in hospital. In the late 1980s Wray moved to Denmark where he married Olive, a student at the University. He died of heart failure at his home in Copenhagen in 2005.

Link Wray's biggest hits

*'Rumble' (16)*

## Other Rock'n' Roll Personalities

**Paul ANKA**

Paul Anka was born on July 30th 1941 in Ottawa, Canada. In 1957 his first record 'Diana' went to No.1 on both the U.S. and the Canadian charts.
Not really a Rock 'n' Roller, Anka was more of a Pop singer, later branching out into Jazz. Up to 2011 he had made 27 good selling albums and was the subject of a Canadian documentary called 'Lonely Boy'. He had a No.1 hit record of the same name. He also composed the Buddy Holly hit song 'It Doesn't Matter Anymore'.

Paul Anka's biggest hits

*'Diana' (1); 'You Are My Destiny' (7); 'Lonely Boy' (1); 'Put You're Head On My Shoulder' (2); 'Puppy Love' (2).*

**Frankie AVALON**

Frankie Avalon was born September 18, 1940. His record 'Venus' stayed at No.1 on the Hot 100 for 5 weeks, and 'Why' was also a No.1 hit record. Avalon also starred alongside Annette Funicello in 37 'beach' type comedy films.

Frankie Avalon's biggest hits

*'Venus' (1); 'Why' (1)*

## Bill BLACK and Scotty MOORE

### Scotty MOORE

Winfield Scott Moore was born 27/12/31. He is best known for being Elvis Presley's guitarist from the early Sun Records days until Presley departed for RCA. Moore is ranked 44th in the Rolling Stone magazine list of the 100 greatest guitarists of all time. He was inducted into The Rock 'n' Roll Hall of Fame (sidemen) in 2000.

## Bill BLACK

Black plays the fool with Elvis & Scotty

William Patton 'Bill' Black (17/9/26 – 21/10/65) was the double-bass player for Elvis Presley with his friend Scotty Moore. Not only a superb bass player Black was a top line comedian, often dressing up as a hillbilly with straw hat and baggy pants and chequered shirt to entertain. He was born in Memphis and it's no surprise that he was part of a band that featured Johnny and Dorsey Burnette, Paul Burlison and Scotty Moore.

Bill Black had several successful hit records when he formed his own band Bill

Black's Combo in 1959. After a long illness he died of a brain tumour in 1965

Bill Black's Combo biggest hits

*'White Silver Sands ' (9); 'SmokiePart II' (17); 'Don't Be Cruel' (11)*

## Johnny CASH and the TENNESSEE TWO (LATER THREE)

As in the case of Ray Charles, Johnny Cash (born J.R. Cash – he was never christened Johnny as his parents couldn't agree on names for him) can't really be classed as a Rock 'n' Roller, but was so much a part of that culture in the 50s and 60s I feel it would be wrong to leave him out. He was one quarter of the Sun Records 'Million Dollar Quartet' along

with Elvis Presley, Carl Perkins and Jerry Lee Lewis.
Cash was born 26/2/32 in Kingsland, Arkansas, but grew up in nearby Dyess Colony. His father had been given some government land to grow cotton.
In 1951 Cash enlisted in the U.S. Air Force and was trained as a Morse Code Intercept Operator at Lansberg, Germany. It was during his time there that he decided that when his service time was up he would become a Country singer.
Cash was honourably discharged in 1954, and he and his wife Vivien Liberto moved to Memphis. He formed a friendship with Luther Perkins, a guitar picker and Marshall Grant who played bass. They plucked up the courage to ask Sam Phillips at Sun Records for an audition. Eventually they won Phillips over and their first single 'Cry, Cry, Cry/ Hey Porter was released on June 21st 1955. In 1960 Cash recruited W.S. 'Flook' Holland as a drummer to 'fill the sound out a bit', and the band's name was changed from 'The Tennessee Two' to (surprisingly) The Tennessee Three.

Cash stayed at Sun until 'Wide Open Road'/'Balthazar' was released on May 1st 1964 then departed for Columbia Records with whom he stayed for 30 years. He joined Rick Rubin's 'American' label in 1993 where he recorded six acclaimed albums until his death from diabetic complications on September 12th 2003.

Johnny Cash's biggest hits (Sun Records only)

*'Cry, Cry, Cry (14); 'So Doggone Lonesome' (4); 'I Walk The Line' (1); 'There You Go' (1); 'Home of the Blues' (3); 'Ballad of a Teenage Queen (1); Guess Things Happen That Way' (1); 'Ways of a Woman In Love' (1); 'Folsom Prison Blues' (4); 'Big River' (4);*

## Ray CHARLES

Born Ray Charles Robinson on 23/9/30 in Albany, Georgia. Charles, (he dropped the Robinson surname) is not strictly a Rock 'n' roller, he is an R&B and Blues singer/pianist, but he did have a great influence on many R 'n' R artists. Frank Sinatra once called Charles "The only true genius in show business". Rolling Stone ranked Charles No.10 on their list of 'The Greatest Artists of All Time'.

Ray Charles recording career began in 1952 with Atlantic Records (The

Midnight Hour/Roll With My Baby). Charles had several hits on the label, including some instrumental Jazz albums, Blues, Gospel and R 'n' R. He had formed his own band and backing group which he called 'The Raelettes'. He reached his peak whilst at Atlantic with 'What'd I Say' although the Jerry Lee Lewis version outsold him.

Ray Charles' biggest hits

*'Mess Around' (3); 'It Shouldn't be Me' (5); 'I Got A Woman' (1); 'Come Back Baby' (4); 'A Fool For You' (1); 'Mary Ann' (1); 'Drown In My Own Tears' (1); all US R&B charts. 'What'd I Say (6 Top 100, 1 R&B); all on Atlantic label. 'Georgia On My Mind' (1); 'Hit The Road Jack' (1); 'I Can't Stop Loving You' (1) on ABC label. 'Seven Spanish Angels' [with Willie Nelson] 1.*

## Chubby CHECKER

Chubby Checker (real name Ernest Evans) was born 3/10/41 in Spring Gulley, North Carolina. He is most famous for his 'dance craze' songs particularly 'The Twist'. Checker is also a fine impressionist and entertains his audiences with impersonations of Fats Domino, Jerry Lee Lewis, Rick Nelson, Frankie Avalon and Elvis Presley. Billboard magazine named 'The Twist' as the biggest hit record of all time. Checker records Public Service Announcements (PSAs) for the US Government, the occasional ‘Psychedelic Album, and appears in various US sitcoms.

Chubby Checker’s biggest hits

*‘The Twist’ (1); ‘The Huckelbuck’ (14); ‘Pony Time’ (1); ‘Let’s Twist Again’ (8); Limbo Rock (2);*

**Eugene CHURCH**

Eugene Church (22/1/38 – 3/4/93) was raised in St Louis, Missouri. He released four singles 'Pretty Girls Everywhere' #6, 'Miami' #14, made the charts but 'Good News' and 'Mind Your Own Business' failed to score. Church left the popular music field to pursue Gospel and Secular music.

He died from cancer at the age of 55.

## Sam COOKE

Samuel Cooke (22/1/31 – 11/12/64). Cooke was given the soubriquet the 'King of Soul', and had 30 Top 40 hits between 1957 and 1964.

He was fatally shot by the manager of the Hacienda Motel on the 11th December 1964. The court brought a verdict of 'Justifiable Homicide' but the circumstances of what happened have been the subject of numerous investigations.

In 1986 Cooke was inducted as charter member of the Rock 'n' Roll Hall of Fame In 2008 he was voted as 4th Greatest Singer of All Time by Rolling Stone magazine.

Sam Cooke's biggest hits

*'You Send Me' (1); 'Chain Gang' (2); 'Twisting The Night Away' (9);*
*'Another Saturday Night' (10); 'Shake' (7).*

## Other Personalities involved in or affected by Rock 'N' Roll

**AMERICAN BANDSTAND**

American Bandstand was one of, if not the, most popular music performance shows on American television. It ran from 1952 to 1989 but in its heydays (1952 to 1956) it was hosted by legendary dj Dick Clark, who also produced the show. Most of the big names appeared on the show including Jerry Lee Lewis, Freddy Cannon, who appeared on the show 110 times, and Donna Summer. The artists lip-synced their songs, they never performed live.

Clark, (Richard Wagstaff Clarke) was born 30/11/29 and died 18/4/2012 after suffering a heart attack during surgery for an enlarged prostate gland.

**The ARCHIES**

The Archies were a fictional group used in the animated tv series 'The Archie Show'. They were popular from 1968 to 1978. They had a #1 hit with 'Sugar Sugar' in 1969. The vocals on the song were by Ron Dante. The follow-up song 'Jingle Jangle' made #40. Other releases were less successful.

**Mae Boren AXTON**
Composer of the Elvis Presley hit 'Heartbreak Hotel'.

**Hank BALLARD AND THE MIDNIGHTERS**
Born John Henry Kendricks in Detroit, Michigan. Ballard formed the group Hank Ballard and the Midnighters. They had a few hits. Ballard composed 'The Twist' which was a No.1 hit for Chubby Checker.

**BIHARI BROTHERS**
Four brothers of Hungarian descent, Lester, Julius, Saul and Joseph. Formed record companies in Los Angeles and Memphis (Meteor Records) where they had an agreement with Sam Phillips to market recordings made by Phillips before Sun Records was up and running.

**Otis BLACKWELL**
Otis Blackwell (16/2/31 – 6/5/2002) was one of Rock 'n' Roll's most influential songwriters. His compositions include

'Fever' a hit for Peggy Lee, 'Great Balls of Fire' and 'Breathless' for Jerry Lee Lewis, and 'Don't be Cruel', 'All Shook Up', and 'Return To Sender' for Elvis Presley. He received numerous awards. He died of a heart attack in Nashville in 2002.

**Gary U.S. BONDS**

Real name Gary Levone Anderson. He was born 6/6/39 in Jacksonville, Florida. His first three releases were under the name 'U.S. Bonds', but this apparently caused some confusion, some thinking it was an advertisement; and others a group not a solo artist. After the three releases he became Gary U.S. Bonds. His first hit was 'New Orleans' which topped out at #6, then his only #1 'Quarter To Three', He had several other chart hits including 'School Is Out', 'School Is In' and a couple of Twist hits. He made a comeback in 2004 and had a big selling album called 'Back in 20'.

**Jackie BRENTSON**

A member of Ike Turner's band and vocalist on 'Rocket 88', said to be the first ever Rock 'n' Roll record

**Felice & Boudleoux BRYANT**

Joint composers of many country and pop hits including 'Bye Bye Love' and 'All I have To Do Is Dream' for the Everly Brothers, 'Blue Boy (Jim Reeves) and 'Raining In My Heart' by Buddy Holly.

**Dave BARTHOLOMEW**

Bandleader, composer and arranger. Bartholomew operated mainly in the New Orleans area. He had a long and successful partnership with Antoine 'Fats' Domino. He was indicted into the Rock 'n' Roll Hall of Fame in 1991.

**Brook BENTON**

Brook Benton, real name Benjamin Franklin Peay (19/9/31 – 9/4/1987) was one of the most popular singers of rock 'n' roll, rhythm and blues and pop music. His biggest hits were 'It's Just A Matter of

Time' (#3), 'Endlessly' (#12), 'The Boll Weevil Song' (#2), and the Tony Joe White composition 'Rainy Night In Georgia' (#4).
He also had two top ten hits with Dinah Washington – 'Baby, You Got What It Takes' (#5) and 'A Rockin' Good Way' (#7). Benton died from pneumonia at the age of 56.

**Paul BURLISON**
Paul Burlison (4/2/29 – 27/9/2003) was a founder member of the Rock 'n' Roll Trio with Johnny and Dorsey Burnette. It was his interest in boxing that got him into contact with the Burnette brothers, and it transpired that they all had an interest in music, hence the 'Rock 'n' Roll Trio' was formed. The trio moved to California, but had little success with recordings until Johnny and Dorsey persued solo careers which did bring hit records for both, whilst Burlison returned home to start his own electrical contracting company. He returned to music in the mid 80s where he became a member of a Rock 'n' Roll Trio

tribute band. He died from colon cancer in September 2003.

**James BURTON**

James Burton was born 21/8/39 in Dubberly, Louisiana. He earned the nickname 'Master of the Telecaster' due his expertise with the model of Fender guitar he uses. He has provided guitar backing for the likes of Bob Luman, Elvis Presley, Johnny Cash, John Denver, EmmyLou Harris, Merle Haggard, Jerry Lee Lewis, Roy Orbison and many others. He has been inducted into the 'Rock 'n' Roll Hall of Fame', the 'Rockabilly Hall Of fame' and the Musicians Hall of Fame.

**'Ace' CANNON**

Texas born saxophone player noted for his 'riffs' in the Coasters 'Yakety Yak' and 'Charlie Brown'.

**Sanford CLARK**

Born Tulsa, Oklahoma 24/10/35 had crossover hits with 'Son of a Gun' and

'The Fool' written by Lee Hazelwood for Jamie Records

**Jack CLEMENT**

5/4/31 to 8/8/2013. Producer for Sam Phillips at Sun Records. His claim to fame is probably the fact that he was the first person to record Jerry Lee Lewis at a time when his boss Sam Phillips was away from Sun Records. He also composed several hits for Johnny Cash ('Ways of a Woman In Love'; 'Guess Things Happen That Way'). He was inducted into the Country Music Hall of Fame on 10/4/13. He died from liver cancer on 8/8/13.

**Floyd CRAMER**

Floyd Cramer (27/10/33 – 31/12/97) was one of the 'Nashville Sound' musicians. Cramer was a fine pianist who invented the 'slip note' method of sliding an out of key note into the correct note. He was born in Louisiana and moved to Nashville in 1955. Cramer joined Chet Atkins 'Nashville Sound' as a session pianist and played on thousands of recordings by the likes of Elvis Presley, Don Gibson, Jim

Reeves, Roy Orbison and The Everly Brothers. He made several albums in his own rite and had big hits with the singles 'On The Rebound' and 'Last Date'.
He died from lung cancer at the age of 64.

**Arthur 'Big Boy' CRUDUP**
Singer and writer of Elvis Presley's first hit 'That's All Right Mama.
Crudup (24/8/05 – 28/3/74) came from Forest, Mississippi. He sang and played gospel and blues music in and around Clarkesville, Miss. He eventually got a record contract with RCA Victor in 1940. Due to an argument over Royalties, Crudup stopped recording in the 50s and returned to his former 'profession' of bootlegging and farm work. Crudup died of a heart attack in Northampton, Virginia in 1974.

**King CURTIS**
Born Curtis Ousley on 7/2/34 Ousley was a virtuoso saxophonist who performed under the name King Curtis. It is his sax that can be heard on great recordings by

The Coasters, Buddy Holly and Aretha Franklin.
Curtis was stabbed to death when he challenged two drug dealers near to his apartment on 13/8/71. Franklin, Stevie Wonder and Brook Benton sang at his funeral. He was inducted into the Rock 'n' Roll Hall of Fame in 2000.

**Sonny CURTIS (see also The Crickets)**
Born 9/5/37 in Meadow, Texas. Curtis (the name Sonny is his real name not a nickname) He became a member of The Crickets from 1959 after the death of Buddy Holly. He has composed several big selling songs like 'I Fought The Law' and 'Love You More Than I Can Say'. Sonny Curtis is a member of the Musicians Hall of Fame (2007) and the Rock 'n' Roll Hall of Fame (2012).

**Bobby DAY**
Born Robert James Byrd 1/7/30 in Fort Worth, Texas. Using the name Bobby Day he recorded two songs – 'Over and Over' and 'Little Bitty Pretty One' that

were good, but covered by Thurston Harris and Clyde McPhatter, and did better for them than for Day, but his 1958 recording 'Rockin' Robin' went to No.2 on the Hot 100. Day died of cancer in 1990.

**Tommy EDWARDS**

Tommy Edwards (17/2/22 – 22/10/69) was born in Richmond, Virginia. His big hit was 'It's All In the Game', a multi million seller. Nothing he did since came close to this record. The gold disc was presented to him in November 1958. Edwards died from an aneurism in 1969.

**Paul EVANS**

Paul Evans was born 5/3/38 in Queens, New York and was at his most popular in the 50s and 60s. His biggest successes were 'Seven Little Girls', 'Midnight Special', and 'Happy-Go-Lucky Me'. He also composed several songs recorded by the likes of Elvis Presley, Jimmy Dean and Pat Boone.

**FABIAN**

Fabiano Forte was born on 6/2/43 in Philadelphia. His biggest hits were 'I'm A Man' and 'Turn Me Loose' both written by Doc Pomus and Mort Shuman. His singing career ended abruptly when, along with the payola scandal, it was revealed that Fabian's voice on the records had been electronically 'doctored'. He did return to singing in the 70s and 80s, but did not have anything like the success he had in the late 50s.

**Charlie FEATHERS**

Charles Arthur Feathers was born 12/6/32 in Holly Springs, Mississippi. He started his musical career as a sideman playing various instruments at Sun Studios. He also cut a few records of his own on the Flip label (a subsidiary of Sun). He had a string of popular Rockabilly/Country hits with 'Peeping Eyes'; 'Defrost Your Heart'; 'Bottle to the Baby' and a few others on the Sun and Meteor labels. He made numerous albums both solo and Rockabilly compilations. Charlie Feathers died from a stroke on 29/8/98

**Alan FREED**

Albert 'Alan' Freed was born 15/12/21 in Pennsylvania. He became known as the 'Father of Rock 'n' Roll'. He was probably the most famous DJ ever, and used the soubriquet 'Moondog'. He prided himself on playing records by black artists rather than cover versions by white singers, but his career was destroyed by the Payola scandal. Freed not only worked as a radio DJ but also organized concerts and top-name countrywide tours. His radio programme 'Disc Jockey Jamboree' was broadcast to Britain via Radio Luxembourg.

Freed was arrested and charged with 'Inciting a riot' when he told an audience at one of his shows 'The Police don't want you to have fun'.

Freed's career ended when it was proven that he had taken Payola (money from record companies to play certain records). He was also accused of taking royalties from records of which he had no right, by putting his name on the label as co-composer – particularly in the case of Chuck Berry.

Alan Freed died aged 43 at Palm Springs from cirrhosis.

**Berry GORDY**

Berry Gordy was born in Detroit, Michigan on 28/11/29. He is the founder of the Motown record label. In his early years he worked as a songwriter penning hits such as 'Lonely Teardrops' and 'Reet Petite' for Jackie Wilson, and 'All I Could Do Was Cry' for Etta James. In 1957 Gordy invested the money he'd made from songwriting to form Motown (short for Motor town) and has since produced hit records for almost anyone who is anyone.

The list is almost endless but includes Mary Wells, Marv Johnson, Stevie Wonder, Marvin Gaye, The Four Tops, Martha and the Vandellas, The Supremes, Gladys Knight and the Pips and the Jackson 5. Berry Gordy was inducted into the Rock 'n' Roll Hall of Fame in 1988.

**Wynonie HARRIS**

One of the earliest Rock 'n' Rollers, Wynonie Harris was born 24/8/15 in

Omaha, Nebraska. He had 15 top 10 hits between 1946 and 1952.
His biggest hits were on the King label, a cover version of ‘Good Rockin’ Tonight’ and ‘All She Wants To Do Is Rock’. Harris recorded for several labels between 1954 and 1964. His final recordings were for the Chess label before his death from throat cancer on 14th June 1969.

**Ronnie HAWKINS**
Ronnie Hawkins (b 10/1/35) is an award winning rockabilly artist. He is sometimes known as ‘Rompin’ Ronnie’, ‘Mr Dynamo’ or simply ‘The Hawk. Hawkins has made more than 25 albums and has hits with songs such as Chuck Berry’s ‘Thirty Days’ which he renamed ‘Forty Days’, ‘Hey, Bo Diddley’ and ‘Suzie Q’. In recent years Hawkins has recovered from pancreatic cancer, a fact that he puts down to all manner of things including faith healers, psychics and herbal medicines.

**Lee HAZELWOOD**

Barton Lee Hazelwood was born on 9/7/29 in Mannford, Oklahoma. He spent his teenage years in Port Neches, Texas and studied for a medical degree in Dallas, and served with the U.S. Army in the Korean War. He was a fine composer having written 'The Fool' for Sanford Clark, several Duane Eddy tunes, 'Houston' for Dean Martin and 'Boots' for Nancy Sinatra to which he also lent his growly, baritone voice. In the 1970s Hazelwood moved to Sweden where he recorded several albums, probably the best being 'Trouble Is A Lonesome Town' consisting of songs about a town's characters.

His last album was called 'Cake or Death in 2005. He died from renal cancer on 4/8/2007

**Levon HELM**

Born Levan Helm (he changed his Christian name to Levon as it was easier to pronounce) on 26/5/40. He was born in Elaine, Arkansas. At the start of his career Helm joined Ronnie Hawkins and the Hawks but shortly after they moved to

Canada where rockabilly was more popular, so Helm left and went to various cities and towns playing with several bands. On return to Arkansas he formed The Band and was employed by Bob Dylan as his backing band. This did not work well, and Helm returned once more to Arkansas. It is said that he spent two years working on oil rigs in the Gulf of Mexico. The Band finally took off in the late sixties and had several big hits with 'Up On Cripple Creek (10), 'Don't Do It' (11), and many others.

In the 80s Helm became a solo artist. In 2007 Helm produced his first album since 1982, a concept album called 'Dirt Farmer' with songs by Steve Earle, Paul Kennerly and others. It won a Grammy in the Traditional Folk category. Levon Helm died from cancer on 19/4/2012. Over 2000 fans attended at public wake at Helm's Barn studio complex 0n 26/4/2-12.

**Clarence 'Frogman' HENRY**

Born on March 19th 1937 in New Orleans, Louisiana, Clarence 'Frogman' Henry was an R&B singer influenced by 'Fats'

Domino. His voice had a distinctive 'croak' which he used to advantage on his hit records 'Ain't Got No Home' and 'You Always Hurt The One You Love' and 'I Don't Know Why I Love You (But I Do') all of which were top selling hits between 1956 and 1961.

**Elmore JAMES**

Elmore James was born 27/1/18 he was a great blues singer and became known as 'King of the Slide Guitar'. During the 1950s he recorded for the Bihari Brothers Meteor label and Leonard Chess' Chess records. George Thorogood, Jimi Hendrix, ZZ Top and Eric Clapton have covered songs by James and all claim to have been influenced by him. He died from a third heart attack in Chicago on 24/5/63.

**Etta JAMES**

Etta James was born 25/1/38 as Jamesetta Hawkins in Los Angeles, California. Her singing career started in 1954. She encompassed several genres including

Blues, Jazz, Gospel, R&B and Rock 'n' Roll. She was inducted into the Rock 'n' Roll Hall of Fame in 1993, and the Rockabilly Hall of Fame in 2001. She was nominated for 16 Grammy Awards winning three times. She recorded for the Chess and RCA Victor labels plus some smaller labels. Etta James had 23 records in the Hot 100 and Rolling Stone magazine voted her No.22 in their top 100 Greatest Singers of All Time list.

**JAN and DEAN (JAN and ARNIE)**

Jan and Dean were a Rock 'n' Roll duo very popular in the 50s and 60s and consisted of William Jan Berry (3/4/41 – 26/3/2004) and Dean Torrence (10/3/40). They could be called the forerunners of surf music in the style carried on by the Beach Boys. Their most successful songs were 'Surf City' (#8), 'Dead Mans Curve' (#10) and 'The Little Old Lady From Pasadena' (#3).

Torrence also won awards as an album sleeve designer. When Torrence was conscripted, Berry recruited Arnold Ginsburg to partner him on a track called

'Jennie Lee' (named after a voluptuous lady in a night club) as Jan and Arnie. The song peaked at No.3 in the 'Billboard Hot 100' .

Berry was involved in a horrendous car crash in 1966 just a mile or so away from a section of road called, ironically, Dead Mans Curve. He was in a coma from two months and it took over a year for him to regain the use of his right arm and recover from some brain damage. Torrence still tours occasionally with the Surf City All Stars.

**Roland JANES and James VAN EATON** – Jerry Lee Lewis' long time guitarist and drummer. Also session musicians at Sun records. Janes (the guitarist) passed away 18/10/2013 of a heart attack.

**'Blind' Lemon JEFFERSON**

Lemon Henry Jefferson was born blind on 24/9/1893. He was very popular and his recordings sold very well, but he was not that influential with younger singers of his day who found him nearly impossible to imitate.

He was a bigger influence on the later singers, BB King, Robert Johnson, Lightnin' Hopkins and T-Bone Walker. It is reported that on December 19th 1929 he was being escorted to deposit a large amount of money (Royalties) at the Union Station, but was attacked and robbed by the person escorting him and died from the resulting heart attack.

**Waylon JENNINGS**

Strictly speaking Jennings was a top Country singer not a Rock 'n' Roller. He was instrumental, with Willie Nelson and Tompall Glaser as being an originator of the 'Outlaw Movement' in Country Music in which artists could use there own backing bands and groups instead of studio musicians. He was recruited by Buddy Holly (his mentor) to play bass guitar on the 'Winter Dance Party' tour. It was Jennings who gave up his seat on the 'plane to The Big Bopper. (See also Buddy Holly and the Crickets).

**The JORDANAIRES**

The Jordanaires were a superb vocal group. They were formed in 1948 as a Gospel group, but are better known as the backing singers on most Elvis Presley's recordings and on concert tours. Over the years the group has had 13 different members. The best-known four that backed Presley were Gordon Stoker (1$^{st}$ tenor), Neil Matthews (2$^{nd}$ tenor and lead), Hoyt Hawkins (baritone), and Ray Walker (Bass).

Neil Matthews died in 2000, Gordon Stoker died 2013. The Jordanaires have now been disbanded.

**The KALIN TWINS**

Hal and Herbie Kalin were twin brothers born 16/2/34. Hal died in a car accident on 24/8/2005, and Herbie from a heart attack on 21/7/2006.

They were typical 'One hit wonders', that one hit being 'When' which went to No.5 in the U.S. Hot 100 (No.1 in U.K.)

**Ernie K-DOE**

Born Ernest Kador Jnr on 22/2/36 he adopted the stage name Ernie K-Doe and is best known for his No.1 hit 'Mother-In-Law'. He never had another hit record, but did become a t.v. personality, sometimes for the wrong reasons. Ernie K-Doe died in 2001.

**BB (Riley) KING**

Riley B King (known as BB King) is, strictly speaking, a Blues man, but has had a tremendous influence on some Rock 'n' roll singers. Eric Clapton, George Harrison, Jeff Beck and Jimmy Page all admit to being influenced by King, and have borrowed some of King's techniques.

King was born on a cotton plantation near Berclair, Mississippi 16/9/25. His career began in 1946 when he followed his friend Bukka White to Memphis, Tennessee working as a DJ at a radio station and singing in clubs and bars. He became known as the 'Beale Street Blues Boy'. He became more popular with rock fans after he opened the show for the

Rolling Stones American Tour in 1969. He appeared on the Pyramid stage at Glastonbury on 25$^{th}$ June 2011. He is the subject of a Morgan Freeman documentary film.
King was given a honorary Doctorate of Music at Yale University, and was inducted into the Rock 'n' Roll Hall of Fame in 1987. He is ranked No.6 of the all time greatest guitarists by Rolling Stone magazine.

**LEIBER and STOLLER**
Jerome 'Jerry' Leiber (25/4/33 – 22/8/2011) and Mike Stoller (13/3/33) were a top songwriting duo. Their hit compositions include 'Hound Dog', 'Jailhouse Rock', 'Kansas City', 'Stand by Me', and 'On Broadway'. They also wrote 'Searching', Charlie Brown, and 'Yakety Yak' for the Coasters, and 'There Goes My Baby' for the Drifters.
They were inducted into the Songwriter Hall of Fame in 1985 and the Rock 'n' Roll Hall of Fame in 1987.

**LONDON RECORDS**

A subsidiary of Decca Records that specialized in releasing discs from smaller American labels like Sun, Imperial, Atlantic, Big Top etc under the one label in the U.K.

**John D. LOUDERMILK**

Born 31/3/34 in Durham, N.Carolina. Loudermilk learned to play guitar at an early age and found work as a handyman at a local t.v. studio. He wrote a song (A Rose and a Baby) which he was allowed to sing on air. Country singer George Hamilton IV recorded the song in 1956. Loudermilk continued to write, and his song 'Sitting In The Balcony' was a hit for Eddie Cochran. Loudermilk was given a contract by RCA Records where he scored a few hits ('Language of Love'; 'Thou Shalt Not Steal'; 'Calling Dr Casey', and 'Road Hog', Tobacco Road). Loudermilk is recognized more as a superb songwriter than a singer and has had his work recorded by many stars including Johnny Cash, George Hamilton IV, Johnny Tillotson, The Nashville

Teens, Jerry Lee Lewis and the Everly Brothers.
Loudermilk was inducted into the Nashville Songwriters Hall of Fame in 1976.

**Frankie LYMON and the TEENAGERS**

Franklin Joseph 'Frankie' Lymon (30/9/42 – 27/2/68) was the boy soprano lead singer of 'The Teenagers'. The original group was mixed race and consisted of Frankie, Jimmy Merchant, Sherman Garnes, Herman Santiago and Joe Negroni, the latter two from Puerto Rico. In 1956 they had their first and biggest hit 'Why Do Fools Fall In Love'. He decided on a solo career in 1957, but at the age of 25 he was found dead at his grandmother's house from an heroin overdose.

**Jimmy McCRACKLIN**

Jimmy McCracklin (13/8/31 – 20/12/2012) was one of the finest exponents of R&B and West Coast Blues, and a great influence of many rock 'n' roll singers. It is said that he wrote over 1,000 songs and recorded 30 albums. He was awarded four gold records. The records are unclear as to whether he was born in Helena, Arkansas or St Louis, Missouri. His biggest singles hit was ‘The Walk’ released on Checker Records (a subsidiary of Chess Records). Jimmy McCracklin died on 20th December 2012 in San Pablo, California after a long illness.

**The MONKEES**

The Monkees were a band ‘manufactured’ for a t.v. series of the same name.
They consisted of Micky Dolenz, Michael Nesmith, Peter Tork, and Davy Jones who was from England. The t.v. series ran from 1966 to 1968.
They had three No.1 hits, ‘I’m A Believer’, ‘Daydream Believer’ and ‘Last Train To Clarksville’. They had several other discs that climbed high into the charts. Jones died from a severe heart attack after horse riding on 29/2/2012

**MURRAY the K**

Murray Kauffman (14/2/22 – 21/2/82) was one of the top disc jockeys and rock ‘n’ roll impresarios of the 50s and 60s.

Murray the K came to prominence at radio station WINS New York when he took over the star spot when Alan Freed was indicted when the Payola scandal (cash for playing certain records) came to light. Murray occupied the 7pm-11pm spot for seven years.

Kaufmann also produced and presented many t.v. and variety shows featuring all the top performers. He was married six times and died of cancer a week after his $60^{th}$ birthday.

**NOR VA JAK Music**

The music publishing and recording company owned jointly by Norman Petty, Vi Petty and Jack Vaughan in Clovis, New Mexico used by Buddy Holly and the Crickets and Buddy Knox. The recordings were forwarded to Coral Records (Decca) for labeling and distribution.

**The OLYMPICS**

There is little documented about this group, They were formed in 1957 and did have at least two big hit records, the iconic 'Western Movies' and 'I Wish I Could Shimmy Like My Sister Arthur'. Maybe they were too similar to the Coasters.

**Johnny OTIS**

Johnny Otis (real name Ioannis Veliotes b 28/12/21 d 17/1/2012) was one of the most talented men in the music industry at the time. He was a Record Producer, bandleader, songwriter, singer, composer, arranger, disc jockey, tv host, talent scout, journalist, author and minister.

Otis is credited with discovering Jackie Wilson, Little Esther, Big Mama Thornton and Hank Ballard. After a full career in music in which he and his band had numerous hit records ('Double Crossing Blues', 'Mistrusting Blues', and 'Cupid Boogie' went to #1 on the R&B charts and 'Willie and the Hand Jive' went to #9 on the Hot 100 charts) Otis became a politician losing a seat for the California State Assembly probably because he used his real name in the campaign, he then became Chief of Staff for Congressman

Mervyn Dymally. He died of natural causes in Los Angeles three days before Etta James passed away. Otis had discovered James in the early 50s.

**Col TOM PARKER** – Elvis Presley's manager after his move from Sun Records to RCA.

**Bill PARSONS**
There is some disagreement between music writers as to whether Bill Parsons actually existed. The single 'All American Boy'/'Rubber Dolly' (a parody of Presley's rise to fame and subsequent enlistment in the US Army) released in 1959 was credited (on the record label) to Bill Parsons, but the vocal was actually by Bobby Bare. Apparently there was a mix-up at Fraternity Records in Cincinnati as to who actually sang on the recording. Bare eventually went to RCA where he became a very successful Country singer whereas Parsons, having released two more singles for Starday Records, both of which failed to sell, retired from music.

**Norman PETTY**
Buddy Holly and the Crickets Manager. See also Nor Va Jak Music

**Dewey PHILLIPS**
A Memphis disc jockey (no relation to Sam Phillips) on station WHBQ. His show 'Red Hot and Blue' was the most popular show on the station. One of the first DJs to interview Elvis Presley on a live radio show.

**Judd PHILLIPS**
Sam Phillips brother and promotions director for Sun Records.

**Sam PHILLIPS (see Page 12)**

**PHILLIPS INTERNATIONAL Records**

A subsidiary of Sun Records mainly used by Sam Phillips to release discs by lesser known artists and L.Ps. Among those consigned to the label were Carl Mann, Charlie Rich and several others whose main output was just one release. There is one quite interesting release on Phillips International, it is No.3559 'In The Mood/ I Get The Blues When It Rains' a piano instrumental by 'The Hawk'. 'The Hawk' is in reality Jerry Lee Lewis, it was his first release since the British scandal.

**Gene PITNEY**

Eugene Francis Alan Pitney (17/2/40 – 5/4/2006) was a singer/songwriter, sound engineer and musician who had great chart success throughout the mid sixties. He was possibly more successful in Britain than in the States.

He had 16 Top 40, and 4 Top 10 hits in the USA, and 22 top 40 hits in the UK. He composed 'Rubber Ball' the Bobby Vee hit, 'He's a Rebel' for the Crystals and 'Hello Mary Lou' for Rick Nelson.

He was inducted into the Rock 'n' Roll Hall of Fame in 2002.
He was found dead in a Hilton Hotel room in Cardiff, Wales on 5/4/2006.
His biggest hits were 'Liberty Valance', 'If I Didn't Have A Dime', 'Twenty-Four Hours From Tulsa' and 'I'm Gonna Be Strong'.

**Doc POMUS and Mort SHUMAN**

Doc Pomus [27/6/25 - 14/3/91], real name Jerome Felder and Mort Shuman [12/11/36 - 2/11/91] were one of the finest and most prolific Rock 'n' Roll songwriting teams. Both were indicted into the Rock 'n' Roll Hall of Fame.
Their compositions included 'Little Sister', 'Yakety Yak', 'Charlie Brown', 'Save The Last Dance For Me', 'His Latest Flame'; 'Turn Me Loose', and 'Viva Las Vegas.

**Lloyd PRICE**

Lloyd Price was born 9/3/33 in Kenner, Louisiana and was known as 'Mr Personality' after the name of one of his million selling records. His biggest hit was 'Stagger Lee' in 1959. 'Lawdy Miss Clawdy', 'Personality' and 'I'm Gonna Get Married' also went to the top of the charts.

He was inducted into the Rock 'n' Roll Hall of Fame in 1998.

**RCA Records**

A flagship recording company, RCA stands for Radio Corporation of America (now owned by the Sony Corporation). RCA started recording in 1929. There are three main labels, RCA Records for Pop, R&B and Country, RCA Victor for Blues, Jazz and Musicals and RCA Red Seal for Classical Music. RCA Records, from a Country and Rock 'n' Roll point of view, is probably most famous for its Nashville Studio. Most of the top country singers have recorded there including Willie Nelson, Jerry Reed, Waylon Jennings, Don Gibson, Charley Pride and many,

many others. They all (with the exception of Jennings who used his own band) used session musicians. Most of the production was by Chet Atkins or Felton Jarvis and the musicians consisted of Floyd Cramer (piano), Atkins (guitar), D.J. Fontana (drums), Hank Garland (guitar), Jerry Scheff (bass), Glen D. Hardin and Hargus 'Pig' Robbins (pianos), Ronnie Tutt (drums) with vocal backing from The Jordanaires or the Anita Kerr Singers.
Hundreds and hundreds of hits came out of RCA Studio 2 Nashville, Tennessee.

**Charlie RICH**
Sam Phillips head of Sun records is recorded as saying 'Charlie Rich was the finest musician who ever walked into Sun Studio'. Charlie Rich (14/12/32 – 25/7/95) was born in Colt, Arkansas. Rich could easily encompass most genres be it Jazz, Rock 'n' Roll or Country, Gospel or Blues. He was known as the 'Silver Fox' because of his locks of white hair.
He started as a session musician for Judd Records, then cut some demo's for Sam

Phillips at Sun, but Sam didn't think they were commercial enough to release. A story goes that Phillips gave Rich some Jerry Lee Lewis records and said 'Come back when you can play this bad'. Rich did return to Sun but Phillips put out his recordings on his subsidiary label Phillips International. Rich had several big hits including 'Lonely Weekends', Behind Closed Doors', The Most Beautiful Girl' and 'Who Will The next Fool Be'. Numerous artists recorded songs composed by Rich. Charlie Rich received several Academy and CMA Awards. He died in his sleep in a motel in Hammond, Louisiana on 25th July 1995.

**Billy Lee RILEY**

Billy Lee Riley (5/10/33 – 2/8/2009) was yet another of Sam Phillips clutch of rockabilly singers. He was born in Pocahontas, Arkansas, and after serving four years in the US Army was persuaded to try his hand at recording. After a few failures he arrived at Sun Studio where Jack Clement recorded several sides for him. The best sellers were 'Red Hot',

'Flying Saucers Rock 'n' Roll' and 'I Want You Baby'. The latter two tracks had backing from Jerry Lee Lewis on piano. Phillips switched his promotion money from Riley to Lewis (to promote 'Great Balls of Fire'). Riley felt let down by Phillips as did other artists at Sun (Hayden Thompson, Warren Smith and Sonny Burgess) who all felt they would have had more hit records had their efforts had better promotion. His album 'Hot Damn! (on Capricorn 1997) was nominated for a Grammy Award.
Riley died from colon cancer on 2nd August 2009.

**ROCK 'N' ROLL HALL of FAME**

The Rock 'n' Roll Hall of Fame and Museum is situated on the banks of Lake Erie in Cleveland, Ohio. Its main aim is to dedicate and archive the history of people who have been influential in the music industry, be they singers, writers, musicians, producers or engineers.
The R'n'R HOF was created on April 20th 1983 by Ehmet Ertegun who was chairman of Atlantic Records. Several venues (Memphis, Detroit, New York

City and Cincinnati) were considered as its home before Cleveland was eventually chosen. During the year the R'n'R HOF host concerts, films, lectures and interviews that help tell the story of Rock 'n' Roll. The institute celebrated its 25$^{th}$ anniversary on October 29$^{th}$ and 30$^{th}$ 2009 with concerts headed by Jerry Lee Lewis, Bruce Springsteen, Ozzy Osbourne, Art Garfunkel, John Fogerty and many others. The first group of inductees, inducted on January 23, 1986, included James Brown, Little Richard, Elvis Presley, Fats Domino, Ray Charles, Chuck Berry, Sam Cooke, the Everly Brothers, Buddy Holly and Jerry Lee Lewis. Robert Johnson, Jimmie Rodgers and Jimmy Yancey. There has been some controversy with inductees as in 2007 when Grandmaster Flash was inducted having polled less votes than the Dave Clark Five. The panel said it thought 'a Rap artist' was needed before 'another Rock 'n' Roller'

**SAM The SHAM and the PHAROAS**
Sam the Sham was really Domingo Zamudio born 6/3/37 in Dallas, Texas.

He was front man of the Pharaohs, and had several hits including ‘Wooly Bully’, and ‘Little Red Riding Hood’.
He is now a motivational speaker,but occasionally does concert performances. ‘Wooly Bully’ incidentally was the name of his cat.

**SANTO and Johnny**
Santo and Johnny were Brooklyn brothers Santo and Johnny Farina. They were of Italian descent. They had one iconic hit ‘Sleep Walk’ which was #1 for two weeks in 1959. They became more popular in Mexico and Europe. ‘Sleep Walk’ is still a very popular instrumental and is played world-wide to this day.

**Warren SMITH**
Warren Smith (7/2/32 – 30/1/80) was born in Humphries County, Mississippi. Smith auditioned for Sam Phillips at Sun Records and his first release was ‘Rock ‘n’ Roll Ruby’ a song written by Johnny Cash. It sold more copies than the first releases by either Presley, Cash or Carl Perkins.

Smith moved to California and Liberty Records having some success, but a bad automobile accident hospitalized him for twelve months. A restart to his career with small labels faltered and he became addicted to pills and this addiction led to an 18 months jail term for robbing a pharmacy. The Rockabilly revival got him an invitation to a festival in London, but he died of a heart attack whilst preparing for the trip.

**Joe SOUTH**

Joe South was better known as a songwriter than a singer but he did have a massive hit of his own with 'Games People Play', and won a Grammy award for his composition 'Rose Garden' which Lynn Anderson took to the top of the charts. South (real name Souter), was a staff guitarist at RCA Records with Ray Stevens and Jerry Reed. He played guitar on several hits for the likes of Aretha Franklin, Tommy Roe, Bob Dylan and many others.

South was inducted into the Nashville Songwriters Hall of Fame in 1979.

He died of heart failure at the age of 72 on September 5$^{th}$ 2005.

**Phil SPECTOR**

Philip Harvey Spector (b 26/12/39) was one of the greatest American record producers, songwriter and, in later years the subject of a murder trial. He was the originator of the 'Wall of Sound' method of recording.

In 1958 he composed, and was a member of the group the Teddy Bears that had a #1 hit with the song 'To Know Him Is To Love Him'. He was a pioneer of the 60s Girl Group phase, recording The Ronettes and The Crystals. He produced records for John Lennon, The Righteous Brothers, Ike and Tina Turner, George Harrison and the Beatles album 'Let It Be'. He was inducted into the non-performer section of the Rock 'n' Roll Hall of Fame in 1989 and the Songwriters Hall of Fame in 2004. He won a Grammy for Harrison's 'Concert for Bangladesh' album.

In 2009 he was convicted of the murder of Lana Clarkson. He is currently serving a prison sentence of 19 years to life.

**Barrett STRONG**

Barrett Strong (b 5/2/41 West Point, Mississippi) was the first artist to have a hit record on the Tamla Motown label, but is probably best remembered for his songwriting with his partner Norman Whitfield. Strong and Whitfield wrote many of the songs recorded by The Temptations. Strong's biggest solo hit was 'Money' which reached No.2 in the charts and was also recorded by Jerry Lee Lewis, The Beatles and several others. He was inducted into the Songwriters Hall of Fame in 2004.

**Ed SULLIVAN**

Edward Vincent Sullivan (29/9/01 – 13/10/74) was an entertainments writer and television variety show host most famous for his 'Toast of the Town' or perhaps better known as 'The Ed Sullivan Show'. Sullivan became known as 'The

Starmaker' but he was reluctant to invite Elvis Presley on to his show because of his 'bad boy' image. However, Presley was too good to miss and Sullivan was forced to invite him on to the show, but Sullivan missed Presley's appearance on the show due to having been in a car accident a few days prior to the show. Guests on the show included The Beatles, The Dave Clark Five, The Jackson Five, The Supremes and many others. Several artists were banned from the show or told to change the lyrics of their songs (One of Dylan's songs was deemed to be possibly libelous and he refused to appear. The Stones were told to change 'Lets spend the night together' to 'Lets spend some time together'). The Doors were also banned.
Sullivan died of throat cancer. He has a star on the Hollywood Walk of Fame.

**SURFARIS**

The Surfaris were a surf rock band from California. They had two big hits in 1963 'Wipe Out' and 'Surfer Joe'. The original line-up was Ron Wilson (drums, vocals),

Jim Fuller (lead guitar), Bob Berryhill (rhythm guitar) and Pat Connolly (bass). 'Wipe Out' rose to #2 on the charts. The maniacal laugh and the words "Wipe Out" at the beginning of the record were by Berryhill's father. They disbanded in 1965, but occasionally reform for special performances.

**TAMLA MOTOWN Records**

The Tamla Motown Record Company was founded in 1959 by Berry Gordy Jnr in Detroit Michigan. Originally, Tamla and Motown were separate labels but were united in 1960. Gordy relocated the company to Los Angeles in 1972 and in 1990 he sold out to MCA, and it is now housed in New York City.

The labels first hit record was 'Money' by Barrett Strong. Other hits on the label have come from (among others) The Marvelettes, Stevie Wonder, Diana Ross and the Supremes, the Jackson Five, Martha and the Vandellas, Gladys Knight and the Pips and many others.

**The TEDDY BEARS**

The Teddy Bears provided the first hit record for record producer Phil Spector. Spector was a member of the group. The record, 'To Know Him Is To Love Him', their only hit, spent three weeks at #1 and a total of 23 weeks on the charts. The group was made up of Spector, lead singer Annette Kleinbard, Marshal Leib, Harvey Gildsein and drummer Sandy Nelson.
It was released on the Dore label in 1958.

**Johnny TILLOTSON**

Johnny Tillotson (b 20/4/39) is from Jacksonville, Florida. He had nine top ten hits in the mid to late 60s. His biggest hit 'Poetry In Motion' just failed to top the Hot 100 charts peaking at #2. His other big hits were 'Without You' #7, 'It Keeps Right On A-Hurtin'' #3, 'Send Me The Pillow That You Dream On' #17 and 'Talk Back Trembling Lips' #7.
Tillotson continues to write and play the odd concert today.

**Ike & Tina TURNER**

Ike and Tina Turner were a husband and wife duo who had hits with ‘A Fool In Love’, ‘It’s Gonna Work Out Fine’, ‘I Idolize You’, and ‘River Deep Mountain High’. The duo was inducted into the Rock ‘n’ Roll Hall of Fame in 1991. Two of their songs, "River Deep - Mountain High" and "Proud Mary", were inducted to the Grammy Hall of Fame in 1999 and 2003, respectively. They were inducted into the Rock ‘n’ Roll Hall of Fame in 1991.

By 1976 Ike had become addicted to cocaine and later that year the couple were divorced. On 12/12/2007 Ike Turner was found dead at his home from a cocaine overdose. Tina has since conducted a highly successful solo career.

**Sammy TURNER**

Born Samuel Black (2/6/32). Sammy Turner had several hits on the Billboard charts most notably ‘Always’ (19); Lavender Blue’, (3), and ‘Paradise’ (46). These hits were on the Big Top label. In the late 60s Turner recorded on the

Motown label but did not score any significant hits.

**Conway TWITTY**

Born Harold Jenkins (1/9/33). Jenkins was advised that his name was "not marketable", and should change it. There are several theories as to how he came to be Conway Twitty, the most popular being that he was scanning a map when he noticed two small towns, one in Arkansas (Conway) and one across the border in Texas (Twitty). He recorded several tracks at Sun Records in Memphis, but none were released so he moved on to MGM Records. In 1958 an Ohio radio station was supposed to play Twiity's MGM release 'I'll Try' which was going nowhere, but played the 'B' side 'It's Only Make Believe' in error. The record eventually went to #1 on the Billboard charts and also #1 in 21 other countries. It proved to be the first of nine top forty hits for Twitty. In 1965 Twitty became a Country singer and emerged with the record of 40 #1 singles, a total only recently surpassed by George Strait. Conway Twitty died on 5th June 1993 shortly after appearing on stage at Branson, Missouri.

**Jerry WALLACE**

Jerry Wallace (15/12/28 – 5/5/2008) was born in Guilford, Missouri.

Wallace was a 'dual genre' singer or 'crossover' singer not unlike Don Gibson, and could score big selling hits in both the pop and country fields. His 'Primrose Lane' reached #8 in the Billboard Hot 100, and he had four songs in the C&W Top 10. His only #1 hit was called 'If You Leave Me Tonight I'll Cry'. He had a total of 37 hits on the Country charts and 17 on the Pop charts. He died from congestive heart failure in 2008.

**Billy WARD and the DOMINOES**

Billy Ward (born Robert Williams in Savannah, Georgia 19/9/21) was leader of one of the most successful groups of the 50s. Clyde McPhatter and Jackie Wilson, who became superstars in their own right were early members of the group. They had five chart hits in the Billboard charts and 12 on the U.S. R&B charts including two #1 hits ('Sixty Minute Man and 'Have

Mercy Baby'). They were inducted into the Vocal Group Hall of Fame in 2006. Billy Ward died in February 2002.

**Muddy WATERS**
The man whose real name was McKinley Morganfield (b 4/4/13) was predominantly a Delta Blues man not a Rock 'n' Roller, but he did influence many of the early late 50s and early 60s Rock 'n' Rollers. Most of his recording work was done by Leonard and Phil Chess of Chess Records, Chicago. Jimi Hendrix, Eric Clapton, Van Morrison and many others say they have been influenced by Muddy Waters. Waters died in his sleep on 30th April 1983.
He won six Grammy awards, was inducted into the Rock 'n' Roll Hall of Fame in 1987 and his portrait appears on a 29 cent US Postal stamp from 1994.

**Sheb WOOLEY**
Shelby 'Sheb' Wooley (10/4/21 – 16/9/2003) was primarily a character actor, but is probably better known for his two chart-topping songs 'The Purple People Eater' and 'That's My Pa'. He

featured in numerous tv westerns ('Rawhide'; 'The Cisco Kid'; 'Kit Carson', 'The Range Rider'), and major films 'High Noon'; 'The Outlaw Josey Wales' and 'Giant'. He was also a regular star voice in The Muppet Show. He released 18 good selling Country and Western albums. Wooley died from leukemia in Nashville in 2003.

# THE TOP 200 RECORDS OF THE 50S AND 60S

1. Johnny B. Goode - **Chuck Berry**
2. Jailhouse Rock - **Elvis Presley**
3. Rock Around The Clock - **Bill Haley & His Comets**
4. Tutti-Frutti - **Little Richard**
5. Whole Lot of Shakin' Going On - **Jerry Lee Lewis**
6. What'd I Say - **Ray Charles**
7. Summertime Blues - **Eddie Cochran**
8. Hound Dog - **Elvis Presley**
9. Long Tall Sally - **Little Richard**
10. That'll Be The Day - **Buddy Holly & the Crickets**
11. Maybellene - **Chuck Berry**
12. Bo Diddley - **Bo Diddley**
13. Shake, Rattle And Roll - **Joe Turner**
14. Blue Suede Shoes - **Carl Perkins**
15. Don't Be Cruel - **Elvis Presley**
16. Bye Bye Love - **Everly Brothers**
17. Great Balls Of Fire - **Jerry Lee Lewis**
18. Earth Angel - **Penguins**
19. Why Do Fools Fall In Love - **Frankie Lymon & the Teenagers**
20. Good Golly Miss Molly - **Little Richard**
21. Be-Bop-A-Lula - **Gene Vincent & the Bluecaps**
22. School Day - **Chuck Berry**
23. Rock And Roll Music - **Chuck Berry**
24. Peggy Sue - **Buddy Holly**
25. Lawdy Miss Clawdy - **Lloyd Price**
26. Lucille - **Little Richard**
27. Roll Over Beethoven - **Chuck Berry**
28. In The Still Of The Nite - **Five Satins**
29. I Only Have Eyes For You - **Flamingos**
30. For Your Precious Love - **Jerry Butler & the Impressions**
31. Blueberry Hill - **Fats Domino**
32. Please, Please, Please - **James Brown & the Famous Flames**
33. Sh-Boom - **Chords**

**34.** Money Honey - **Drifters featuring Clyde McPhatter**
**35.** I Walk The Line - **Johnny Cash and the Tennessee Two**
**36.** Heartbreak Hotel - **Elvis Presley**
**37.** Fever - **Little Willie John**
**38.** The Great Pretender - **Platters**
**39.** Ain't It A Shame - **Fats Domino**
**40.** That's All Right - **Elvis Presley with Scotty and Bill**
**41.** Your Cheatin' Heart - **Hank Williams**
**42.** Sweet Little Sixteen - **Chuck Berry**
**43.** The Train Kept-A-Rollin - **Johnny Burnette Trio**
**44.** Come Go With Me - **Del-Vikings**
**45.** Let The Good Times Roll - **Shirley & Lee**
**46.** Rip It Up - **Little Richard**
**47.** Rocking Pneumonia & the Boogie Woogie Flu - **Huey "Piano" Smith & the Clowns**
**48.** Pledging My Love - **Johnny Ace**
**49.** Sixty Minute Man - **Dominoes**
**50.** Rocket 88 - **Jackie Brenston**
**51.** Yakety Yak - **Coasters**
**52.** All Shook Up - **Elvis Presley**
**53.** Folsom Prison Blues - **Johnny Cash and the Tennessee Two**
**54.** Searchin' - **Coasters**
**55.** You Send Me - **Sam Cooke**
**56.** Mack The Knife - **Bobby Darin**
**57.** Wake Up Little Susie - **Everly Brothers**
**58.** Susie Q - **Dale Hawkins**
**59.** La Bamba - **Ritchie Valens**
**60.** Goodnite, Sweetheart, Goodnite - **Spaniels**
**61.** I've Got A Woman - **Ray Charles**
**62.** I'm Walkin' - **Fats Domino**
**63.** There Goes My Baby - **Drifters**
**64.** Shout - **Isley Brothers**
**65.** White Christmas - **Drifters featuring Clyde McPhatter**
**66.** Keep A 'Knockin' - **Little Richard**
**67.** Kansas City - **Wilbert Harrison**
**68.** Poison Ivy - **Coasters**
**69.** Since I Don't Have You - **Skyliners**
**70.** Jambalaya (On The Bayou) - **Hank Williams**
**71.** Money - **Barrett Strong**
**72.** Speedoo - **Cadillacs**

73. Rumble - **Link Wray**
74. Lonely Teardrops - **Jackie Wilson**
75. Hang Up My Rock And Roll Shoes - **Chuck Willis**
76. Sea Cruise - **Frankie Ford**
77. Rave On - **Buddy Holly**
78. Work With Me Annie - **Hank Ballard & the Midnighters**
79. Shake, Rattle And Roll - **Bill Haley & His Comets**
80. Sincerely - **Moonglows**
81. Crying In The Chapel - **Sonny Til & the Orioles**
82. Story Untold - **Nutmegs**
83. My Babe - **Little Walter**
84. At My Front Door - **El Dorados**
85. Gee - **Crows**
86. Matchbox - **Carl Perkins**
87. C.C. Rider - **Chuck Willis**
88. Only You - **Platters**
89. All I Have To Do Is Dream - **Everly Brothers**
90. Send Me Some Lovin' - **Little Richard**
91. At The Hop - **Danny & the Juniors**
92. Little Darlin' - **Diamonds**
93. Rock-in Robin - **Bobby Day**
94. Honky Tonk - **Bill Doggett**
95. Blue Monday - **Fats Domino**
96. Jim Dandy - **Lavern Baker**
97. Reelin And Rocking - **Chuck Berry**
98. Rebel Rouser - **Duane Eddy**
99. Love Potion No. 9 - **Clovers**
100. Chantilly Lace - **Big Bopper**

---

101. Oh Boy! - **Buddy Holly & the Crickets**
102. Get A Job - **Silhouettes**
103. Book Of Love - **Monotones**
104. C'mon Everybody - **Eddie Cochran**
105. Do You Want To Dance - **Bobby Freeman**
106. Willie And The Hand Jive - **Johnny Otis Show**
107. You're So Fine - **Falcons**
108. Handy Man - **Jimmy Jones**
109. Sea Of Love - **Phil Phillips with the Twilights**
110. Breathless - **Jerry Lee Lewis**
111. Stagger Lee - **Lloyd Price**
112. Tequila - **Champs**
113. It's Only Make Believe - **Conway Twitty**
114. Have Mercy Baby - **Dominoes**

115. Maybe Baby - **Buddy Holly & the Crickets**
116. Young Blood - **Coasters**
117. Little Bitty Pretty One - **Thurston Harris**
118. Not Fade Away - **Buddy Holly & the Crickets**
119. The Fat Man - **Fats Domino**
120. Baby Let's Play House - **Elvis Presley with Scotty and Bill**
121. Mystery Train - **Elvis Presley with Scotty and Bill**
122. Tweedlee Dee - **LaVern Baker**
123. One Mint Julep - **Clovers**
124. Shake A Hand - **Faye Adams**
125. Honey Hush - **Joe Turner**
126. Tears On My Pillow - **Little Anthony & the Imperials**
127. Oh What A Nite - **Dells**
128. My Prayer - **Platters**
129. Dizzy Miss Lizzy - **Larry Williams**
130. Who Do You Love - **Bo Diddley**
131. Brown-Eyed Handsome Man - **Chuck Berry**
132. Ready Teddy - **Little Richard**
133. Honey Don't - **Carl Perkins**
134. I'm In Love Again - **Fats Domino**
135. Little Girl Of Mine - **Cleftones**
136. A Thousand Miles Away - **Heartbeats**
137. Tear It Up - **Johnny Burnette Trio**
138. Blue Suede Shoes - **Elvis Presley**
139. Drown In My Own Tears - **Ray Charles**
140. I Put A Spell On You - **Screamin' Jay Hawkins**
141. Love Is Strange - **Mickey & Sylvia**
142. I'm A Man - **Bo Diddley**
143. Unchained Melody - **Al Hibbler**
144. See You Later, Alligator - **Bill Haley & His Comets**
145. Around And Around - **Chuck Berry**
146. Don't You Just Know It - **Huey "Piano" Smith & the Clowns**
147. One Night - **Elvis Presley**
148. Carol - **Chuck Berry**
149. What Am I Living For - **Chuck Willis**
150. Sixteen Candles - **Crests**
151. Smoke Gets In Your Eyes - **Platters**
152. Bird Dog - **Everly Brothers**
153. Baby What You Want Me To Do - **Jimmy Reed**
154. A Teenager In Love - **Dion & the Belmonts**
155. Splish Splash - **Bobby Darin**
156. I'm Ready - **Fats Domino**
157. I Wonder Why - **Dion & the Belmonts**
158. Charlie Brown - **Coasters**
159. Rock And Roll Is Here To Stay - **Danny & the Juniors**
160. Back In The U.S.A. - **Chuck Berry**

161. Come Softly To Me - **Fleetwoods**
162. Beyond The Sea - **Bobby Darin**
163. Night Train - **Jimmy Forrest**
164. When You Dance - **Turbans**
165. The Wallflower - **Etta James**
166. Whole Lotta Loving - **Fats Domino**
167. Flip, Flop And Fly - **Joe Turner**
168. (Night Time Is) The Right Time - **Ray Charles**
169. Mama, He Treats Your Daughter Mean - **Ruth Brown**
170. Good Rocking Tonight - **Elvis Presley with Scotty and Bill**
171. Come On Let's Go - **Ritchie Valens**
172. Walking After Midnight - **Patsy Cline**
173. I'm A King Bee - **Slim Harpo**
174. Got My Mojo Working - **Muddy Waters**
175. Goodnight My Love - **Jessie Belvin**
176. Day-O (Banana Boat Song) - **Harry Belafonte**
177. Stranded In The Jungle - **Cadets**
178. I Just Want To Make Love To You - **Muddy Waters**
179. Hearts Of Stone - **Charms**
180. Jingle Bell Rock - **Bobby Helms**
181. Too Much - **Elvis Presley**
182. Diana - **Paul Anka**
183. Dedicated To The One I Love - **Shirelles**
184. Silhouettes - **Rays**
185. Honey Love - **Drifters featuring Clyde McPhatter**
186. Lovey Dovey - **Clovers**
187. Hoochie Coochie Man - **Muddy Waters**
188. Dust My Broom - **Elmore James**
189. Dream Lover - **Bobby Darin**
190. It's Late - **Ricky Nelson**
191. Sleep Walk - **Santo & Johnny**
192. Reet Petite - **Jackie Wilson**
193. Don't Let Go - **Roy Hamilton**
194. Sweet Nothin's - **Brenda Lee**
195. Fannie Mae - **Buster Brown**
196. Hey Little Girl - **Dee Clark**
197. Short Fat Fannie - **Larry Williams**
198. The Wind - **Diablos**
199. Rock Island Line - **Lonnie Donegan**
200. Harlem Nocturne - **Viscounts**

# ACKNOWLEDEMENTS

## Photographs Used

**All photographs used in this book were downloaded from individual artists Wikipedia sites.**

## Bibliography

**Books used for information in the completion of this book :-**

**'The Sun King'. Kevin & Tanja Crouch. Piaktus books. 2008**

**'Good Rockin' Tonight'. Colin Escott with Martin Hawkins Virginia books. 1992**

**'Rock of Ages'. Ed Ward, Geoffery Stokes, Ken Tucker Penguin books. 1987**

**'For The Record, Sun Records an Oral History'. Dave Marsh Avon Music 1998**

**'Buddy The Biography'. Philip Norman Pan books 1996**

# HOW TO GET A JOB

www.hellstedt.org

Book Design by HMDpublishing

# Dedication

*To all my coaching clients that I have listened to and that I have learnt so much from.*

*Also, to my friends and especially my children, that always has supported me in my different ventures over the years.*

*Remember that you don't fail until you give up.*

*A dream written down with a date becomes a goal.*

*A goal broken down into steps becomes a plan.*

*A plan backed by action makes your dreams come true.*

*My motto is – What I don't know today, I can learn tomorrow.*

# Foreword

This book is written to help you understand the steps needed to have a better chance to get a job.

Your decision to purchase this book may turn out to be the smartest decision you have ever made.

I have been unemployed, and I have been an employer in my time. That means that I have been on both sides of that fence.

During a time span of approximately 10 month of the Corona look down, I coached around 800 clients one-on-one and hosted about 50 lectures, all digital. One thing I realised was that both leaders an unemployed people need guidance in many times similar things.

In this book I have collected different steps that will build you up to become a more affiant job seeker, with more confidence and with better structure in your quest to find a job.

Best of luck and I hope you find the book helpful.

Gustaf-Wilhelm Hellstedt

# Contents

# SWOT ANALYSIS

## A guide towards getting a job

AND IT IS SIMPLER TO DO THE ANALYSIS THAN YOU MIGHT THINK.

FIND OUT WHO YOU ARE

WHAT ARE YOU GOOD AT

WHAT ARE YOU NOT SO GOOD AT

## • SWOT

I am convinced that you are most likely to succeed in life. The reason I say so is that you are curious and willing to learn, hence you are reading this right now. What you need to do is to use your talent to the fullest extent.

To be able to do so you need to identify your strengths and weaknesses. If you know your weaknesses, you can manage them in such a way that they won't matter in the future.

The best way to identify your strengths and weaknesses, along with highlighting the opportunities that arise from them, is to use the technique SWOT.

Let us get you unstuck from your current situation and begin moving on to the next level with me sharing some harsh reality.

You need to dig deep into yourself to find out who you really are.

Let me explain what SWOT stands for. It is an acronym for the words Strength, Weakness, Opportunities and Threats.

As someone defined it, "SWOT can help you better understand how to play your strengths and manage your weaknesses, as well as uncover opportunities for growth and eliminate threats that could keep you from moving forward."

Strengths and weaknesses are internal factors, while opportunities and threats are external factors. You as a job seeker need to list all personal strengths and weaknesses to identify the opportunities and risks in your career path that you are willing to pursue.

You will uncover hidden opportunities through your strengths. You will understand your weaknesses and reveal the threats by eliminating them so they no longer can hurt your ability to move forward.

When you have completed the SWOT analysis, you will be able to see what separates you from your peers. You will start to understand what your USP – Unique Selling Point is. It gives you a chance to further develop the talents and abilities you will need to achieve your personal goals, whatever they may be.

One thing is for sure, that it will help you in your career.

Enjoy reading and good luck with your SWOT analysis!

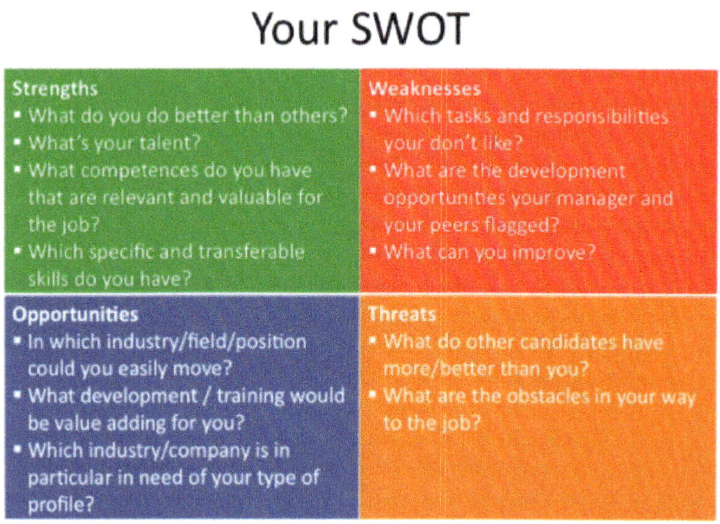


For jobseekers the SWOT analysis starts with an exploration of strengths + weaknesses. Here you focus on who you are as a professional, without outside influences. This in relation to your earlier relative successes or failures.

## • STRENGTHS

Defining your strengths is a matter of looking at your past and current situation and figuring out what were the things you achieved that can be quantifiable.

And also, what did it take to achieve those things? What specific talents and skills do you possess to achieve such outcome?

Understanding yourself is crucial. Remember, most people are skilled in specific areas, however, every person has his or her unique expertise and abilities.

You can prioritise, compare and analyse the strengths and weaknesses in relation to experiences, leadership, personality, professional skills as well as communication skills which can be easily identified in normal routine work. With that in hand, you can then have an intensified focus in your search for your dream job.

Here are some questions to ask yourself when filling out the "strengths" box (or shall we call it your "strong box"):

- What are you naturally good at?
- What skills have you worked to develop?
- What are some advantages that you have over others?
- What traits define you as a professional or individual?
- What former achievements are you most proud of?
- What would your current or former boss or coworkers say are your strengths?
- Do you exhibit values or ethics that others lack?

- Do you have personal resources you can tap into?
- Do you have any networks you can tap into?
- Do you perform a certain skill better than others?
- Have your bosses or coworkers touted any of your skills?
- How does your background set you apart from your peers?

Think of strengths as trying to sell yourself to your employer or selling your services to a client. This box is a crucial and vital part to your SWOT. Read it twice and go through your answers more than once.

Next step, Weaknesses.

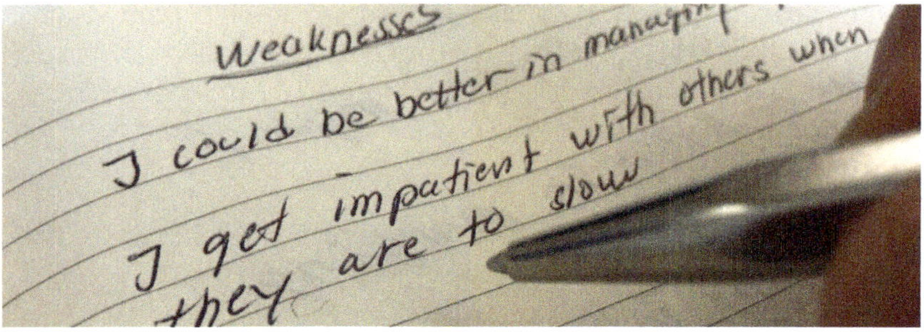

## • WEAKNESSES

Have you been to an interview lately?

Well, then I am sure you been asked to describe your weaknesses. Please, tell me that you didn't answer with "I don't have any!" You'd better come up with something better than that because a recruiter or employer will see right through that and you won't be taken seriously. Try thinking about a mistake you've made or a skill that you are lacking.

I urge you to be honest with yourself. Do not try to avoid anything or sugar coat yourself. One really important note: if you cannot or will not realize your own weaknesses, your personal growth will end. If you lie to yourself at this stage, how do you think that will affect your chances in an interview situation or in a real job situation?

The most important thing is to be able to take an honest look at yourself and admit your shortcomings. We all have them.

We all have weaknesses, but rarely want to admit to them. It's best to begin with a truthful answer to your own questions.

Another way to find out is to ask for feedback from your co-workers, supervisors or mentor. Why not a good friend or a significant other?

Some questions to consider when filling out the weakness portion:

- Where is your education, training, or skills lacking?
- What do you avoid because you lack confidence?
- What are your negative work habits and personality traits?

- What would your current or previous boss and coworkers say are your weaknesses?
- Are you not skilled at delegating tasks?
- Are you self-critical/sensitive?
- Are you shy/not adept at public speaking?
- Are you too competitive?
- Are you not detail-oriented/too detail-oriented?
- Are you not comfortable taking risks?
- Are you too focused/lacking focus?
- Are you taking on too much responsibility?

The point of this box – weakness, is to be completely honest with yourself. Expose all your flaws and deal with them. By doing so, you can accomplish self-awareness and work on your issues. You will evolve and highly increase your success rate of getting a job! Awareness of your weaknesses helps enormously in interview situations. You will also have a chance to reduce or eradicate some of these flaws. Next, Opportunities.

## • OPPORTUNITIES

Would you see an opportunity if it was staring you in the face? To define the word, one can say that it is about a set of circumstances that make it possible to do something, in this case getting a job.

- Is there any new technology you can use for help?
- Is your industry growing? If so, are there job opportunities?
- Can your network or personal connections, help/advise you?
- Are your peers failing at something that can give you the advantage?
- Is there a void in your niche that you may be able to fill?
- Do your hear employers/clients complain about anything for which you could offer a solution?
- Are there any groups, events or classes you can attend off- or online?
- Is there an opening for a job that you could apply for if you took a course or achieved a new skill?

Here, it is time to start thinking what type of job you are looking for, what kind of career field you want to be in. Something you need to do to narrow the scope, or for that matter maybe widen the scope.

What I know is that there are opportunities all around you. On the SWOT chart, opportunities and strengths are connecting factors.

Look at your strengths and ask yourself whether these open up any opportunities – and look at weaknesses and ask yourself whether you could open up opportunities by eliminating those weaknesses.

Some things to think about include: What does your ideal employer look like? What does your next role look like? And what attributes would you like to see from a leadership team and boss? Once you have those answers, you might look for opportunities that match.

Other ways to identify opportunities require you to be proactive. For instance, joining networking groups, classes and utilizing additional resources to step outside of your comfort zone can greatly enhance your development.

Everything is available on-line today. This is a great opportunity! The pandemic has actually created new ways for us to network.

When analysing what your previous tasks have been and what you accomplished, dan these skills be applied in another field of work or another branch?

Finally, I will introduce the last segment of SWOT analysis: Threats.

## • THREATS

Now think about all the things that can go wrong. This is where you can let your internal Gremlin (the little voice in your head that tells you the sky is falling) run wild and list everything that comes to mind.

When making your list of threats, consider external factors that put you at a disadvantage. Understanding potential threats can help you form plans to minimise the risk or turn it into an opportunity.

Threats are factors that pose as a hindrance to getting jobs. Threats coincide with weaknesses. Examples of possible threats could be a competitive field and lack of experience.

When it comes to your threats, you should keep an open mind and not let them deter you. After all, the purpose of creating a SWOT analysis is to help you further in your career, not set you back due to fear or apprehension.

Approach threats in such a way that you combine them with your weaknesses to figure out what external threats could affect your internal threats.

You should ask yourself the following questions:

- Is your education getting obsolete or out-dated?
- Is your industry changing due to factors like technology or the economy?
- Is your age a threat?
- Could any of your weaknesses lead to threats?
- You can't afford to go down in salary?

- Are you facing any family- or home-related issues that may affect your work?
- Could your health be a threat?
- Would a continuous pandemic be a threat?
- Can language be a threat?
- Is your job role changing due to factors like technology or the economy?
- Companies are not hiring people with your major/degree.

To identify threats that could prevent you from finding employment, ask yourself, "What is it that will keep me from having an effective and productive career search?"

While the SWOT analysis process creates anxiety, it helps tremendously. Like preventive medicine, you can fix those threats and hopefully come out with promising results.

## NEXT STEP

Congratulations, you have just gone through the first chapter for the first session out of four in Block 1 in "TBS – Three Block System". You should now have a good idea on how to make a personal SWOT analysis.

The findings you get out of the SWOT analysis will be part of the foundation we have now started to build for a **Brand called You.**

A way to get the job you have been dreaming about.

You can, of course, use every part of TBS separately, but it is absolutely most effectively used all together.

The next session in the series is called **Characteristics.**

## YOUR SWOT TEMPLATE

# Make your own personal SWOT-analysis

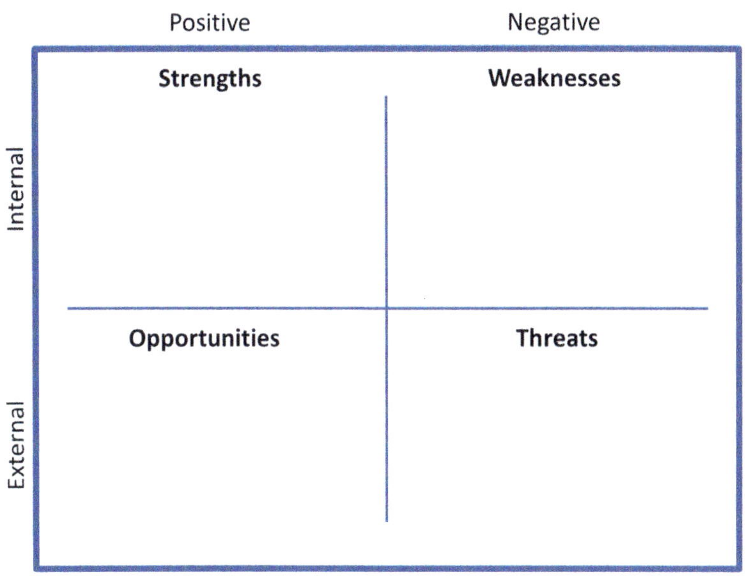

# CHARACTERISTICS

## A guide towards getting a job

WHAT CHARACTERISTICS DEFINE YOU
KNOWING YOUR CHARACTERISTICS WILL HELP YOU LEARN MORE ABOUT THE WHO, WHAT AND WHY ABOUT YOURSELF.

# • CHARACTERISTICS

We continue your journey towards a new job.

By finding out what type of characteristics and qualities define you, who you are will become clearer not only for you, but also for a future employer.

As you might have noticed in previous chapter, an employer can also be looked upon as a client. A client interested in the services you can provide in his workplace to solve any problems within the company. For you that can mean getting a job.

When reading job advertisements, they often have a variety of desired characteristics describing the ideal candidate for the position.

First, I want to explain to you that what they ask for in the advertisement is like the wish list for Santa Claus. It is what they are hoping to find, not always what they receive.

How much can you deliver on that wish list and what is requested? Maybe they can be happy to receive some other knowledge or features as well. We are grateful for other gifts than those on the wish list at Christmas time, correct?

Only as long as the gift fits into the context. But as jobseekers, you do not always know all the contexts, so it is important to show of yourself what you can – characteristics plus the rest including CV. Everything is connected!

Our goal is to make you fit the profile by making you understand the process of becoming an ideal candidate.

Something we do by going through all of the different steps in the TBS – Three Block System. Doing the SWOT was your first step, now we will get cracking on your Characteristics.

## WHAT ARE CHARACTERISTICS?

Let us start with explaining what this actually means.

You need to understand that your personal qualities are the characteristics that make you who you are.

We are looking at the soft skills and knowledge that you possess and are able to bring to your workplace. Your personal qualities define how you will go about applying yourself to a role or a task at hand.

When you learn how to identify and make best use of your personal qualities, you will enable yourself to develop both personally and professionally.

As a professional in any industry, it is important that you understand your own attributes and the impact they have on how you are doing your job as well as how it affects others in your surroundings.

For an employer, a client or a manager, having insight into the attitudes, behaviours and preferences of people that will interact at the workplace, helps to build teams and leads others towards successful performances.

Understanding your own and others' personality traits can help with problem solving, particularly where the problem is rooted in behaviours.

I am a strong believer in that understanding an individual's personal qualities is an important skill that benefits everyone.

Your personality can make the difference between poor and great performance both for yourself and your team, whether or not you are consciously aware of how your personality is affecting your work.

Sometimes it is easy to create efficiency in a business just by moving a person into a different group or to a new task. But to be able to do so one needs to understand the qualities and ultimately the characteristics of the people involved.

When you know more about yourself in this matter you will become much more self-confident about where you fit in the most.

Personal qualities are an important ingredient in defining competence. This area is often overlooked alongside the rather easier to identify skills and knowledge criterion demonstrated by qualifications and training: the hard skills.

There are a number of tools and techniques available to help you get to grips with your own personal qualities. One is to ask friends, family and co-workers past or present, depending on your situation.

Having the support of a coach or mentor can really help you to reflect upon your own performance and approach to work. A good coach will help you to better understand what drives you and how your personality traits can help or hinder the achievement of your goals.

You find your coach at www.hellstedt.org

## • EXPANDED CHARACTERISTICS

I am going to give you a few examples of characteristics that an employer/client is looking for. These are commonly used by jobseekers and are also asked for in advertisements by employers.

To be able to stand out from others using the same words, one trick is to put some more content into the actual word. To paint a picture of how you are or act in reference to the word.

You should try to find at least 5-6 different characteristics that define who you are and how you work. Never use more than three in any job seeking situation. You can use them when someone asks the standard question in an interview situation "Tell me three good things about you".

Prepare for the second question, "What are your weaknesses?"

"Tell me three negative things about yourself."

It can be counter-intuitive to put yourself down or admit to personal shortcomings, but the questions negative connotation doesn't require an outright negative response.

Instead, a creative approach to admitting your failings can position you as an honest and forthright candidate.

If you are clever (you are after reading this material) you have prepared that answer the same way. You pick out three characteristics that sound a bit negative, but in your description of them they come out on the good side.

I will give you an example af a less-than-perfect quality that you can change into something good.

Bad in time management

The words do not sound positive. It answers the question of something negative you had to say about yourself.

Let us now change that with an extended answer.

Bad in time management – I struggle with time management on occasions, but I have taken a couple of courses in the subject and found some tools. I now use electronic alarms and a detailed calendar plus I always build in an extra 30 minutes

You will read more about similar answers in Block 3, session 4 – Interview situations. This gives you a good indication on how to use the idea of extended characteristics.

Let us continue with finding more qualities to extend.

To do so we will look at requirements in a real job advertisement.

The words come from an advertisement on LinkedIn for a smaller company with 50 employees and now they are looking for a new Account Executive. I have just copied two out of ten different characteristics they asked for. *Remember what I wrote about the wish list for Santa Claus.*

You are:

- Organised
- Analytical

In your cover letter answering the advertisement, you might want to answer that "I am a well organised person".

First, we use just the plain word, your quality.

Secondly, we put an explanation to the word where it becomes a clear personal characteristic for any reader.

| well organised |
|---|

Just the empty word doesn't say much, correct? So, let us try it in a different way.

| Organised – I am ambitious, enterprising, structured, driven, goal-oriented, flexible, observant and see both details and wholeness, like to organise and plan. Thrive at a high pace with varying tasks. |
|---|

Being "organised" is of course a very good quality. But it can be interpreted in many different ways. So, what you can do, if this word fits you as one of your main characteristics, is to put an explanation to it. Like the example above and make it personalised only for you.

Another example of a useful characteristic found in the advertisement was:

Analytical

Let us do the same thing with this word. When you expand it with an explanation on how you interpret the word from your point of view, it changes and becomes so much more useful.

Analytical – I see several solutions to a problem and have a good eye for detail. I have the necessary patience and understanding that is required to establish a sustainable, long-term customer relationship.

You are now creating a visual picture of yourself for the reader.

**USEFUL EXAMPLES**

**Communicative** - I am comfortable at balancing and efficiently interpreting all levels of multicultural encounters due to my keen respect and understanding of cultural diversity.

**Taking responsibility** - I have experience arranging a wide variety of events and activities. I am reliable and goal-oriented with a positive attitude. These traits allow me to carry out and complete tasks with professional quality.

**Determined** - I always do a thorough investigation before a given task. When it is done, I act quickly and decisively without losing focus in action in case something unforeseen should happen.

**Goal-oriented** - I have always enjoyed it best when I see clearly that there are both individually set goals and common group goals. I thrive the best when I see that the opportunity for me to develop exists within the organisation.

**Reliable** - I strive to always honor my word, keep agreements and deliver promised results.

**Service-oriented** - I am a naturally social, humble and positive person with a talent for making customers happy and managing various contacts in a constructive manner, even in conflict-filled starting positions.

**Enterprising** - Coming up with tips on what can be made easier and simplify everyday life is something I am good at. I have many ideas and find it easy to plan my work tasks.

**Organised** - I usually see the world in the form pieces of a puzzle and have a very good ability to fit the right piece in the right place.

**Service-oriented** - I want the customer to be satisfied. I give that little extra, even if it's not always needed.

**Dutiful** - My confident and independent way of working contributes to both customers and employees feeling comfortable working with me.

**Enthusiastic** - I create a positive atmosphere around me and take on new tasks and challenges with joy along with the desire to involve both myself and others.

**Orderly** – I am careful with documents and am well organised. I am aware of the importance of being orderly, as workflow becomes much more efficient then.

**Team player** - I am a person who appreciates good working relationships that provide support and encouragement. I am usually patient and calm and show openness to people around me. Being a good listener is natural for me and I am there for my co-workers when needed.

**Thorough** - I follow the routines that exist, as I know how important it is that they are followed in a professional way.

**Driven** – I am very ambitious and determined. I work hard to achieve the goals set and always find new ways to reach them.

**Initiative** - Problems are there to be solved. As a person, I like to take initiative and solve tasks.

**Experienced** - My long professional career has given me experience from several different organisations and industries which enables me to easily get a quick and good overall view of different situations.

## ● NEXT STEP

Congratulations, you have just gone through the chapter for the second session out of four in Block 1 in "TBS – Three Block System". Halfway through the first block.

You should now have a good idea on how to work with your personal qualities and characteristics.

The lessons learned from this will be continuing to build and create the foundation we now have started to build for a Brand called You.

A way to get the job you have been dreaming about.

The next session in the series is called The Pitch.

# ELEVATOR PITCH

## A guide towards getting a job

AND IT'S SIMPLER THAN YOU MIGHT THINK.

CREATE THE PERFECT ELEVATOR PITCH

BE READY FOR THE SPONTANTEOUS MEETING

## • ELEVATOR PITCH

Originally, an elevator pitch or elevator speech, is a short description of an idea, product or company that explains the concept in a such a way that any listener can grasp the meaning in a short period of time.

This description typically explains who the concept is for, what it does, why it is needed, and how it will get done.

In our case, we want to use it when explaining an individual person - you. The description generally explains an individual's skills and goals. It clarifies why you would be a productive and beneficial person to have on a team or within a company or project.

An elevator pitch can be used to entice an investor or executive in a company or explain an idea to a founder's parents. The goal is simply to convey the overall concept or topic in an exciting way.

Time to convert that into explaining who you are and what you can do for your future employer.

The name, elevator pitch, reflects the idea that it should be possible to deliver the summary in the time span of an elevator ride or approximately between thirty seconds and one minute.

The first two sentences of any elevator pitch are the most important and should capture the attention of the listener.

*In* short, a pitch is a persuasive speech you use to introduce yourself. The purpose is to explain your value while clearly sparking interest in who you are and what you do.

In a previous chapter, I mentioned USP – Unique Selling Point. It is here you will need to use USP in a very short timeframe to get the attention of the listener. Something that might lead to a proper interview and ultimately your dream job.

Sound scary? Awkward? Impossible?

Don't worry, we will break it down and make it possible for you to create the perfect pitch for yourself.

It is easier than you might think.

Enjoy your reading

## • WHAT IS A PERSONAL ELEVATOR PITCH?

Let us explore. An elevator pitch, as I explained in the foreword, is a short but easy-to-understand explanation of you, your product, or your company. In this case, you are selling your services such as what you are good at, what you have experience in, what you are educated to do and what you really want to do.

A personal elevator pitch needs to be a compelling introduction of yourself, what you do, and what sets you apart from others in your field. It's intended to quickly captivate your audience and help open up a dialogue.

A pitch consists basically of only a few parts that are broken down into three questions requiring specific, straightforward answers:

**Who are you? - What have you done before? - What do you want?**

These questions need to be converted in statements and delivered in 30-60 seconds.

It can take some time to get your pitch right. You will go through several versions before creating one that is as good as you want it and that also sounds natural in a conversation.

Most importantly, it needs to sound good not only to you, but to your coach or to the people you have selected as your test group.

We all know that first impressions are important. Especially when you are looking for a new job.

"You only have one chance for a first impression."

Different studies have concluded that within the first seven (7) seconds of a meeting, people will have a solid impression of who you are. There is some research that suggests all it takes is a tenth of a second to start determining traits like trustworthiness.

That is not enough time to talk about the weather or charm the person in front of you with stories that have nothing to do with your job interview. You don't have the luxury of banking on a second meeting to clear up any misconceptions.

Findings in a study about 'The Art of First Impressions' revealed that seven of ten people form a first impression of somebody before they even speak. The study consisted of 2000 people which equates to 69% of the test subjects.

So, this is what you are up against. But we will sort you out and get you ready.

## • THE PITCH BROKEN DOWN

We started already on page 5 breaking down what a pitch is.

**Who are you? - What have you done before? - What do you want?**

Now let's see if we can break this down to something useful for you.

Start your elevator pitch with something that grabs attention of the listener is an important tip.

**Example of a 40 sec pitch:**

Your hook can be a question, such as, "Are you aware how many business owners waste time and money because they don't have time to organise their day in an efficient way? I can save you time so you can focus on what you do best, run your company."

Follow that up with, "I've been an executive assistant for the last five years and during this time I have come up with a system on how to quantify efficiency".

And then we continue with what you want.

"If you employ me as an assistant my goal will be for you to work less and accomplish more."

Your send off is an important cause for action.

"I'd love the opportunity to put my expertise to work for your company. Would you mind if I set up a quick call next week for us to talk about any upcoming opportunities for your team?

If we hook up on LinkedIn here and now, we can communicate that way."

Saying **"work less and accomplish more"** would most likely have a business owner asking how you intend to do that. That is a very appealing statement.

Did you notice what I did with the part **"Who you are"**? I converted it to a mission statement **"I can save you time"**.

What is the most important thing in life and something you can never get back? Yes, you are right, it is time. The greatest gift of all time you can give anyone is just that, time.

I also covered **"What have you done before"** in a quick and easy way, giving some credibility to the pitch.

It leads to stronger connections.

Look again at the example listed above. Included are several jump-off points allowing you to dive into deeper conversations.

First paragraph: you can always be more efficient, although it is a challenge.

**"I can save you time"** is also a challenge that can start questions = interaction.

The middle paragraph states what type of position you have had and for how long. Again, it can create interaction. "Where did you work?"

The system I hinted at that I had created will for sure create some curiosity.

**You describe what you are looking for without being too pushy.**

Again, look at the example above. It ends with the person stating, "is looking for a position as an assistant". This is to the benefit of the employer. The person doesn't directly ask for the role, so it doesn't come across as pushy.

**It will make you stand out.**

By having a crisp, concise personal elevator pitch, you'll stand out from the pack.

Can't stress enough the importance of a course of action included in the pitch.

In this example I used "setting up a quick call" and using LinkedIn as a communication platform, something that actually serves more than one purpose.

Your profile on LinkedIn should be more or less a mirror image of your CV. This subtle verbal message has allowed you to give the receiver just that- your CV. You have delivered the desired connection to your host on a subconscious level. Clever!

All of this accomplished in about 40 seconds.

Remember all the things you came up with when doing the SWOT analysis earlier? That data will now come into use when you create your pitch.

The elevator pitch goes beyond sharing what it is you do and what you want. Instead, the goal is to intrigue your lead so that they want to know more.

Be ready to answer questions: you need to keep the conversation going.

Always have a business card handy, preferably a digital version and that includes LinkedIn.

Don't get upset if your elevator speech doesn't get you what you want immediately.

## • AND THERE IS MORE

You will most likely need to create more than one pitch, to be used in different scenarios.

It's a good idea to have one general pitch that you can use at any moment, but you should practice tailoring your pitch for unexpected encounters.

For example, if you are approaching start-up companies, you could include in your pitch why you are especially excited about working for start-up businesses.

The more personalised your 'why' is, the more likely you are to get a positive result from the conversation. It shows your depth of interest and respect for the listener's time.

When pitching in other circumstances the things that motivate you in front of a start-up company might not apply for a company that has been in business for decades, so they won't understand why you would like to work for them with the same pitch.

### EXPRESS CONFIDENCE

Even the best elevator pitch can lose its effectiveness if your delivery lacks confidence. That makes sense, correct?

Keep your chest high, shoulders back and smile when delivering your pitch. Use a strong speaking voice to show confidence in your experience and what you want in the future. Look the listener straight into his or her eyes.

There is a possibility that your audience won't be open to hearing your pitch. Yes, it can happen!

If it's not the right time or the person you are speaking to doesn't seem receptive, gracefully drawback.

If you have asked for an in-person meeting and they have said no, you can ask if they would prefer email or a phone call. If you get the sense at any point that the conversation is an inconvenience, leave the interaction with empathy for your audience.

You could request to hear about their career path and give them the chance to share their pitch or you could ask for an introduction to someone else, if appropriate.

Remember that developing an elevator pitch one step at a time makes it simple to create a speech that can be used in any professional situation.

Elevator pitches can be helpful as you take them into your next networking event or interview, both digitally and IRL. Your elevator pitch could be the beginning of a new opportunity, so draft, review, refine and deliver with confidence.

Ask yourself this question as you start writing: What do I want my audience to remember most about me?

Very important! Keep in mind that your pitch should also be of interest to you, after all, if you don't get excited about what you're saying, neither will your audience.

Your pitch should bring a smile to your face and quicken your heartbeat. People may not remember everything you say, but they will likely remember your enthusiasm.

If you feel your pitch is boring and uninteresting, I guarantee you that it is just that!

## PRACTICE

Like anything else, practice makes perfect. Remember, how you say it is just as important as what you say. If you don't practice, it's likely that you'll talk too fast, sound unnatural, or forget important details in your pitch.

Set a goal to practice your pitch regularly. The more you practice, the more natural your pitch will become. You want it to sound like a smooth conversation, not an aggressive sales pitch.

Make sure that you're aware of your body language as you talk, which conveys just as much information to the listener as your words do. Practice in front of a mirror or better yet, in front of friends until the pitch feels natural.

As you get used to delivering your pitch, it's fine to vary it a little – the idea is that it doesn't sound too rigid or like it's pre-prepared, even though it is!

## WHY DO I NEED AN ELEVATOR PITCH?

There are many uses for an elevator pitch. Some of the most common, except when being used in an elevator...include:

In a Cover Letter:

Use your elevator pitch as a way to either help you brainstorm the main points you want to touch upon in your cover letter or use it within the actual text of your statement as a way of getting off to a strong start.

Using your pitch in this format is a fantastic way to highlight what drives you and what makes you special.

During an Interview:

Often hiring managers will ask you to tell them about yourself during an interview. Having an honest, memorable, and well-thought-out answer can capture their attention and show that you know you can be a valuable asset to their organisation.

It can also help open a meaningful dialogue about what you're looking for and whether this career opportunity will be the right fit for you.

At Networking Events:

You're likely to meet dozens, if not hundreds of people, at networking events. Having prepared authentic statement about yourself can help break the ice when starting a conversation.

It can also help those you meet remember you and your accomplishments long after the attended event.

On social media, use your elevator pitch to help build your personal brand, such as LinkedIn or other professional networking platforms.

As you see, your pitch can be used in many different scenarios, so put your effort into getting it right. Remember that you will be talking about a subject that should be easy for you to discuss, you will be talking about you.

This is why we began with a SWOT analysis on yourself. Identifying your strengths, weaknesses, opportunities and threats. All of this falls into place when constructing your perfect pitch.

You never know when an opportunity opens up for you. You have a shot at pitching in front of your most desired potential employer.

Always be prepared and ready.

## • NEXT STEP

Fantastic, keep pushing. You have just finished the third chapter out of four in Block 1 in "**TBS – Three Block System**". Good work!

I am sure that you now understand the importance of the pitch, how to use it and most importantly – how to create it.

We continuing to build and create a **Brand called You.**

You still have eleven more sessions.

Plenty of knowledge for you to read and implement.

We are well on the way to get you the job you have been dreaming about.

The next session in the series is called **Curriculum Vitae, the CV.**

This session will be the last in block 1 and is extremely important.

# CV - CURRICULUM VITAE

## A guide towards getting a job

THE MOST IMPORTANT DOCUMENT

YOU HOLD THE KEY

TO YOUR OWN SUCCESS

## • CV

Your CV is the most import document you will need in your future job search. If you don't have one, WHY?

If you have one, let us take a look at it and see how we can optimise it. I am sure that it can be improved.

But what does CV actually mean, what language is this - curriculum vitae, and what is the correct translation of that?

The language is Latin, and the correct translation is "course of life" which is often shorten to just CV, "life". It is an extensive or complete summery of your career, including qualifications, education and other significant information.

It is typically the first information a potential employer will receive from you as an applicant for a job. That is why it is the most important document for you, that is why you need to spend time in creating it in the best possible way.

CV is the fourth and last session in Block 1 in TBS – Three Block System, in how to get your dream job.

Previously, you have conducted a SWOT Analyses to identify your strengths, weaknesses and also highlight the opportunities and threats.

After that, you worked on understanding your personal qualities, your characteristics that make you who you are.

Third session was all about how to construct the perfect pitch.

A persuasive text to help introduce yourself. A way to explain your value and clearly spark interest in who you are and what you do.

All of these together, combined with your education, certificates and work experience, will form the foundation of your CV.

It is very easy to forget what you have accomplished over time. Documenting your achievements on a regular basis is important. Always make sure that you update your CV with the following information:

- Key projects that you have led or worked on and the impact that they had on the business
- Process improvements where you have decreased costs or increased efficiencies
- Ongoing qualifications with the name of the course and when you completed it
- New skills that you have developed

Enjoy your reading

## • SOME GUIDELINES

Throughout this session some things will be repeated.

There are several important rules when it comes to visually creating something that will attract interest when reading your CV document.

Roughly simplified, it comes down to how to distribute air and letters. You don't want a document so packed with information that it becomes unreadable. The reader won't be able to see the forest through the trees.

If there is too much text, it will become too difficult for the eye to find so-called insertion points, putting your documents at risk to be registered as "difficult" and not being read.

Another simple rule is that your documents must be consistent in typography. All headings need to have the same font, size, color, line spacing and line width. The same applies for the text. It needs to be consistent all through your document.

The reason for this is that you want to make it easy for the reader and at the same time, arouse interest. If the flow for the reader is good, without a lot of interruptions, your document will be easy to digest, and it will also be easier to remember you.

Many ask what length the CV document should be? I say that in general no longer than two pages.

That said one size doesn't fit all. For example, a school drop-out or recent graduate with minimal experience may only need to use one side of A4.

Although not used as often, a three-page or more CV might be needed for those in high-level roles or for people who have gained a lot of experience or worked in multiple jobs over the last five to ten years. For example, some medical or academic CVs may be longer depending on your experience. While it's important to keep your CV concise you should also avoid selling your experience short. If you have important experience, it should be in your CV.

To save space, include only the main points of your education and experience. Stick to relevant information and don't repeat what you've said in your cover letter (session eight). If you're struggling to edit your CV, ask yourself if certain information sells you. If it doesn't, leave it out. If it's not relevant to the job you're applying for, delete it. If it's old detail from ten years ago, summarise it.

## COMMON ISSUES WHEN WRITING A CV

When writing a CV there can be a few difficult issues that may need to be thought about so that you portray yourself in the best light, but without being untruthful in any way.

**Ensure it is consistent with other online platforms:** It is necessary to ensure that your CV is consistent with any online platforms where experience and CVs are posted. LinkedIn is a prime example. Whilst they should not be exactly the same in terms of wording, they should have the same dates and basic facts, etc.

It is likely that prospective employers will do a little more research on those they are considering for a particular position, so it is well worth ensuring they are consistent with each other, otherwise it may set off warning bells.

**Career gaps:** In real life, career gaps can often occur, but it is an issue that many people worry about when writing their CV. They can arise for a variety of reasons e.g., raising a family, taking care of sick relatives, medical emergencies, sabbatical for travelling or global pandemics.

These can be addressed by adding a single line in the CV giving dates and stating the reason. By addressing it in the CV, it gives the interviewer the reason for the gap. Interviewers are real people themselves and they realise that life happens. By addressing it up front it takes away the impression that you might be hiding something.

**Career not moved**: In recent years, people have been far more mobile in their jobs. In some areas, people can move every couple of years while others may stay with the same company for many years.

Some recruiters may consider a person who has been in the same job for a long period of time as lacking dynamism and motivation. For anyone who has been in the same job or with the same company for a long time, it is worth highlighting how your responsibilities have grown or how the job has changed and how your contribution has increased.

Successfully done, this can show reliability and loyalty, which are two good characteristics for anyone employing new people.

**Ageism:** Ageism is an issue that many countries are trying to legislate against, it should not be a consideration when interviewing a candidate for a position. Despite this it can, and in my experience, will influence people looking at CVs. They may put the CV to one side if they think the person is older than they want.

To help overcome this, there are several methods to help overcome the issue. Whilst it is not normal these days to put age and date of birth on a CV, there can be other tell-tale signs that recruiters or hiring managers can use to gain a good view of the age of the candidate.

It is wise not to put elements into the CV that may lead the recruiter to think that you are a dinosaur. Don't put elements into the CV that describe long forgotten technology, unless there is very good reason. Also, emphasize skills that link your knowledge to modern technology and those that will be relevant in the modern environments.

Today, it is very easy to find out someone's age via social media. Let the recruiter first read your CV without revealing your age. If they are interested a little bit, they will Goggle to find your age. At least they are interested.

**CVs are useful for anyone seeking any form of employment:** permanent positions, contract work and often consultancy work. A CV is vital for many forms of job seeking.

As companies often receive vast quantities of CVs, it always helps to make yours stand out by presenting a very positive first impression.

This will help improve the chance of being offered an interview. Even at the interview, a well-presented CV will give the interviewers a more positive first impression which helps tremendously.

Follow the basic guidelines for the CV by spending time thoroughly presenting your experience and formatting the CV so it looks professional. This is always time well spent!

## • PERSONAL STATEMENT

### WHAT IS A PERSONAL STATEMENT?

It's known as the opening statement or executive summary.

A personal statement is a concise paragraph or summary which details what experience and knowledge you can bring to a company.

Strategically placed at the top of your CV, the personal statement is your opportunity to really sell yourself to employers and to highlight the relevant skills and experience you possess.

While effectively convincing recruiters that you're a good fit for the role, a personal statement gives you the chance to show off your strengths and share your career goals.

The personal profile is essentially a snapshot about you that should excite and entice the employer to want to pay closer attention to your CV. It's the sales pitch that highlights your best features.

**Do I need a personal statement on my CV?**

While your CV doesn't necessarily need a personal statement, employers spend only seconds looking at CVs. With this in mind, a personal statement can give you an invaluable opportunity to make your application stand out to employers and set yourself apart from the competition.

If you'd like to include a personal statement on your CV, it might be best, as a graduate, to focus on your educational background and the career path you'd like to embrace. If you have relevant experiences, use these to make your personal statement unique.

If you're struggling with what to write, break your personal statement down into three parts. Focus on:

- who you are
- what you can offer
- your career aims

There is no hard and fast rule. However, personal statements are generally displayed as a single paragraph without a title or subheading.

You'll need to keep it consistent with the rest of your CV formatting, meaning that the font size and type will need to be the same throughout your document.

Also, consider the voice you'd like to use. Personal statements can be written in either the first or third person, but you'll need to maintain this voice throughout, so don't switch between the two.

Remember, avoid copying and pasting ready-made examples. Instead use them as a guide to craft your own tailored CV personal statement.

## INCLUDE KEYWORDS, NOT BUZZWORDS

Keywords are specific statements or required skills taken from the job advert. Keywords will ensure that your CV not only passes an initial screening from the recruiting software, known as an Applicant Tracking System (ATS), but they also show the hiring manager that you understand the responsibilities and experience required for the job. Alternatively, buzzwords are simply seen as fluff, acting as useless and cliché adjectives that take up valuable space in your personal statement.

**Example Personal Statement, keywords highlighted:**

"**Startup** veteran for 10 years, including businesses rated the UK's fastest-growing. **Strategic advisor** with a specialism in **fast-growth forecasting, initial finance** and operations function setup in **SaaS, e-commerce, fintech and blockchain** businesses. Proven **team builder**, creating an **FP&A function** from scratch and leading first hire to full **CIMA qualification**."

**Another example:**

"CIM qualified VP Marketing with experience growing market share and penetrating new markets for world-class luxury goods brands. Fluent in French, I have held country leadership roles in Belgium and Singapore and possess strong Digital Marketing skills. London-based, I am now seeking a Chief

Commercial Officer role with an entrepreneurial, fast-paced luxury brand with international growth."

Only three sentences in this personal statement and they pack a punch.

It's clear that the applicant is an expert in digital marketing, the inclusion of the French language capability and markets worked in, convey that the applicant has international experience, and an ATS will instantly match this person with roles in London. Also, note that the statement is keyword-dense as well.

## • PREPARATION - POINTERS

There are several key points that should be adopted when preparing a CV.

Things to do:

- Use positive language

- Concentrate on your achievements
- Always be concise
- Keep to two A4 sides of paper
- Check thoroughly for spelling and other mistakes, and check again
- Review the CV and ask the opinion of another person

Things not to do:

- Never say anything that is not true and you cannot back up
- Never leave any gaps in the career history, it will cause interviewers to question what is being hidden
- Don't make the layout very fancy, keep it clean, simple and attractive

## • PREPARATION - IMPORTANT CONTENT

When wondering how to write your CV, here are a few key items that it should contain.

**Contact information:** Include your full name, address, phone number and email address.

When providing your email address, make sure the one you use looks professional. Some of the more humorous ones may not be appropriate and will give the wrong impression of you.

**Personal details:** As the description implies personal details including nationality and whether a driving license is held may also be included. I suggest you leave out your date of birth. In some countries, it is not appropriate to put in your age and the recruiter is not allowed to ask the age question. It can also damage your chances for an interview (if you are a dinosaur like me).

**Skills:** This section includes a highlight of your key skills. It is often scanned by prospective employers looking for keywords therefore it is a very important element in the CV preparation.

**Professional experience:** The work experience section of the CV backs up the skills section, which all employers will want to see. This can be a little tricky for new graduates, so be sure to include any relevant experience including vacation jobs. Everything counts.

Include the organisation where you worked, the job title, the dates you were employed and a summary of your experience and achievements.

To make it easier for the recruiter to find the most relevant information first, work experience should be set out in reverse chronological order, e.g., most recent experience first.

This area of the CV should focus on achievements and successes and highlight proven abilities. Again, it needs to be truthful, but also represent yourself in a positive light.

**Academic history:** List all schooling from high school through postdoctoral (if applicable). Include the title of the degree you earned, the year you graduated and the name of the school.

**Awards and honours:** For each award, add the name, year received, the organisation that gave you the award and any pertinent details (such as how often it's presented).

**Other education:** Naturally when preparing a CV, you include a list of qualifications and brief educational details. It can be courses you have taken that can have relevance for the employer.

**Publications and presentations:** For publications, provide a full citation including your co-authors, date, summary, volume, page, DOI number. For presentations, provide the title, date and venue where you presented.

**Qualifications and skills:** List a combination of hard and soft skills you've developed throughout your career. Foreign languages are important to include.

**Professional associations:** List the organisation's name, location or chapter and the dates of active membership.

**Grants and scholarships:** Provide the name of the grant or scholarship, date awarded and the institution that provided the award.

**Licenses and certifications:** Include the name of the license or certificate, the date you earned it and the institution that awarded it.

Consider also mentioning your proficiency level such as Basic, Intermediate, Advanced or Expert for every skill on your list.

**Other relevant information:** At times you may want to include other supplementary information including hobbies, interests, etc. Sometimes this is thought to be a bit superfluous, but it can give the interviewer a fuller picture of you.

This section should be kept short, and if space on the CV is at a premium, then it may be best to omit it.

**References:** It is normal for prospective employers to contact references before commencing any new employment. In some cases, this has been done before the interview, so be aware of this.

Accordingly the names and contact details for referees are often included on a CV. Another way is to write "References upon request".

I suggest having two references, if possible.

Normally one is required from the previous employer. I would suggest you add another, a personal reference. Someone that maybe hasn't worked with you, but can vouge for what kind of person you are.

Important, make sure to inform your references that you are sending out your CV with them listed as references. They need to be aware of what you're doing and have time to prepare.

## • SAMPLES

There are many types of CV templates to choose between. Make sure that you select one that complies with what you have learnt, and you feel confident using.

I recommend the site Visual CV to find a good template. Alternative you create your own from scratch.

https://visualcv.grsm.io/gwhellstedt

# NAME
# LAST NAME

**JOB YOU'RE LOOKING FOR**

name.lastname@gmail.com
+34 999 999 999
City - Country
skype
url.linkedin
@twitter

## ABOUT ME

Xxxxxxxxxxxxxxxx xxxxxxxxxxxxxx xxxxxxxxxx xxxxxxxx xxxxxxxxx xxxxxxxx xxxxxxx xxxxxx xxxxxx xxxx xxxxxxx xxxxx xxxx xxxx xxxxxx xxxxx xxxx xxxx xxxx xxxx xxxx xxxx xx xxx xxx xxx xx x xxxxxxxxxxxxxxxxx xxxxxx.

## SOFTWARE

| | |
|---|---|
| Excel | ★★★★★ |
| PowerPoint | ★★★★☆ |
| Word | ★★★★☆ |
| Photoshop | ★★★☆☆ |
| Xxxxxxxxxxxxxx | ★★☆☆☆ |
| Xxxxxxxxxxxxxx | ★★☆☆☆ |

## REFERENCES

- ✓ Spanish
- ✓ English
- ✓ German
- ✓ French

## WORK EXPERIENCE

00-00-00
(City-Country)

**NAME OF THE COMPANY**
Job occupied
Missions or tasks realized:
xxxxxxxxxxxxxxxxxxxxxxxxxxxxxxxxxxxxxxxxxxxxxxxxxxxxxxxxxxxxxxxxxxxxxxxxxxxxxxxxxxxxxxxxxxxxxxxxxxxxxxxxxxxxxxxxxxxxxxxxxxxxxxxxxxxxxxxxxxxxxxxxxxxxxxxxxxxxxxxxxxxxxxxxxxxxxxxxxxxxxxxxxxxxxxxxxxxxxxxxxxxxxxxxxxxxxxxxxxxxxxxxxxxxxxxxxxxxxxxxxxxxxxxxxxxxxxxxxxxxxxxxxxxxxxxxxxxx

00-00-00
(City-Country)

**NAME OF THE COMPANY**
Job occupied
Missions or tasks realized:
xxxxxxxxxxxxxxxxxxxxxxxxxxxxxxxxxxxxxxxxxxxxxxxxxxxxxxxxxxxxxxxxxxxxxxxxxxxxxxxxxxxxxxxxxxxxxxxxxxxxxxxxxxxxxxxxxxxxxxxxxxxxxxxxxxxxxxxxxxxxxxxxxxxxxxxxxxxxxxxxxxxxxxxxxxxxxxxxxxxxxxxxxxxxxxxxxxxxxxxxxxxxxxxxxxxxxxxxxxxxxxxxxxxxxxxxxxxxxxxxxxxxxxxxxxxxxxxxxxxxxxxxxxxxxxxxxxxx

00-00-00
(City-Country)

**NAME OF THE COMPANY**
Job occupied
Missions or tasks realized:
xxxxxxxxxxxxxxxxxxxxxxxxxxxxxxxxxxxxxxxxxxxxxxxxxxxxxxxxxxxxxxxxxxxxxxxxxxxxxxxxxxxxxxxxxxxxxxxxxxxxxxxxxxxxxxxxxxxxxxxxxxxxxxxxxxxxxxxxxxxxxxxxxxxxxxxxxxxxxxxxxxxxxxxxxxxxxxxxxxxxxxxxxxxxxxxxxxxxxxxxxxxxxxxxxxxxxxxxxxxxxxxxxxxxxxxxxxxxxxxxxxxxxxxxxxxxxxxxxxxxxxxxxxxxxxxxxxxxxxxxxxxxxxxxxxxxxxxxxxxxxxxxxxxxxxxxxxxxxxxxxxxxxxxxxxxxxxxxxxxxxxxxxxxxxxxxxxxxxxxxxxxxxxxx

## EDUCATION

Year
City-Country
**Diploma xxxxxxxxxxxxxxxxxxxxxxxxxxxx**
University or school

Year
City-Country
**Diploma xxxxxxxxxxxxxxxxxxxxxxxxxxxx**
University or school

Year
City-Country
**Diploma xxxxxxxxxxxxxxxxxxxxxxxxxxxx**
University or school

## • NEXT STEP

Perfect, you have now completed the first block out of three in TBS.

You are starting to see how everything is connected.

Next block will set you up with knowledge of how you can set up goals, analysing advertisements, doing cold calls and most importantly – writing a cover letter.

We are, step-by-step, getting closer to the end goal. And for me that is for you to feel confident with how to find and get your dream job. Having a CV and a Cover Letter that you feel confident sending out to employers and recruiters. That you feel good about how to create a Brand Called You.

You still have plenty more sessions.

Keep up the good work and keep going.

# SMART

# A guide towards getting a job

TIME TO SET YOUR GOALS,
YOUR SMART GOALS

HOW GOAL ORIENTED ARE YOU

AN INTRODUCTION TO HOW TO SET
YOUR GAOLS, THE SMART WAY

## • SMART

In the first session's Block 1, I began my text by stating how convinced I am that you are most likely going to succeed in life. My motivation behind that statement is that you are curious and willing to learn.

I am even more convinced because you have started on Block 2. My goal for you has not changed. I am here to give you the necessary tools so you can use your talent in its entirety. We are quickly getting there.

In this session I will teach you about how to set goals, really SMART goals.

Specific ⟷ Measurable ⟷ Acceptable ⟷ Time-bound

S.M.A.R.T. is a so-called mnemonic acronym. A guide in the setting of objectives, for example, in personal development. In your case, the objective is to find you your dream job.

I don't know your specific situation, but I believe you are looking for a job, hence you have taken on this book and TBS - Three Block System course.

Were you one of the thousands laid off over the last year and currently out of work? Maybe you are stuck in a rut thinking about a career change?

Whatever your current situation, setting SMART goals for a job search will help you find a new position.

Setting goals is more than having aspirations. That is not enough here. Statements like "I will find a new job" or "I will start my own business" are not enough. We need to be more specific.

Setting goals means creating a written plan that includes reasonable and measurable long-term and short-term objectives. It means setting SMART goals.

A dream written down with a date becomes a goal.

A goal broken down into steps becomes a plan.

A plan backed by action makes your dream come true.

Step by step you are learning how to analyze who you are and putting that into action. Now we move along with setting the goals for how and where to implement what we did in Block 1.

This is also a very important session since your goals will be your way forward. "If I don't know where I am going, how can I know when I am there?"

Enjoy reading and good luck with your SMART goals.

## • WHY SHOULD WE SET GOALS?

1. Nothing happens by chance.

Great discoveries and fantastic inventions did not become a reality because people just dreamed or did a little unplanned work or waited for someone else to get to grips with things. Vasco Da Gama, da Vinci, Pasteur and Edison all had one thing in common - a goal. Same goes for Richard Branson, Elon Musk and other well-known entrepreneurs of our current time.

A strong will and a concrete elaborated plan. It is only by finding a purpose and then creating a path to a goal that you will succeed in changing something seriously. The fact that chance leads us on the wrong track from time to time does not have to mean anything negative. On the contrary, the coincidences that appear become meaningless with-out a goal. With a goal in mind, coincidences instead turn into important small pieces of the puzzle.

Achieving goals, no matter how big or small, always strengthen self-confidence. It cannot be said too many times.

3. People with a goal feel better. They are happier, healthier and more positive. You will also find things easier and becoming happier when you know what you want and have something concrete to strive for - and not least when you start realizing your goals.

To "just take the day as it comes" is an old stupid philosophy of life. The hip era, however, ended in the 70s.

4. Lack of time is a recurring explanation for why we do not have time to set any goals. No matter how you turn things around, the day will always have 24 hours. Have you ever considered that it is through better planning and by having

clear goals that you learn to make better use of time? In this case, that is exactly what is happening!

5. What matters is not what your goal is. The important thing is that you set one (or more) goals and sub-goals. It is also not so important if you succeed 100% in reaching your goal. It may sound strange, but the most important thing is that you have set a goal that you strive for. Even if you only get halfway there, you have still reached twice as far as if you had done nothing at all.

6. Setting goals is a fantastically effective way to channel energy. It will be much easier to gather and use your powers if you know what you are striving for.

7. Many people claim that they do not know what they want. It's just bullshit. Most people know very well what they want.

You're on this program for a specific reason or am I wrong? You want a job, right?

So not only do you set goals, I want you to set SMART goals.

## • WHY SPECIFICALLY SMART GOALS?

The answer is that there is a principle behind the name.

It is therefore not the case that you have to be smart to set such goals. On the contrary.

By making the goals SMART, you increase the chances that you will be able to achieve them in the long run.

The word SMART is as you know a game of letters. Each letter has its own meaning, and all letters represent important ingredients for the goal to be as good and effective as possible.

The whole concept of SMART goals is therefore about you formulating goals that you have the best chance of succeeding in achieving.

### SPECIFIC

The first cornerstone of the SMART goals concept is that the goals must be specific.

That a goal is specific means that it is very precise and well defined. It cannot be misinterpreted in any way.

For example, a non-specific goal could be to "apply for a job". A corresponding specific goal would be to "apply for a job as a salesperson".

You should always set specific goals as they are easier to follow and easier to see if you have achieved them or not.

## MEASURABLE

Goals should be measurable. As we mentioned in the previous point, it is therefore important that it is easy to know when you have met the goal.

If your goal is to "apply for a job as a salesperson", then it is very difficult to know when you have actually achieved the goal. It is not enough to just apply for one job.

We need to be clearer than that here. Your goal should be measurable. Your aim can be to "apply for 10 jobs as a salesperson every week" instead of just "apply for a job as a salesperson".

Now it is measurable. How close did I get to my goal this week?

## ACCEPTABLE OR ATTRACTIVE

It is very important that you can stand behind your goals and accept the meaning of it. In that way the goals become both acceptable and attractive.

This point becomes even more important because if it is not attractive to try to achieve the goal, you will not work to achieve it.

## REALISTIC

It is very important that your goals are reasonable and realistic.

But at the same time, the goals must not be too easy. Strive to set goals that are challenging, but within a realistic reach so that you feel it is all possible.

I will "apply for 100 jobs as a salesperson every week" becomes unrealistic. Remove a zero and it will be feasible, in other words, it will be realistic.

## TIME-BOUND

When setting goals, it is important that there is a clear start and end date. Without it, the goal becomes insignificant in your mind, it won't be important.

We repeat, it is very important to set a specific time when the goal must be met. If you do not do this, you lose the effect of fighting to reach the goal in time. At the same time, it is easy to constantly postpone the goal. Set a date on all your goals.

This is the definition of SMART. Of course, you can break it down further if you want.

But let me give you an example of a goal that picks up the whole definition of SMART:

-I will send 90 job applications as a receptionist or customer recipient by April 1 to receive an income by June 1.

It is specific and measurable, but also attractive and realistic.

Why 90 applications? If we divide it by the number of weekdays from January 1 until April 1, which is 90, there will be 1 application per day.

That number can be met, it is possible to send out one application per day.

Something to consider:

It is important when formulating your goals that you use terms such as:

- I will start...
- I will apply...

Then you know what to do, you can take control.

But if you put in writing: I shall stop.... It becomes an avoidant goal.

Let me simplify it for you with an example:

I should eat two healthy apples a day instead of saying I should stop eating junk food every day. In that way it becomes a positive goal instead of an avoidant, a negative goal.

You can also use both activity and effect goals.

Such as: I will call 30 different companies (activity) and send out 10 CVs or get one interview (effect).

Super simplified:

I will...  Before...  To...

An action... A deadline... A purpose...

Remember that when you write down relevant goals, focus and direction will be created in the job search.

Tips on how to achieve your goals:

If you always start from the SMART model, you will have significantly more use for your goals. There are a few more things that can be useful when working with your goal. Here are a few more points.

***Always write down your goals.***

By having the goals on paper, the chances increase that you will actually succeed. An ordinary lined paper usually works well to write the goals on.

***Go through the goal twice a day.***

First when you wake up in the morning and then before you go to bed. This means that your subconscious is constantly processing the goals, which you eventually will have incredible use for.

***Reconcile your goals.***

Have someone review your goals. A friend, someone close or a job coach. This helps make it even more motivating to strive towards the goal.

Questions you can ask yourself.

- What do I want to achieve?
- Why is it important for me to achieve this goal?
- What do I need, what resources are required and what is missing, to accomplish what I am set out to do?

Now you know why your goals need to be SMART.

**YOUR TEMPLATE FOR HOW TO PRIORITISE**

## • DO YOU FEEL UNFOCUSED? HARD TO KNOW WHAT TASK TO TAKE ON?

Here is a matrix that can simplify life.

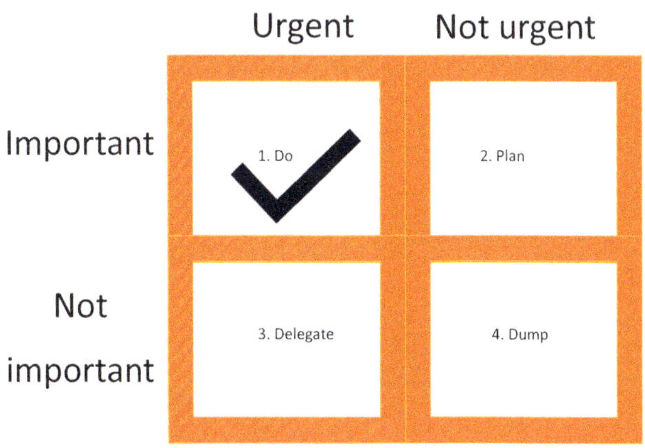


## LET ME EXPLAIN THE MODEL.

We divide our tasks into how important and how urgent they are.

We then create four fields. In order for you to be able to decide if it is important, it is crucial that you keep track of your goals. Decide for whom it is important? Is it for you or for someone else?

In box 1, it is both important and urgent. This is where the tasks that we usually call "ad hoc solutions" end up. Things we may have forgotten or things that require an immediate response, such as sending a CV before the application deadline expires or someone wants it within an hour.

Box 2 is just as it says, about the tasks that are to be planned. For example, complete your SWOT and your Pitch.

In other words, the strategically important tasks, the ones that lead you towards the goals. Sometimes it is difficult to create time when we are stressed. That is why it is so important to plan, set SMART goals.

In boxes 3 and 4, the information is not important and varies in urgency.

Which box should you focus on?

Box 1, we need to give immediate attention, but most of the work is done in box 2.

It is in box 2 that we get the right things to happen that play a significant role in our future job search.

It takes insight into what actually are the 2s for you. Being disciplined is key. Follow a schedule and actually take the time to do your homework. As I usually say, "Applying for jobs is a job in itself".

By consciously working in box 2, you reduce some tasks that can easily end up in box 1.

So why do we sometimes end up in boxes 3 and 4? Well, here we feel really good when we get things done. Easy tasks that are not important and most likely, in no hurry to get done.

It is a bit like getting a lot of likes on social media. In this case, it also creates stress because we lose time. Time for the things we really need to accomplish, like the important tasks.

Keep in mind that it can be easy to get confused and mix-up important and urgent.

Analyze what you spend your time on everyday day.

Divide your goals into sub-goals. "When eating an elephant, take one bite at a time." Clearly, no one is encouraging dining on these fantastic animals, but it's good advice about how to tackle a huge, overwhelming task or project.

## REMEMBER!

Goals help you focus.

Goals help you see your progress.

Goals motivate you.

Goals allow you to take control of your life and future.

Goals help you get the life you want.

## • NEXT STEP

Very good, you have finished the first session in Block 2 in "TBS – Three Block System". You are now far on the way towards being halfway through. Still a few more steps to pass.

The SMART system will be a very good tool for you to work with. Use it! The whole program is set up in such a way that each session is useful by itself, but of course, you get the best result using it all together.

There is also a deeper thought process behind the order of things.

The next session in the series is Add Analysing. You will learn about how to analyse different adverts for jobs. What are the key words, what is it they are looking for?

# JOB AD ANALYSING

## A guide towards getting a job

HOW TO UNDERSTAND AND INTERPRET AN ADVERTISEMENT FOR A JOB

HOW WELL DO YOU UNDERSTAND WHAT

THEY ARE REALLY ASKING FOR?

## • AD ANALYSING

Ad Analysis, what is it? How is it done? What can I get out of it as a job seeker?

There are multiple frameworks used for Ad Analysis in business. We will explore a couple of them to see what can be used in the purpose of understanding what they are looking for in the world of job advertisements.

To begin with, a job ad is a way for a company to ask the market if there is anyone out there who can fit a specific profile to come work for them?

The meaning behind the text in the ad reveals that the company has come to the conclusion, via an internal analytical process, that there is a demand within the company for a new employee.

They have created a wish list for the desired features this person should have. What experience, education and personal characteristics they think are needed to assimilate to the work environment and actually achieve results.

Again, you will need this wish list to be able to analyse and understand what is important and how you will be able to stand out from the rest of the applicants for the position in question.

I have simplified some of the analysing principals and that comes in handy in the job seeking case. We will dive into that shortly.

The idea for this session is to give you specific knowledge to understand and extract information from a job advertisement so you can respond with an answer that makes you stand out from the other applicants. Most importantly, it shows the employer that you have what they are looking for. That you fit the profile.

Sounds easy, but that is not always the case. By using this TBS step by step method, we build up the knowledge of not only yourself and who you are, but we also make you understand what it is the employer is looking for.

Let us continue into the world of ad analysing!

## • TBS ADVERT ANALYSING MODEL

In this model, I use two main principals.

Some of them include 5Ms, Gunn's Principles, etc., which are normally used in business. This model is slightly different though.

When I was analysing ads, I kept it as a policy to simplify the procedure. Hence, the framework I follow does not have a name as such, so I call it the TBS job-advert analysing model.

This framework has 2 basic elements: **Strategic** and **Tactical**. Let's talk about them as well as their components.

Whenever a company decides to hire and to run an ad for this position, there are certain objectives in its mind that it wishes to achieve.

The first rule of analysing any ad, for any reason, is to identify the objectives - I used to call it the **'Basic Insight'** behind the ad.

The first thing you look for in an ad is the key or basic insight, which often requires some browsing about in the company's current operations.

Always Google the company, read about them online, do your research. It pays off in the end, I promise.

Basic insights:

1). Company has a new big order. Needs more staff

2). Company loses staff due to unknown reasons. Needs to rehire staff.

3). Company is branching out. Needs more staff.

4). Company is in a growth and expanding phase. Needs more staff.

Understanding the reasons gives insight for your coming career at that particular company. What kind of company is it? What are their core values?

This is information that can be crucial for you to know. It is also information you can find out if you get an interview. The more you know before you apply for the job means a more detailed Cover Letter you will be able to write.

If it is a larger company, there is quite often something in the online news feeds, a webpage, FB or LinkedIn that can give some sort of indication to what might be going on within the company. Even smaller firms usually post company news on the social media which can be helpful in building your portfolio about them.

It is recommended to expand your investigation of the company via Google. Search for information about the Managing Director of the company. The extra search can reveal useful information that can be both positive and negative.

If you find out that the company has a big yearly turnover of staff, be careful. I once worked for a company that had a nearly 40% yearly turnover of staff. Such workplaces are extremely toxic and should be avoided.

Google will help you fill up the "Basic Insight".

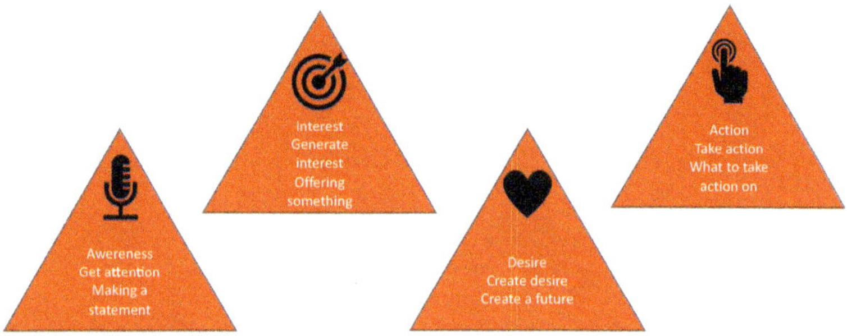

The second strategic element is the '**AIDA** Target'. There are four basic objectives of any ad campaign - **Awareness, Interest, Desire** and **Action**, also commonly known as AIDA. After viewing the ad, it should become clear to you which one the company is targeting. It can easily be identified after you understand the message.

- What specifically are they making clear in the ad for you?
- What is most important for them when employing a new co-worker?
- What statement do you see in the ad?
- After reading the ad, what is it you are most aware of?
- What are they offering?
- How are they trying to generate interest for the position in question?
- What makes you feel you want the job after reading the ad?
- Do you feel there is a future for you in company? Why?
- Do you feel a desire to get this job? Why?
- What is it you now need to take action on?
- What is the next step?

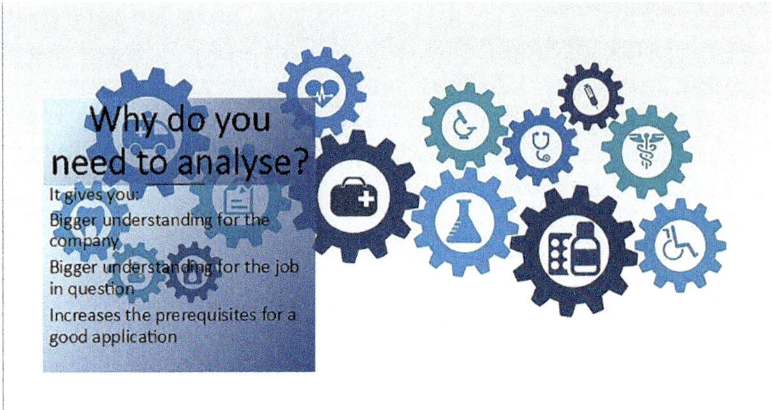


**The more you know and understand about the company hiring staff, the better you understand if this is something for you**

- What impression does the ad give?
- Can you read between the lines?
- What are the main tasks of the work?
- What skills and experience are required?
- What is negotiable?
- What kind of person are they looking for?

The general impression can give you a good insight into the culture of the company. Reading between the line is important. Sometimes it is good to analyse and see what it is they are not saying.

Finding out the main task for the position shows what the company is thinking about for the future.

The type of skills and experience required can vary for the same position at different companies. It tells you about their priorities.

Some ads list what is most important and least important.

If you find yourself lacking some experience or education needed for the job, it might be up for negotiation if it is something that you can study while working there. In some cases, further studies are not necessary.

What pictures do you see in front of you, what kind of person are they describing in the ad? Is it you or almost you?

Job ads normally consists of four parts and why that matters.

1. Job description

   Gives you information on how the company looks upon the position. Same title can have different description depending on the employer's point of view.

2. The company's requirements for the person they want to hire.

   Gives you information on what they expect from you.

3. Description of the business

   Gives you information on how they see themselves. When doing research on the company, you might come to a different conclusion.

4. Contact information

   Gives you information on where they are located and how they want to be reached.

## • PUTTING IT ALL TOGETHER - HOW AND WHY

Analysing adverts thoughtfully saves you more than just time. It will sustain your morale, give you more time to focus on the jobs you do have a chance of getting and improve your success rate in getting an interview.

Everything we cover now will help you write both your Cover Letter and CV in such a way that you will become more attractive for a future employer.

Listed below are seven repetitions and conclusions on what to do and why you should do them.

**1. Do a thorough review of each advert that is of interest to you.**

Read it through several times until you get a real feel and an understanding of what's being described. A typical job advertisement consists of:

- A statement about the organisation and how it perceives itself in the market.
- A statement about the job in terms of what is involved and daily tasks.
- A list of the selection criteria for any prospective applicant.
- Application details for the job in question.

**2. When you get a feel for what the job is about and what is expected from you as an applicant, set about reading "between the lines", to uncover what is not openly stated.**

In doing so, try to deduce if there is one particular crucial need or if there is anything else you can interpret from the words in the advert.

It's also useful to read the advert critically and ask yourself if they "have left anything out? Anything not covered when you feel that it should have been, could affect your suitability.

- It's a good idea to prepare specific questions about the things you either don't understand or don't see clarified in the job advertisement.

  Phone the contact of the company or agency and ask these questions. The answers will form part of your assessment of the advertisement and your own suitability.

- When phoning, take care not to "get interviewed" as part of the call.

Make it clear that you are only seeking more information and even make an excuse to get off the phone and call back later if it seems that you're already getting interviewed. **EXTRA IMPORTANT.**

- Also consider future needs and drivers of this job. What else will the company potentially need from this role down the track?
- Consider what skills and experience you have that would be ideal for this position which are not mentioned in the text of the advert.

  You'll need to pitch these to the employer who may not be aware of the relevance, but don't dismiss them for this reason.

**3. Once you've worked out what the job is all about, take a highlighter pen and mark every clause or phrase where it states what the actual requirements are. EXTRA IMPORTANT.**

**4. Read the advert again carefully to see if these needs are essential or merely desirable.**

This is known as a "filter". It is a way to eliminate applicants so that those interviewing don't have to expend additional time interviewing people lacking the relevant skills and qualifications. Time savers.

- When you analyse the advert, some phrases will stand out. These all shout 'IMPORTANT' at you, so look for similar phrases that you can match yourself against. Examples of what to look for include:
  - "it is essential that you...", or
  - "you must have...", or
  - "you will have..."

- Other advertisements are not so firm. In this case, the advertisement is saying "desirable" but not essential.

  Such advertisements may say:

  - "you should have...", or
  - "some knowledge of...", or
  - "ideally...".

- You should be able to meet more than 60 percent of the essential requirements which form the backbone of the job if you are to be seriously considered. **EXTRA IMPORTANT.**

  It is optimal to be able to meet all of the essential requirements, but there is some leeway for lateral skills and experience.

- The desirables are nice-to-haves and the more of these you meet, the better, but they are not the main issue.

  However, you can cover these in the Cover Letter to increase your chances of getting an interview.

**5. Look for the crucial need. EXTRA IMPORTANT.**

This one is the killer and the one you must have as it will knock you straight out. If you don't have it, then don't proceed.

- If you do have it... make sure it's the **first thing you mention in your response. That says**, "this candidate understands what we need".

**6. For your own sake in terms of future fulfilment in the job, consider what outcomes you will be expected to achieve in this job and whether you feel capable of this.**

Also look at what opportunities and possibilities are in the job and whether you have the skills and personal qualities needed to make the most of these opportunities.

Finally, but importantly, what challenges or barriers do you see as part of this job? Do you think they are surmountable or likely to become a dealbreaker? Being honest now can save a whole lot of pain later. You might see the potential difficulties, yet rationalise that on-the-job training will overcome it. On the other hand, you might feel that no amount of training will change your inability to handle deadlines, pressure, or multi-tasking, etc.

**7. When you have completed this analysis and you still see a good match, go ahead and draft your response letter.**

You should try to follow the style of writing shown in the advertisement by using similar phrases and words. However, don't just regurgitate their advert back to them; they want to know that you've really digested the job and you're able to phrase your suitability to it in your own words.

## ● EXAMPLE

This is just one example on how you can highlight text in a job advert. The ad is from LinkedIn.

- What are the main tasks of the work?
- What skills and experience are required?
- What is negotiable?
- What type of person are they looking for?

Use different colors. Now you can start implementing what you have learned in this segment.

We are looking for a Customer Success Manager to our office in Stockholm! 🤩

Your key role is to help the customers to maximize their adoption of LeadDesk solutions. The role is to be a hands-on expert and a project manager during the most critical phases of our customers' journey.

A successful Customer Success Manager is able to juggle between problem-solving, consulting, coordination, communication, and sales-like priorities in her/his daily work.

The ideal candidate has the ability to influence internal and external stakeholders, including senior business executives and entrepreneurs, and has a passion for helping us and others succeed. You think clearly and solve problems fast.

This is a challenging and rewarding role, where you see how LeadDesk software is delivered into the heart of our customers' workflows. You will get to work in an open, collaborative, and international team environment.

**What we'd like to have from you:** 💪

- Customer relationship experience (e.g., enterprise/SMB sales, project management or consulting)
- Experience in project management
- Prior experience in working with technology, ideally software-as-a-service (SaaS) products with a reach beyond the IT department
- Fluent communications skills in written and verbal Swedish and English
- Positive can-do attitude and enthusiasm in learning new

**We consider an advantage:** 💡

- Some level of technical knowledge is needed to succeed in this role
- Familiarity with modern web tools, technology & SaaS software

**What's in it for you?**

- The opportunity to work in an inspiring fast-paced environment in a venture capital-backed SaaS company
- An international work environment with great team spirit and colleagues full of positive thinking – LeadDesk currently employs 10+ nationalities in seven countries
- A culture where we do things together to help our customers and ourselves succeed
- Possibility to influence your role and career path
- Centrally located office facilities in Stockholm.

**How to apply** 📝

We will fill the position as soon as we find the right person. Could it be you? Great – we can't wait to meet you! Please apply promptly by sending us your application, CV and salary request. You can also apply with your LinkedIn profile.

**If you have any questions regarding this position, please contact Rebekka Gotter: rebekka.gotter (a) leaddesk.com**

Candidates for this job vacancy may be subject to background checks. By sending your application, you consent to having your background checked during the recruitment process for criminal convictions.

*About us 👋*

*LeadDesk is the Software behind Sales and Customer Service Superstars. We believe that happy agents are the key to better business.*

*We are a listed growth company. Currently, we are the market leader in the Nordics - aiming next to be the market leader in Europe. We are well on the way and already have over 20 000 happy agents in 34 different countries making millions of contacts every day.*

*LeadDesk is a company with a truly international vibe - we have 12 offices in seven different countries (Finland, Norway, Sweden, Denmark, Germany, Spain, and the Netherlands) and over 10 different nationalities working at our Helsinki headquarters alone.*

*We do everything with high ambition and a drive. We want to get things done and keep up the startup-like dynamic of constant development and being one step ahead. Therefore, we are constantly looking for people that share out ambition and drive to join this exciting journey!*

## • NEXT STEP

Perfect, that was the second session in Block 2 in "TBS – Three Block System". You are getting closer by the session...

The session you just finished is kind of ground-breaking. If you do not do a comprehensive analysis, you will not be able to create a top-of-the-line application.

With the tools you now have achieved through the different steps you have all of the possibilities to create an application that is accurate and stands out. The TBS system will give you the best tools to get your dream job. It will be up to you to apply your knowledge into your applications.

From here we will now move over to something slightly different, the Cold Calling List.

There is more than one way of finding opportunities within the job market. And that is exactly what we are soon getting in to after this.

# COLD CALLING LIST

## A guide towards getting a job

ALL JOB OPPORTUNITIES WILL NOT BE ADVERTISED

HOW YOU CAN FIND THE HIDDEN TREASURES -CREATING YOUR OWN OPPORTUNITIES

## • COLD CALLING LIST

In this session we will find out another way of discovering opportunities for you in the job market and in your job search.

Some estimate that as much as 80% of new jobs are never listed but are instead filled internally or via networking.

You want to tap into this hidden job market and there are a few ways of going about this.

In this book, we will show you how to create your own wish list of companies you would like to work for or can consider working for.

By creating a cold calling list and filling it up with 50-100 companies that you would consider working for, greatly increases your chances of employment.

It is not only about writing down a list of potential companies of interest, but going the extra mile by doing basic research on each and every one of these companies.

The strategy here is to do it a little more strategically. This list will become a manual for your work ahead with cold calls to companies of interest.

In this session, we will go through the process together.

We will show what kind of headlines you will need and how to properly use your Cold Calling List.

The idea is to give you a new way of reaching into the job market by identifying companies that have not made public a vacant position in their company.

We will also try to help you get over your fear of cold calls, since eliminating this fear is crucial when searching and applying for work.

You continue to build up your skills and knowledge on how to approach the best path towards your dream job.

In previous sessions you have worked mostly on deepening your knowledge of who you are while using different kinds of analysing methods.

This session is about identifying how to find where to implement that knowledge.

Let's get cracking on that list now!

## • WHAT TO DO, AND HOW TO DO IT

The goal is for you to use the newly created list to unveil hidden jobs, specifically, jobs that are not advertised. As I have stated already, approximately 75-80% of all job openings are estimated to be filled without an ad being published.

### *1. List of Companies*

What I want you to do is to write down the name of at least 50 companies of interest, but preferably 100 companies.

At the top of your list is the Number 1 company you want to work for. This company is the most attractive and has piqued your curiosity.

The company with the least attraction is at the bottom of your list. I will explain more about the numbers later.

### *2. Location*

Write down where they are, geographically, address.

### *3. Contact details*

Find out which people at each company who are the right contact persons for you. If the company has multiple offices, you need contact persons at more than one location.

Head of HR, Manager Director, Head of Sales, Office manager...Who is it you need to talk to, list them here.

Collect e-mail addresses and phone numbers. Most of these you will find via Internet.

### *4. Service*

What position are you applying for at the different companies? Research how they are organised, use their webpages to find out more.

### *5. Company information*

Compile information about the company. You need to be able to answer questions about why you are applying to them, why you want to work for them.

***6. Call***

Contact the companies. Start with the last company on the list. That is, the least attractive. Then you get the chance to practice your sales pitch so that you don't make a fool of yourself at the dream company – No1.

Most often it takes 5-10 calls to companies to fine tune your presentation and build up your confidence.

Note: You should not call if you don't have your Pitch done. The pitch is one of your key components in this process!

***7. Agenda***

Have the purpose clear and one goal for the call.

Most often, the goal is a personal meeting, and the purpose may also be to establish a good contact with the company (even if they don't have an opening right now).

Your main goal should be to get an interview.

Secondary objective would be tips and/or other contacts.

***8. Log***

After each call, keep a short log of who you spoke to, what you said and when the call was made.

Write down the outcome of the call. Documenting the conclusion will make it easier to reconnect next time you call them.

The conclusion includes a set date for your next contact with them.

### 9. Learning

After each call, write down what you did well during the call and what you need to improve on for the next time.

Then make the changes you need to your pitch, test it and pick up the phone and call the next company on the list.

If you do this, you have control over who you contacted, when you contacted them, when to contact them again and you will receive tips about jobs at companies that aren't on your list, but can be added.

Chance favors those who are prepared!

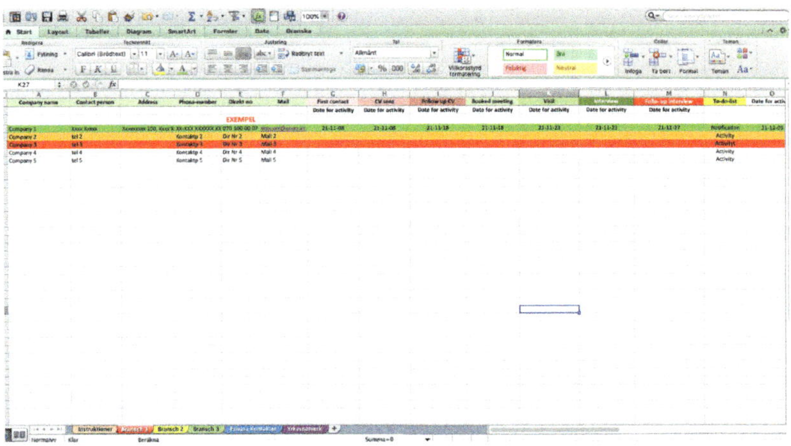

## • HOW COMPANIES PARTLY RECRUIT

**As you now understand, the Cold Call List is not too complicated.**

What you do now put that collected data into a ledger. Excel is a very good program to use for this purpose.

If you think about it, 100 companies are not so many when you start calling. How many calls a day can you do, 10? In ten days, you have called all the companies on the list. Once complete, you repeat the process with a new list.

When you have written down your favorite companies of interest, you come to a point where you wonder which companies should be on your list.

All of the companies you have listed up to this point have a competitive edge in the market. These are companies that work with similar products in similar ways. Map them out and put them on your list as well. All of a sudden, the list has expanded.

Why the company list and how companies recruit

9 out of 10 jobs were not advertised due to the fact that it is not cost effective to recruit due to the lengthy recruiting process. Smart employers prefer active jobseekers. Using their own networks to find new employees.

There are many studies about the benefits and the overall impact of networking. The results of these studies have varying results, but all agree that it's definitely a popular way to get a job.

Some experts say that 70% of people ended up in their current position thanks to networking, while other experts say the results lie between 80%-85%.

When people are asked how they landed their current job, the most common answer is via networking.

In one survey, conducted by LinkedIn and the Adler Group, "active candidates" were separated out from "tiptoers" and "passive candidates," those who looked for work in more casual ways.

Regardless of the individual attitudes and approaches job seekers brought to the table, networking was the most popular way to get a job. For "tiptoers", networking beat the odds 3 to 1. For even more casual job seekers, dubbed "passive candidates," networking dominated other job-search methods on a scale of 7 to 1.

Later in the TBS program you will have a session specifically about networking.

Use color to mark the different companies in your list according to this model here and it becomes clearer where to put your focus.

- **Warm companies** with identified employment need within 1 week - 1 month, those who say they need to employ in the near future, in the role you are looking for.
- **Lukewarm** companies with identified employment need within 1- 2 months, alternatively those who say maybe, not now but later.
- **Cold companies** with identified need for employment within 2 -3 months, alternatively a clear NO, to be followed up in 3 months, then maybe again.

## FEAR OF COLD CALLING

"I can't sell myself". Have you ever heard someone say this before? This phrase is the most common cold calling obstacle for job seekers.

You are NOT going to sell yourself, I repeat that – you are NOT going to sell yourself.

And now you are confused.

What is it you are set out to do?

You are looking for a job. You want to get employed at this company you are about to call. To begin with, you want to get the chance to come in for an interview.

You call them up and you say: "Hi, my name is (your name) I have this great body and I am offering you to have it, the hole body or just parts of it. It is up to you. I am willing to chop off an arm or a leg for you. Whichever you prefer".

That is selling yourself.

Obviously, this is not the way to go about it. It's just your imagination running wild.

**What is it we are really offering an employer?**

You are going to sell the synergy between your skills, attitude and knowledge = your ability.

Synergy between Knowledge, Skills & Attitude

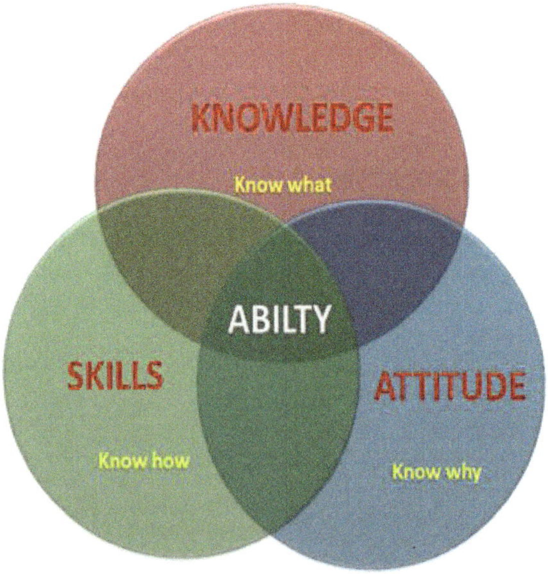

Of course, it is not your physical self you are selling.

It is the combination of your schooling, education, life experience, work experience –

all that has formed you to the person who is making the phone call.

You are applying for this job for a specific reason

and that is because you believe that you can actually do the job well.

As you can see, it is not yourself you are selling it is your abilities, your skills – know how, knowledge – know what, and attitude – know why.

You are offering the employer a service, a service provided by you, but still, it is a service.

When you go from thinking that you are selling yourself to selling a service it becomes easier and clearer. You will not talk about your personal life as you are going to talk about this amazing service that you can provide to the company you have called.

The really good part is that you know all about this service and what it can do for this company. By utilizing this service within the company, it will make life better for both the company and its employees. This service is so outstanding and can't be found anywhere else.

## • NEXT STEP

We have now finished the session about cold calling, a very important step for you in your quest towards the dream job.

We are getting closer to the end of the middle block in TBS, only two more block before entering the final block.

The next session will give you incite on how to create your cover letter. You have built up your awareness on who you are, explored what you can do and how to use this in your communication.

With your CV and cover letter combined with a great pitch, you have the right tools to contact future employer. You know how to analyse job advertisements and make cold calls. After the next session, you will have the ability to create the cover letter built on what you have previously learned.

Moving on through the different chapters we will explore other interesting areas of job searching. We will examine how to create and utilise different kinds of networks. As you now know, most jobs are landed via networking.

Our last session will be about interviews and various useful techniques to succeed. We like to say that the Interview Session is the similar to an exam. The knowledge you have gathered over the course of this program will help you complete the Interview Session.

You can always reach out and contact us if you have any additional questions.

We also offer coaching both IRL but also digitally.

You can read more on the webpage: www.hellstedt.org

You can also wright to us: **contact@hellstedt.org**

# COVER LETTER

## A guide towards getting a job

WHO ARE YOU AND WHAT DO YOU WANT

TIME TO EXPLAIN WHO YOU ARE AND WHAT YOU CAN DO FOR THE EMPLOYER

## • COVER LETTER

According to a CareerBuilder study, over 49% of HR managers consider a covering letter the second-best thing to give your resume a boost, number one being customising your resume.

A cover letter is important as about 26% of recruiters consider them critical in their decision to hire.

Another study on employer preference suggests that 56% want applicants to attach a cover letter to the resume.

The recruiter or employer will notice right away if you have put some effort into your application or not. They will see straight through the transparency if you use the same standard application documents for multiple employers.

Your cover letter will feel like an impersonal and general job application. An employer will not spend time reading this type of application. If you really want the job, you need to go all in and adjust your documents according to the requirements of each job position. Show that you are genuinely interested in their company, particularly this open position you are applying for.

You have a lot to win if you work through the content, language, and layout. In this session, you will learn how to create your cover letter step by step. As stated above, a cover letter should always be adapted to the job that you are applying for.

The first step that will prepare you for writing your cover letter is to go over the previous sessions. They will provide you with material that you will use while following this step-by-step cover letter-session.

And yes, there is system in doing all of this. I will show you that you don't have to rewrite everything for each application.

In the content of the previous chapters, you will find useful learning to be implemented here, hence step-by-step.

- Session 1 – SWOT
- Session 2 – Characteristics
- Session 3 – The Pitch
- Session 4 – Curriculum Vitae, the CV
- Session 5 – SMART
- Session 6 – Ad Analysing
- Session 7 – Cold Calling List

Are you with me? Let's do this!

Don't worry, we will break it down and build it up together to create the ultimate cover letter.

## • WHAT IS A COVER LETTER?

This lesson will help you understand the purpose of a cover letter, identify the main parts of a cover letter, find out what makes a cover letter effective.

Prospective employers use your resume to learn about your education, skills, and work history, as well as who you are and how to reach you. But that is mostly your past. Your cover letter has a slightly different purpose, it is more about your future and your abilities.

Remember what I wrote on page 96 and 97 in Cold Calling List?

"But what is it we really are offering an employer?

You are going to sell the synergy between your skills, attitude and knowledge = your ability."

As the name implies, a cover letter is a document that introduces you and accompanies your resume (your work history). It is what a hiring manager will see first. That is why it is important. It will be the text that that will entice the employer to look further into who you are and what you can do for them.

In today's competitive job market, hiring managers may get hundreds of resumes for only one position. Going through all of them is very time consuming. To alleviate the time strain, most hiring managers will quickly read over or scan cover letters to decide which resumes to read more closely.

**Another very important knowledge is that the hiring manger or recruiter normally only sees maximum 1/3 of your cover letter in their list of applicants on their computer, the beginning of your letter.**

The cover letter is your opportunity to attract.

You will be able to demonstrate:

- Why you are interested in the position.
- Why they should be interested in you, highlight some of your top skills.
- That you have knowledge about the organisation in question.
- That you have done your research.
- That you understand what is expected for the position.
- That you can express yourself.
- That you are grateful for their time and consideration reading your application.

In the first third of your cover letter, you must show that you are the perfect fit for the job. To do so, review session 6 – Ad Analysing. Find out what the most important skill the employer is looking for and make sure that you have that and write it in the beginning. That gives the reader the incentive to read more.

## • WHAT ARE THE DIFFERENT PARTS OF A STANDARD COVER LETTER?

### THE BASICS

A cover letter is basically a formal business letter that acts as an introduction to your resume. Because it is a formal business document, it should be in block business letter format. In this format, text is left justified (aligned on the left-hand margin).

- Date: This is the date the letter is written. We recommend using the Month Day, Year format, such as December 7, 2021. That works in most countries.
- Address: For the address, you should provide your home mailing address followed by the physical address you want to submit. If you don't want to write a physical address, write just your city and country.
- Greeting: The greeting is an important part of your cover letter. It establishes who you are sending the resume and cover letter to. I recommend that you try to find the name of the hiring manager to use here. If you can't find a name, use a generic term like Staff Selection Team or Hiring Manager.
- Body 1: The body should be divided into three sections. The first section is the intro and the part that needs to attract interest for the reader to continue through the full extent of the letter.
- Body 2: The body 2 is the main part of your cover letter and presents you as the best possible candidate for the job (what you can do). Most of this part can be reused for

all your cover letters, regardless of which company you are applying to.

- Body 3: The 'send off'. Where you have a statement that shows that you have read their homepage and the ad carefully. This needs to be a rememberable statement.
- Close: Use a polite and professional phrase here, such as Sincerely, Respectfully, or Kind Regards.
- Signature: This area should contain your name, a written signature in addition to another way to contact you (such as a phone number or email address).
- Enclosure line: Use this line whenever you include a separate item in the same envelope or email message. It will tell the recipient to look for the enclosed attachment, which will usually be your resume, but could also be samples of your previous work.

If you're sending a cover letter via email, you don't need to include the date, return address, or mailing address at the top of the page. Just include your own address and other contact information, such as your email or phone number, below your name in the signature area.

**Grand opening and more**

## • THE OPENING – THE MOST IMPORTANT PART

### WRITE A CATCHY OPENING PARAGRAPH

Here's the brutal truth:

These few sentences at the beginning of your cover letter will determine whether the hiring manager will read on. The attention span is very short, remember that this person has hundreds of applications to go through.

You need to make your cover letter attract and hold the hiring manager's interest. What is it the reader is looking for?

To find an applicant that fits what they are looking for as quickly and effortlessly as possible. Let's help them find you.

You need to get the hiring manager exactly what she is looking for. You must show that you are going to satisfy the company's *specific needs*.

And all of this needs to be included in the first third of your cover letter.

**Let us break it down and simplify this.**

"Marketing manager

The Gate Advisory is looking to recruit a dynamic, strategic, and sales focused individual to lead the advisory's marketing and communications strategies and the development of our brand as our new Marketing Manager.

You should have proven marketing experience, a passion and care for our local communities and be someone who can formidably advocate for the values and work of the Gate.

Leading on all of the Gate's marketing and communication strategies, and the development of our brand, you will be able to demonstrate a strategic, and sales-focused mind set. We are looking for someone with proven marketing experience, a passion for clients and who can be a tireless advocate for the work of the Gate.

The role requires strong organisational skills, a 'can do' attitude, good computer literacy, and a willingness to learn and adapt on the job working in a busy working environment.

The Gate is run by a small and dynamic team. We seek out individuals who care about their colleagues, the work and the experience of our client members.

Address your application to:

Catherine Adams

catherine.a@gateadvisory.co.uk

Mark your email: Marketing Manager"

- **Address the cover letter directly to the hiring manager. If the person's name is not stated in the ad, call up the company and ask.**

  *Dear Catherine,*

  *Dear Miss Adams,*

  *Dear Ms. Adams,*

  *Dear Mrs. Adams,*

  **Miss:** Use "Miss" when addressing young girls and women under 30 that are unmarried.

  **Ms.:** Use "Ms." when you are not sure of a woman's marital status, if the woman is unmarried and over 30 or if she prefers being addressed with a marital-status neutral title.

  **Mrs.:** Use "Mrs." when addressing a married woman.

  **Mr.**: Use "Mr" for a male of unknown age and status.

  **Sir.**: Use "Sir" to be correct and show respect.

In this case it is difficult to know age or status of the person to address. We use her first name instead in this sample since the overall feeling in the letter gives away that it is ok – "small dynamic team", "care about their collogues".

**"Dear** Catherine**,"**

- **Personalise your introduction to the company and the job position.**

- **Introduce yourself and identify the job for which you're applying.**

  You have now used up the first important sentences. By using the name of the hiring manager, you have already made this personal. You continue by having a very short, personalised introduction and show that you have taken to heart what position it is and what is required, the highlights.

  Here is the challenge – introduce yourself as the perfect candidate.

  That can be your headline if you like.

  *"Highly experienced and skilled marketing expert applying for the position as Marketing Manager."*

  What you have done is acknowledged the job position, "Marketing Manager", and also showed that you have what it takes to fill the position, "Highly experienced and skilled marketing expert".

  By doing so you have already in the first sentence showed that you are a person of interest. You haven't wasted their time.

  And you continue in the same manner.

- Mention your most relevant work experience that makes you a good candidate. After analysing the ad, you know exactly what words to use. You state your abilities by using words from their ad and applying them to yourself.

  *"After working over 10 years with brand development, marketing and sales strategies plus growing a company from no 40 in its market till no 1, it's time to take the leap and make the journey once again. These are areas of interest I am passionate about: growth, communication, and organisation."*

- Show them you are enthusiastic and excited about the chance to work with them.

  *"These are areas of interest I am passionate about: growth, communication, and organisation."*

- Be sincere and direct.
- Don't waste their time with irrelevant sentences.

In this example we have created an opening that gives the reader incentive to read further. We stated the necessary fact already in the headline and then in the first paragraph.

This opening model can be applied for all kind of positions and branches.

The cover letter can successfully be divided into three sections, and we have just covered the opening.

We now move on to the middle section which is the part where you can elaborate more around your experience and what you want.

This part can be more or less unchanged, constant, throughout your different cover letters. For that reason, you write it in more general terms.

We started with the heading, salutation, and opening paragraph that was to get them hooked and make them read more.

The second paragraph is where you write why you are the perfect fit by explaining more about your background and experience. This paragraph should be mostly about how your previous experiences will help your future employer press ahead with their plans.

Job seekers impress employers by identifying transferable skills related to new positions. People often apply to new positions, so it's likely you'll not have the exact experience requested. But employers would rather know how your past experiences will inform future decisions.

Here you can also say something about what you hope for in the future. Let them get to know you a little bit more.

You end this paragraph by explaining why the company is a perfect fit for you. This specific part you customise for each cover letter.

Lastly, you write your send off, the closing paragraph.

Your cover letter shows that you have relevant skills. You've explained your motivation and abilities. What could possibly go wrong?

Well, you can mess up the last section, the sendoff.

And it's the decisive part.

It must amplify the general impression you've made with the previous paragraphs. It must make the hiring manager *excited* as she starts reading your resume.

This you do by providing value.

Tell the hiring manager or recruiter that you're looking forward to meeting in person (or on digital meeting) and discussing **how your experience and knowledge can help your future employer in fulfilling their goals.**

Example:

> "I would welcome the opportunity to further discuss your digital marketing objectives and show you how my success at my previous employer can translate into digital and online marketing growth for Gate Advisory"

Only thing missing now is the formal closing at the very end.

Write "sincerely" and follow it with your full name. Adding your handwritten signature is optional, but it's recommended for more formal cover letters. You can add your signature in a digital version, since 98% of the applications are sent in a digital format.

If you're not a fan of the well-worn, "sincerely," feel free to use any of the following synonyms:

**Sample cover letter signoffs:**

Sincerely or Sincerely yours

With best regards, Best regards, Kind regards

Thank you

Yours truly

Thank you for your consideration

Respectfully yours.

It's a good idea to repeat your basic contact information, such as your LinkedIn profile, email address and telephone number below your sign-off.

## • NEXT STEP

Congratulations, you have now finished session eight and the second block in, TBS. Really good work!

It is all coming together and the tools for analysing not only yourself but also the market and advertisements you now have.

The pitch is in place and so is your CV. After this session you can start producing your cover letters to go with your CV.

Your next step is the last session in Block 2, the last and final step in creating a Brand called You and the journey towards your dream job.

You will explore another way to communicate with your job market by learning how to create and sustain your network. It is not always what you know, but who you know that makes the difference.

You will also get more insight on interview situations. What questions to expect and what questions to ask, plus much more.

If you have questions, don't hesitate to contact us, we can help you.

Your coach can deepen your knowledge and train you.

# NETWORKING

## A guide towards getting a job

"IF YOU WANT TO GO FAST, GO ALONE. IF YOU WANT TO GO FAR, GO WITH OTHERS."

SOMETIMES IT'S NOT ABOUT WHAT YOU

KNOW, BUT WHO YOU KNOW

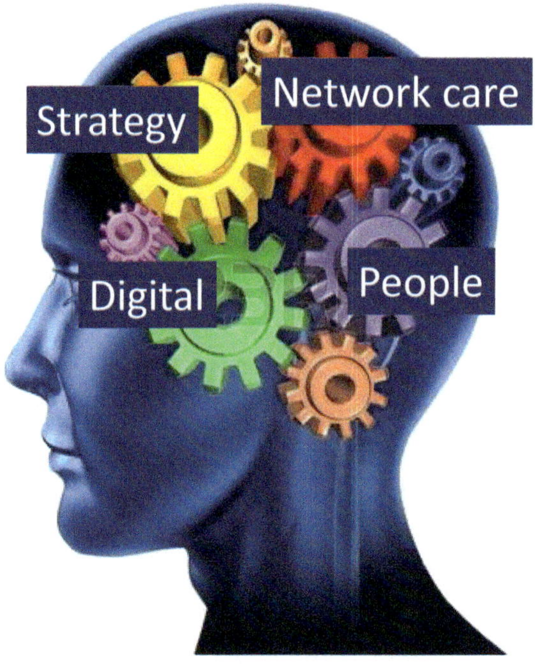

## • NETWORKING

I will start with a very true statement:

**"Take care of your network, and your network will take care of you."**

Networking is not only about collecting business cards or having "friends" on social media. You need to do Network Care by keeping contacts alive and being available, but first you need to have a network to care about.

Now we will examine some basic ideas around today's networking.

There are 6 different key questions that you need to ask yourself:

What is a connection? Why are you connecting? Who are you connecting with? When to connect? Where to connect? How to connect?

These questions need to be answered and understood for you to become successful in networking. They are the foundation of all professional networking.

Networking successfully is about being a person who has something to give. It is important to understand the reason for why you are doing what you are doing.

Over the years I have met so many people who just collect business cards without having any idea or plan on how to utilise the connection they just made. Without understanding how you can be accessible and at the same time finding connections that can be relevant to you, you will be at a loss.

Don't waste peoples time when you meet contacts that spark an interest. Be prepared, have a plan, have a strategy, and make sure you can deliver a good pitch.

Same strategy applies online. Always be obtainable and have a plan for your interaction with people.

*Networking is a continuous connection exercise to expand and broaden your personal professional community. Networking is a selfless two-way connection to help you meet others and for you to further connect them.*

I am looking forward to connecting with you! When you do send your request to me, for example, on LinkedIn, remember to be ready!

Enjoy your reading

## ● NETWORK EXPLAINED

Network = The sum of all of your contacts, wherever they are coming from and whatever type of relationship you have with them. They are all a part of your network.

Your mother and father, siblings, distant relatives, childhood friends, school bullies, teachers, neighbors, former or present colleagues, the arresting officer (😇)...they are all a part of your network.

It is not always easy to define your network. We often have different groups of contacts. Contacts from study time, contacts from a previous workplace or industry, etc. All of this together makes up your network.

Today's world with social platforms like Facebook, LinkedIn and Instagram have made it easier to expand our network globally.

Everybody that you, in one way or another, have been in contact with is included. But it can also include people that belong to the same club, workplace, family, residential area, Facebook group, LinkedIn group etc.

I divide the concept of network into two categories:

A). direct network – direct contact

B). indirect network – secondary contacts/via others

Category A is clear and self-defined. Category B refers to people you are connected to via different clubs, associations, groups online etc.

Grouping your contacts into different buckets in the two categories can help, for example:

friends

relatives

previous clients

influential and powerful executives, current colleagues and

"friends who are real connectors"

Then you need to figure out how best to allocate your attention to these "buckets".

Priorities aren't always obvious. There may be people you keep in touch with for no other reason than that you enjoy their company or you share similar interests. You need to think about the ways in which your relationships make you better off in the pursuit of a job.

Can this person help you connect with an employer?

The first task for you is to map out who you know in category A. If you wonder why that is necessary, continue reading and it will be explained to you.

## THE 6 HANDSHAKES RULE

Formulated in the first half of the 20th century, the theory of 6 Handshakes Rule is that you can connect to literally anyone in the world through a maximum 6 social connections.

The idea of 6 Handshakes Rule originated with Frigyes Karinthy, a Hungarian author who, through his short story "Chain Links", illustrated the 6 degrees of separation.

The theory proved that the population of the earth was closer than it was than ever before, was stated as follows:

"We should select any person from the almost 8 billion inhabitants of the Earth – anyone, anywhere at all. He bet us that, using no more than five individuals, one of whom is a personal acquaintance, he could contact the selected individuals using nothing except the network of personal acquaintances.

For example, "Look, you know Mr. X.Y., please ask him to contact his friend Mr. Q.Z., whom he knows, and so forth."

On this note, I hereby claim that it works.

Common expressions such as "I know a guy who knows a guy" and "a friend of a friend" take on another meaning when you relate it to the 6-Handshakes Rule.

In today's modern world, it is difficult to write or even think about anything that doesn't have a touch of technological or social media influence.

If you are thinking that technology and social media are far more colossal than just Facebook, then you are right. Keep reading and I will try to give you some perspective to help you grasp the endless realm of modern technology's borderless world.

My own experience has taught me that technology eases the process, shortens the path, and speeds the time required to support this rule.

Microsoft researchers also agree with the validity of the theory.  A total of 30 billion electronic messages shared between 180 million people in various countries, confirms their findings.

Researchers have concluded that 2 people are considered acquaintances if they have sent one another a message. 180 billion different users in the database, according to this study, could be connected to each other with an average distance of 6.6 links.

My goal is that you expand and work on your network. According the findings in Microsoft's research, your next job should be found within the group of people you are connected to.

With this knowledge in hand, you understand the impact of your total Network, correct? If not, I cannot help you...

**What is Connection?**

Human connection is explained as an energy exchange between people who are paying attention to one another. It has the power to deepen the moment, inspire change and build trust. It is up to you to expand and deepen the connection. How you do it depends on your intentions.

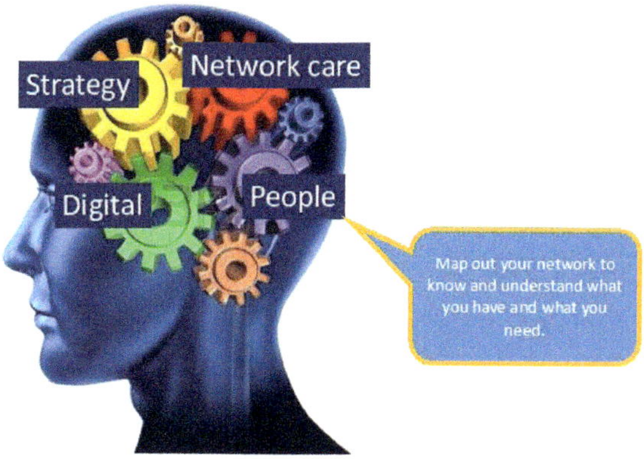


## ● PEOPLE

In the previous chapter you have been reading about what a connection is and the 6 Handshakes Rule. It is all about the people we are surrounded by. The purpose is to find a job, now it's time to figure out how all these people can help you and how you can help them.

A lot has already been covered concerning this subject so we will keep it short.

What is it you need and who's got it? If we go back to your cold calling list (session 7), you will find a list of company's you are interested in working for. How can you reach out to these businesses? In some of the previous sessions, I discussed the importance of doing research on these companies to identify the manger director, head of HR etc.

Which people are the smartest to bet on in your network? Are there people who work in your field, in your industry, or people with valuable contacts? The answer may vary.

After mapping out your network, you will be able to see who relates to which company or who knows someone that does. What contacts are you missing? Who do you need? Where can you find this person? I bet he or she is on LinkedIn, so go ahead and follow, start interacting.

If I am networking with a specific purpose (at a trade show, or to learn about some businesses I would like to work for), I research who will be there to put myself in the right place so that opportunities will arise.

Secondly, I aim to sell without selling because I intend to add value to my relationships and expect nothing in return, so don't start off by asking for a job!

This isn't easy, but if value is derived from a purposeful place, it will be rewarded in droves. When building relationships, remember that both sides should have meaning and value.

I don't build relationships just to close a deal or get a job, but rather I take the time to create a meaningful relationship by getting to know the people personally.

Lastly, always find something to learn. Whether it be about a new innovation or even a new restaurant, this provides for a more authentic approach and a great way to start a new friendship.

Don't be afraid to ask (to connect, for a meeting, an introduction, etc.), the worst that can happen is that someone will say no.

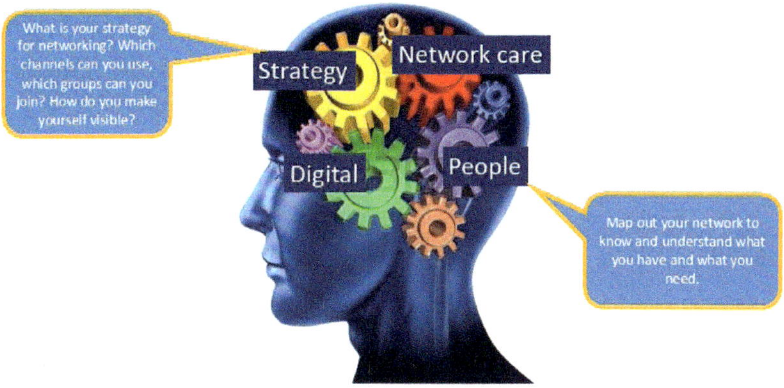


## • STRATEGY

To be successful you need to work out a networking strategy. If you randomly start contacting people it will take forever to reach your goals, if ever.

What is it you need? Or rather, who is it you need? Who do you know already that has contacts within your favorite businesses on your CCL (Cold Calling List)? Who do you know that has a contact within that company you just saw advertising for your dream job?

What is your plan for reaching out to businesses and future contacts?

Two different scenarios to consider, "in real life" or digitally?

In general, being social puts you in the starting position. You will start hearing where people from a certain industry gather for drinks after work or where decision makers in the different industries are moving. The next trade fair, conference, lecture and more.

These are places where you need to be, to meet with representatives for the industry you are interested in.

Google, ask friends and acquaintances, if you want the information, you will find it.

Call or write to someone you want to get to know better and if possible, suggest a lunch or coffee. If it is not IRL, do a Teams/Zoom meeting. Do not give up just because they can't meet with you in real life!

Get in touch and tell people you're looking for a job. Always think long-term. The next time a job vacancy appears in your network, someone might be thinking about you. Become what I would call "Top of Mind".

There is a stigma around being unemployed, get over it. If you don't tell people you are looking for a job, they will not be able to help.

Before all your meetings, be prepared. In session three you received instructions for how to create your pitch. Now is the time to use it, have your pitch ready and deliver it when you meet a contact that can be useful. Your pitch can be tailored for different circumstances and definitely for meetings like this.

What is your strategy going into the places mentioned above? Are you looking for a specific contact only to broaden your network? Are you hoping to meet someone to book a meeting? Maybe you meet the "right person"? What is your strategy, your goal for that meeting?

Go back to session 5 and reread about your SMART goals.

Opportunities are all around you. We meet people all of the time. It could be the cashier at the supermarket, the person sitting next to you on the train or someone you meet at a function.

True story from my past.

I was going to a flea market, but the premises were packed with people, so I waited outside and started a conversation with a lady.

We talked about the current work situation in society in conjunction with people who are frequently buying and selling at flea markets.

I told her that I was looking for a job as substitute teacher.

As it happened, she was in charge of all hiring of substitute teachers in four different schools around my city.

You never know who you might meet!

*My strategy was to bring up that I was currently looking for a job as a substitute teacher. I always steer conversations into a direction that give me the opportunity to talk about it..*

**Have a strategy.**

How is it with your digital strategy?

Which platforms are you networking on today?

Remember how this session started and the questions I asked?

A. What is a connection?

B. Why are you connecting?

C. Who are you connecting with?

D. When to connect?

E. Where to connect?

F. How to connect?

A and B - Has been answered in the first chapter.

C to F are even more interesting and will continue here.

Many questions in the beginning, let us sort them out. First question is, "Which platforms are you on today? It's important we exclude all the normal jobsites and concentrate on social media.

LinkedIn is the most important social media platform to be on as a jobseeker. Facebook and Instagram are also very useful, even TikTok can be used.

LinkedIn has a job search part where you can look for and apply to available positions.

However, we are going to focus on Networking and not the LinkedIn job search application here.

When you are building your network, we have discussed the importance that it includes people you have met in all sorts of circumstances.

LinkedIn is the perfect place to look them up.

This is the place for professional work-related networking. Here you can read what they have done in the past and where they are working today.

If a CV covers your past, LinkedIn should tell you more about the future.

You can read about the companies you are interested in, follow up with reading about and connecting with the CEO, head of HR or anybody else of interest in the company.

You can connect with people on Facebook as well, but that can easily become more personal than professional. If they have an open

Instagram account, you can follow them there as it is considered less personal than Facebook.

You will find a diversity of information on social media.

I recommend you begin following and connecting with friends and family. If you have them on Facebook, make sure you also have them as connections on LinkedIn.

And when you start following other people of interest to you, remember that there are different ways to approach them.

In most social media venues, you find different groups to join. Find groups that relates to the type of job you are interested in. Follow and start commenting on posts within the group. It is here you will have a better chance of finding people who are working at the different companies that you yourself are interested in working for.

The best way is to read what the person of interest is writing about on social media. If the subject is "likeable", then click "Like" on their post. After doing that a few times, the next step is to comment on what they are writing. If you have a different opinion, say so. Argue your case, have a discussion, as long as your opinion is not radical.

Make yourself known to the person of interest. By interacting in this way, you will get noticed and you are now actually building a relationship with that person. After doing this for a bit of time, you can write him/her a private message. You message can be something like this:

*I have been following you for a while and I like what you are writing here on LinkedIn. Also, I have looked at your company website and it seems to be a very interesting business with really good values* (show that you actually know what you are talking about*)*.

*My background is xxxx xxxx and I think that I can contribute to your business with my knowledge within xxxx xxxx.*

*It would be an honor if we could have a quick conversation over Teams/Zoom during the week. Would Thursday at 10.00 work for you or Friday at 11.30?*

*Sincerely*

This is only one of many examples of how you can interact.

In the message you remind him/her of your presence by giving tribute to the persons writing. He/she might remember you if you have commented on some specific posts. You show interest for the business by making the person understand that you have really studied the business website.

You state that you think you can contribute to the business, perfect if you can be specific. You offer two different times for a short on-line meeting. Very common answer to the offer is either a yes to the first suggested time or they offer another more suitable time.

This a very good and productive way of networking. I personally use this approach more or less on a daily basis.

If you want the meeting then take the initiative and be proactive by proposing times, sending the calendar invite, visiting them or sending the follow-up

This method works in a similar way for Instagram, Facebook and even TikTok. Anywhere on social media where you can like and comment a post, do it!

Make yourself known to your person of interest. Communicate and build a relationship with them.

**Simple strategy.**

- Decide which social media suits you best. I suggest LinkedIn.
- Start following businesses on your interest list.
- Start following people of interest to you.
- Interact with the people you are connected with on social media.
- Book meetings.

Through the digital world, we can retrieve loads of information about businesses and people. This is your way to prepare yourself for meetings and interviews, finding job openings, applying for jobs and showing who you are by having a good LinkedIn profile and interacting with your contacts.

Cultivate your existing network! You know people who know people. Ask you network if they know people they might refer you to. Be specific and targeted about what you're looking for and people will often open up their networks for you.

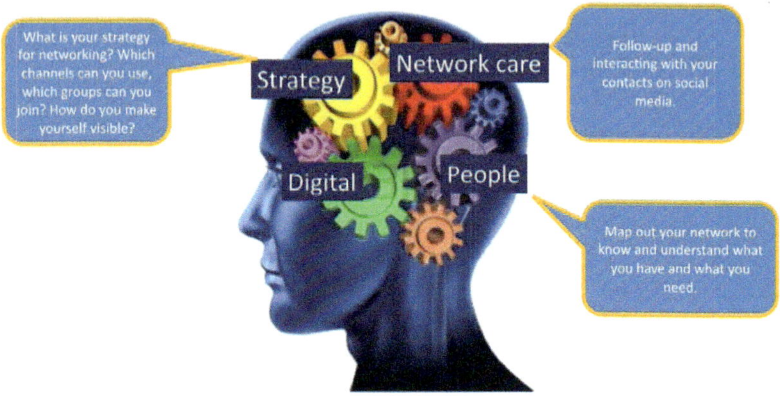


## • NETWORK CARE

Following up with your contacts is a subject we have already reviewed in great detail but let me add some additional tips.

How do you take care of your network? Depending on the extent of your network, this task can be a challenge. If you have a very big network, social media is the best place to show that you do care.

We get constant reminders about other people's birthdays via Facebook and LinkedIn, use that to send a message or write something on their page.

By liking and commenting you show interest. Send a private message once in a while asking them how they are.

Invite them to have a phone, Teams/Zoom conversation.

Invite them to have a coffee or lunch with you.

Yes, common knowledge, I know. Do you take action? Are you actually doing it? Remember that social media is a community, ecosystem and an intertwined connection of interests.

Some people have an intuitive knack for making connections and always have their antennae out for interesting new people to meet.

Others intellectually understand the value of cultivating robust relationships and broadening their circle, but struggle with deep-seated anxieties about feeling inauthentic, scrutinized or appearing self-serving in their approach.

Given how essential a healthy network is to professional success and advancement, it's important to develop a repertoire of effective network-building strategies that work and that you can feel good about, no matter which category you fall into.

Be the owner of what you do, who you are, mistakes you've made, why you're on this current path which has the ability to change at a moment's notice. Humility and honesty go a long way.

*Being your honest self and not being afraid to show vulnerability are fundamental to building real connections. While most strangers bond over common experiences or shared interests, I often find that people who have diverse viewpoints or experiences from mine leave the most lasting impression.*

If you approach your network only when you need help, you have less of a chance of getting a good response. It is the give and take that requires thought, maintenance and continuity all the time.

Do not forget: Write your own posts to stay visible.

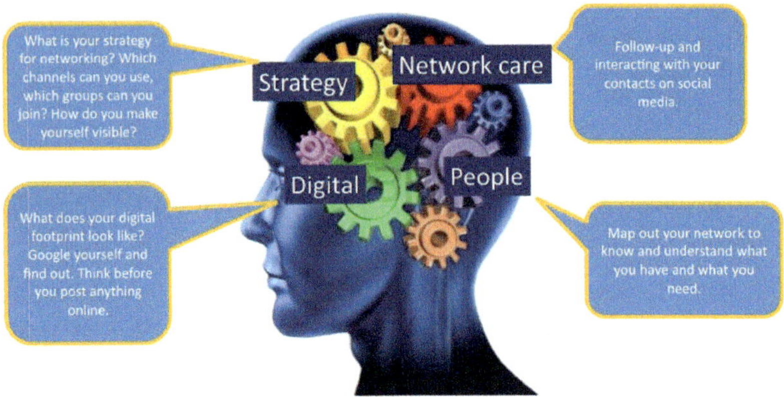


## • DIGITAL

When was the last time you Googled yourself?

Do that right now before reading further.

What did you find?

When networking it is vital to know what others find when they Google you. What does your digital footprint look like?

I will give you an example. As a jobseeker, you have just sent out a personal letter along with a CV.

The recruiter or employer Googles you and discovers that what you have written in your personal letter and CV does not mirror what they find online.

Your LinkedIn does not verify what is stated in your CV and the content in your cover letter does not match the crazy things they just found out about you via Instagram and TikTok.

If you really want a job, stop posting stupid things online.

Stop showing off your drinking habits on Facebook and Instagram.

If you have radical political views, keep them to yourself if you want a job.

Sure, it is fun to have a cat, flower or something else along that line as your profile picture, but it also says something about you as a person.

It is all about making choices. You can continue to post your radical views, post whatever crazy and stupid things you spend your time doing. Have a weird profile picture if you like.

That is your choice. It will also be the choice of the recruiter and employer to choose a different candidate that looks more serious to represent their company.

**Your digital footprint**

You may be wondering, "What is a digital footprint? Why should I care about it?"

Every email, post, photo and click you make online leaves a trail. Even by downloading my program, you're adding to your ever-growing on-line string of little breadcrumbs. It's permanent. It follows you for life and it's not going anywhere because it's your digital footprint.

Whether or not your information is shared intentionally, it's being gathered by employers, advertisers, and companies from which you shop. You are constantly being monitored and your search information is being gathered and filed away.

This information is called your digital footprint, and it is becoming more important and valuable than ever in today's digital economy. While there's no official definition of the term "digital economy," it can be summed up as the entire ecosystem built from our online connectivity. In this newfound era, your digital footprint can no longer be ignored. Especially as a jobseeker.

Your digital footprint is anything that is about you or put out by you online. That includes social media, your own website, articles about you or written by you and posts you have written and commented on. It spans all time and doesn't just include what's found at the top of the page, it icludes information that is both easy and hard to find.

You should keep in mind that anything you place online, whether text or images, has the potential to be available online forever.

Take note that your digital footprint isn't just things you actively put online like photos or Facebook status updates, it's your information that is being scraped from more passive online activities as well.

Your digital footprint is data that's created through your activities and communication online. This can include more passive activities, such as if a website collects your IP address, as well as more active digital activities, such as sharing images on social media.

How is your digital footprint used? In multiple ways, but we will focus on the present – job hunting.

Your digital footprint is used by employers both current and prospective. It is especially important to care for your digital footprint if you're job hunting, as Googling is now a central part of the hiring process.

As I have written earlier, an online background check by recruiters and employers is a common practice these days.

In worst-case scenarios, individuals could lose their job offer if employers come across something inappropriate.

### How can you manage your digital footprint?

So how can you manage your digital footprint? Here are a few places to start:

- Google yourself: Take inventory of what's out there. Search for your name every few months, so you're aware of the information others have access to.

- Set up Google alerts: I recommend setting up a Google alert for your name. The tool will then send you occasional alerts of every post that has your name in it.

- Think before you post: Never put a temporary emotion on the permanent internet. Anger is temporary; online lasts forever. Pause before you post: Think twice, post once is the advice.

- Careful with the pics: Limit your sharing of questionable images. Fifteen minutes of humour is never worth a lifetime of potential humiliation. Was it really that funny?

### Benefits of a digital footprint

When they're done right, a digital footprint can provide you with a really great first impression. You're now aware that employers are following your trail, so take advantage of it.

A strong online presence can be a great career asset in today's competitive job market. Many employers are performing online searches, in addition to reviewing resumes and cover letters.

This is done as an attempt to learn more about prospective hires, including their interests, industry involvement, yet more importantly, their ability to effectively market themselves.

If hiring managers are impressed by the content they find, like thought-provoking commentaries or links to industry articles, they may be more inclined to reach out to individuals for an interview.

Take charge of your digital footprint.

## • NEXT STEP

You have now finished Block 2 and your next session is the "TWS – Three Way Communication System" in the last block.

The sessions have become a bit longer and we are rapidly getting towards the end. Only a few more sessions and you will have all the tools you need to be successful in your job hunting.

I urge you to go back and reread all of it and start implementing the things I have written for you. If you don't act, nothing will change. And change is the key to your success.

If you continue doing what you always have been doing, you will end up at the same place again. You must find a different way to approach what you are doing to get a different result.

Please, reach out if you have questions and don't hesitate to contact us.

I am happy to coach you, if that is what you feel you need.

You can read more on the webpage:

**www.hellstedt.org**

You can also wright to us:

**contact@hellstedt.org**

# TWC

# A guide towards getting a job

THREE WAY COMMUNICATION SYSTEM

TO FOLLOW UP IS ONE OF THE KEYS TO CREATE OPPORTUNITIES

## • THREE WAY COMMUNICATION

What on earth do I mean by TWC – Three Way Communication System?

It is rather simple really.

It is about how you contact a recruiter/hiring manager/ employer.

What do you do when you see an advertisement? What is your first response after you have analysed the text? If done correctly, your analysing should give you a good understanding of what the hiring company is looking for. What were your thoughts after reading the advertisement? Did you have any questions after reading through it?

The idea of TWC is to properly utilise your questions after reading the advertisement by calling up the hiring company. This is your opportunity to contact and introduce yourself to the recruiter.

If you initially don't have any questions, make sure you take some time to come up with some **intelligent** questions to ask. I want you to create a relationship with the recruiter through your phone call. That is **step 1** out of 3. By the way, you work in the same way with your Cold Calling List.

If contact via the phone call was done correctly, the recruiter looking through the application forms will remember your name.

We must use every tool we have to get through the "noise" out there. By asking relevant questions about the job, you show genuine interest and you also retrieve vital information to be used in your application.

Not only that, but you can also refer to your conversation with the recruiter in your cover letter showing that you have a relationship with the company.

This is **step 2** out of 3. When sending in your application, you are no longer an unknown. You will be remembered if you made a positive impression on the recruiter with the initial phone call.

**Step 3** is your follow up phone call after a brief waiting period to ask your follow-up questions in conjunction that you have now applied for the job.

All together it becomes a system – TWC.

Three-way communication: you call, you send in your application, and then follow-up with another call.

Not complicated and for some of you, it is natural to do it this way. Surprisingly though, a lot of job seekers just send out a CV, nothing more. That is like putting a message in a bottle and hoping for the best.

As you know, after going through the nine previous sessions, all is connected and gives you the insight on how to be an efficient and successful job seeker.

Enough said, time to start with session 10 - TWC

## • NOT COMPLICATED

The basis of the idea around TWC is to contact companies either when they have published an advertisement for a job or through a cold call. You simply call a company from the list of prospective employers. This wish list is your Cold Calling List.

Another option is that you have contacted an employer through your network. Remember what you learned in the previous session.

In all cases, you should call an employer keeping in mind that the initial goal is to be asked to submit your CV. After the CV is submitted, follow up the submission with another call after a brief waiting period. Of course, the final goal is to get an interview, but I have chosen to divide the process.

It would be great progress if the call turns into an interview or an invitation to one. That would be an enormous bonus!

**Understanding the recruiting process**

This is mainly done through:

- ▲ Ads
- ▲ Recruiters
- ▲ Network
- ▲ Internal

Advertising is mainly done through:

- ◈ Job search sites
- ◈ Social media

**The 10 biggest job search sites in the world are:**

- **Best Overall:** Indeed
- **Runner-Up, Best Overall:** Monster
- **Best for Employer Research:** Glassdoor

- **Best for Remote Jobs:** FlexJobs
- **Best for Experienced Managers:** The Ladders
- **Best for Startup Jobs:** AngelList
- **Best for Connecting Directly with Recruiters:** LinkedIn
- **Best for Up-to-Date Listings:** Getwork
- **Best for Recent College Graduates:** Scouted
- **Best for Hourly Workers:** Snagajob

Don't forget that every country has it own local unemployment agency that also have listings of available jobs. There are also other local job search sites.

**The social medias mainly used are:**

- LinkedIn
- Facebook
- Instagram

Concerning recruitment companies, you need to do your own research as well, since that can be very regional, differs between countries. Some are also global.

**Here are the 10 largest recruitment companies**

- Randstad
- Adecco group
- Manpower Group
- Recruit Holdings Co Ltd
- Allegis
- Hays

- Persol Holdings
- Robert Half
- Kelly Services
- Express Employment Professionals

One thing that is important to understand is that 8 out of 10 jobs are not advertised. Hence the importance of cold calls.

Working on your network is vital. Your cold calls won't be so cold when you call people in or get a contact thanks to your network.

9 out of 10 jobseekers only respond to ads via email. This is an opportunity, be smarter. There are so many job seekers that only send out their CV, nothing more. Make up your mind, are you willing to put in the effort?

Being organised and treating job seeking as a job is the way towards success.

Another thing to consider is that to recruit takes time and costs money, that's why smart employers prefer active job seekers. And that is why TBS – Three Block System becomes most effective path to a job.

*The Phone Call* is the scariest moment in the job search in comparison to *The Interview*. Most people find it unpleasant to call an employer about a job. So unpleasant that they never do. Anyone who actually dares to pick up the phone and make the call has the advantage.

Many times, the reason for the uneasy feelings created by the thought of cold calls is insecurity. After going through the TBS model, you can feel much more secure in what you are doing and trying to achieve.

One way of avoiding the anxiety is to be well prepared. And we are preparing you step-by-step. You have worked on figuring out who you are, what your characteristics are, constructing your application papers and so much more. You have a strategi for your job search and the knowledge to go through with it.

**You are far too smart to be the only thing standing in your way.**

## • MORE FOCUS ON THE CALL - PHONE FRIGHT

There is a variation on "cold calls" that is not quite as chilly.

The expression for these calls comes from a sale method called Social Selling.

Here is additional information on the subject.

What is Social Selling? This is when you combine your sales/presentation skills with your existing network and the capacity with social media. You work by taking advantage of your network and communicating in a personal and trusting way. You achieve more!

**LinkedIn is usually the best**

Technically, LinkedIn is usually the best tool for Social Selling. LinkedIn is good to use because the contacts you make become naturally linked to your professional role. You establish new contacts and take care of your existing contacts based on sharing relevant content that your recipients find enriching and interesting.

## CALLING

### 1. Dare to start

According to me, a warm call is when you call a person you have already had contact with before, you may even know each other a little or you've received an introduction through an acquaintance.

A cold call is when you call a completely unknown person, a stranger, to introduce yourself. That can be significantly more nerve-racking. Although it can be difficult to pick up the phone and apply for a job, there are no shortcuts – just start practicing. The more calls you make, the more comfortable you'll be.

Remember what I wrote in session 7 – the Cold Calling List? For practice, start calling the companies you are least interested in.

**2. Don't tell me too much.**

The most important thing when making cold calls is to focus on the right thing. Invest in selling your services (not yourself) with the goal to get a meeting or interview.

Don't get into long explanations about your résumé or why you would fit perfectly into the company. You do not get a job directly over the telephone, therefore the goal is to submit your CV or get a meeting/interview.

**3. Learn to handle a no**

Think of yourself as a seller selling services = your abilities. Prepare for the fact that you will get many that say **NO**, when you start calling.

But a good salesman also knows that the more **NO** you get, the closer you are to a **YES**. When a company has no need for your abilities at the moment, you may still have the opportunity to submit your CV for future recruitments.

**4. Follow up**

Even if your aim is to be booked for an interview, it does not mean that your work ends once you've succeeded in acquiring the interview. One of the most important parts of the process is to follow up on your calls and meetings that you have worked so hard to get.

Do not accept the typical phrase "don't call us, we'll call you". Don't be afraid to follow up on what you have started. Dare to pick up the phone after some waiting time even if you received a **no** the first time.

When asked why 99 percent of the population hates receiving and making calls, there are many answers. Generally, people have phone fears. You don't even dare call the insurance company or the bank when you have a question. Many are afraid of being rejected. Another reason is the malicious picture we have of phone sales. The creepy salesman that calls in the middle of dinner... The recipient of the call is adverse and from the calling perspective it is difficult to get a **no** all the time.

**Remember to make the cold call relevant.**

The starting point for success is that you must know why you are calling. What is it you want to achieve? What message is it you want to convey? What is it you want to "sell"?

Take a few more minutes to prepare. Do research, ad analysis – if there was an ad to begin with.

If you make a North Pole (freezing) call, no ad, then you need to keep track of it, research the business you're calling and familiarize yourself with the company.

Today, when everyone has websites, the research becomes easier. Use your knowledge to try to find triggers and identify problems you can solve for the prospective employer. You need to individualise the cold calls since you can't say the same thing to everyone.

The foundation for this is your Pitch and Cold Calling List

(Session 3 and 7).

What do you know about the businesses on your list? Have they just received a large order? What does your trend/ competitive intelligence say? How are they organised? Have they hired a new HR manager or a new CEO – the opportunity lays in that they are reorganising.

Do your research and analysis!

Timing and relevance are important success factors. How do you know when it's an appropriate time to call?

– It's up to the recipient whether they want to answer or not. Don't have the mindset that you are disturbing them by calling, make sure you have something relevant to convey. If you have that mindset, you'll be more persuasive in the conversation.

It doesn't matter whether or not if you are a good salesperson, you are going to get a lot of **NO's**. If the answer is that they don't have time right now, then see it as an opportunity.

Ask them:

Is there any time that's better suited for a conversation? Make a suggestion, "- Is it better to call you tomorrow at 11?"

Is there anyone else at the company that I can contact instead?

It gives you an opening for a call with number two. You have now acquired an important reference. "Hi, my name is Gustaf-Wilhelm Hellstedt, just spoke to your HR manager, John Doe. He suggested I should talk to you about a position in the company..."

"Hi, my name is Gustaf-Wilhelm Hellstedt, I spoke a short while ago with your CEO, John Doe. He thought it would be good if we had contact regarding a possible job opening in your department..."

You can still get a **NO**. They simply do not have any vacancies. But it has opened for you to have contact again. Accept the no and move on to the next company on the list. Getting no is part of the game. There's no reason to take it personally.

## • FOLLOW-UP

Companies probably get a lot of "cold" emails and they are rarely followed up with calls.

Sure, you can email any employer, but at some point, you'll have to pick up the phone. The success factor is to combine text with verbal.

- Be relevant, that's the most important thing.
- Be hearty and quickly get to the point.
- What is the value you offer? Be sure to get it out in one sentence, do not lose yourself in irrelevant details.
- Lower the voice mode and talk slowly. If you're stressed, you usually talk too fast.

**Before the call:**

**A.** Set aside time.

Instead of making cold calls just now and then – which also makes them easy to postpone – set aside a set time of the week, such as a half-day when you can call, being undisturbed and focused.

**B.** Set goals.

Decide how many calls to make and log the outcomes of the call and you'll see how many people you've reached (which wasn't a switchboard or answering machine), how many appointments you booked and how many companies asked you to call back and how many companies requested resumes by email.

The latter parameters are also good because there may well be new opportunities for follow-up. The log will help you see what hit rate you have.

**C.** Have a good basic list - the Cold Calling List.

Make sure your list has the most relevant companies possible by segmenting it, based on industry, turnover, number of employees, or other variables that prevents you from spending time calling businesses that don't suit you.

**During the call:**

1. Ask if you are interfering – or do not ask. One of the worst of cold callings big questions. Should you ask that question if you want something/selling something (your abilities), asking if the person you are calling has time to talk. My conclusion is that it does not affect the end result. The important thing is to choose what suits you best and does not prevent you from moving forward.

2. When receiving a **no**, set a new time. If the person does not want or can't talk, be sure to decide a time or day for a new call. This also applies if they ask you to come back after Christmas, weekend or vacation. Add to your calendar. Ask if there is anyone else at the company you should talk to? Who is the right person?

3. If they ask you to come back in a year – call in six months. I they ask you to come back in a week, call in four days, otherwise you risk missing your window of opportunity. If it takes too long until the next follow-up, a lot can happen during that time, so stay one step ahead.

4. When the call is made, start from the **three I's**. **Introduction**: a short, concise introduction where you either open with information about who you are as well as what you want. Include 'The Pitch' from the beginning. A relevant problem based on existing problems you can solve for them.

Create **Interest**: ask relevant questions, prove your abilities.

Then take the **initiative** for a meeting: give the person two options for dates and time when you can have a meeting, then send an invitation via Outlook, preferably with a short summary of your call.

**Introduction - Interest - Initiative**

5. Create recognition. You can easily show that you understand the company's problems, especially if you notice that the individual you're talking to doesn't want to be so open.

Example: "In connection with expansion, there is often a need for logistics solutions..." is an effective way of formulating.

6. Create control of the progress of the call by preparing a few bullet points to cover. If your first question receives a negative answer, have one or more follow-up questions prepared so that you are the one who takes the lead of the call.

7. Be prepared to change the topic. If you notice that the counterparty is negative, have another topic prepared. Make sure to have done your homework and research concerning the company and its development.

Have you had contact with the company before, thus not a real "cold call", what has happened since the last time? For example, "The last time I had contact with you, we talked about you waiting for a bigger order that would provide opportunities for me to....".

## • AFTER THE CALL

A. Keep a record (Cold Calling List), a log, of all your calls, even if the employer is not responding. It is a way for you to know when you can call again.

One tip is to call maybe three times in a week If you aren't getting a response and then let it go after five unanswered calls. It may be better to reach them by email. Some choose not to answer a call from an unknown telephone number or they are simply very busy. Be receptive to the situation.

B. Combine contact with networking. Other ways to attack your market/companies that aren't as direct is to listen to acquaintances who might be working at the company. It can provide new opportunities to find someone to contact at the company.

C. Work in a structured way. Use business intelligence by keeping your list of potential companies up to date and monitor the businesses you are going to call.

Schedule your calls. Always write down the results of the calls. Write down when you plan to contact them again and add it to your calendar.

D. Always follow up. Timing is important, the company can change its mind for various reasons and be more receptive the next time. To avoid the follow-ups feeling nagging and pointless, keep careful notes on developments, what's happening at the company, business intelligence.

E. Get in touch more times than you think you need to. You don't know what's going on behind the scenes. There are always changes at companies such as people quitting, new sales/orders, new guidelines etc.

Be proactive! If they say they are going to come back to you... don't just sit around and wait. Get back in touch!

## RESEARCH

Start from the "cold calling list", where you segment, for example, by size, turnover and industry. This is where your cold list comes into use. The cold list is for the companies where you have no direct connection or network. To simplify it, it's just a company you are interested in but have never had contact with.

Once you've sifted through several companies that fit the segment you're interested in, start your research.

You open a word document, and then look for the following information that you add to the document:

- Do they hire - do they advertise for people? What roles? Look for information about this, via Google, LinkedIn and the prospects website.
- What do their finances look like – many financial statements are made public.
- What does their website look like? What information do I get from it?
- Do I have mutual friends with decision-makers? Has anyone who works there, worked with someone I know, gone to the same school, known to an acquaintance of someone who's a cousin of someone's sister...?

**Social media and Internet**

- Do they write any content? Do decision makers have their own blog somewhere? Do they have a business blog? Where do their decision-makers hang out on social media? Are they on Soundcloud, Youtube, Facebook, Twitter, LinkedIn?

- Decision makers - Google the individuals, look for pictures and personal information. Find mobile numbers and emails, as well as personal information such as hobbies, family situation etc.
- Other triggers found online - have they recently received a price or have they bought up a company? Have they recently hired a new person in the role I want to apply for? Have they just landed a big business deal? Business intelligence!

**8 tips – succeed with the phone call**

1. Overcome fear

Phone fright - the fear of calling and exposing yourself to the risk of making a fool of yourself. Remember that taking risks builds confidence and the rush afterwards is so nice that you can't wait to plunge down the cliff again. The key is to stop thinking of it as a well-timed way to position yourself. See it for what it is: a perfectly natural way to get answers to relevant questions.

2. Choose the right time

To call after submitting your application to ask "if it has arrived" or "how many applications they have received" is just annoying and unprofessional. Make sure you ask the relevant questions, such as "Is there anything else that needs to be submitted?"

3. Have a clear purpose

Don't ask just for the sake of asking – it's a shallow question and allows you to be perceived as a difficult person.

Be proactive. Call to get more information about job requirements and what expectations the company has for the person they are going to hire. Such conversation makes you appear interested. It's information that can give you a head start – you can get many tips on what to focus on and highlight them in your cover letter and CV.

4. Ask smart questions

"Can you tell me more about the job?" could be a kamikaze question.

Examples of good questions: "-It says here that there are four to five requirements for this position. Where will the priority be?" or "What do you see being the biggest challenge for the person who gets the job?" If you don't know, it creates challenges in putting the right message in the cover letter. Another could be: "What is the background of the person (people) currently working in this position?"

It can be really interesting and useful for you to know this information.

5. Keep it short

Don't rush, but don't ramble on too much either. If you chatter on for ages, you just show that you don't understand the value of time – time is money. Feel free to use a stopwatch and round off before you have reached five minutes. It's longer than you think.

6. Stand up

When you call, that is. The diaphragm is then stretched, which makes you breathe more freely allowing your voice to sound stronger. If you prefer to walk around with the handset, make sure you don't walk so fast that you get out of breath.

7. Remember names

It leaves a positive impression if you thank "Anna" for her time. Make a note of who you are talking to. It's even better if you remember the receptionist's name, too. The receptionist is the gatekeeper who can connect you with anyone at the company.

8. Practice

If you have multiple calls to make, start with the least important and work your way up to the company where you most of all want to work. Practice brings skill, so your presentation will get better and better with each call.

| **Goal for the call** | **Preparations** |
|---|---|
| Ideally: Come to an interview<br><br>Minimum - Send CV<br><br>Make an impact so the employer<br><br>remembers you. | The Pitch<br><br>Application documents - CV and Cover letter/email<br><br>Prepare a script (use one<br><br>if you need one)<br><br>Find the right contact person |

**Be your own employer**

Set goals for the day/week – create routines

Pep yourself up – be your own best friend

Start ringing early in the day – after a few calls, the uncertainty releases

Forget bad calls

Forget a bad day – a fresh start every day

Reward yourself after a good day/week

## • NEXT STEP

When I started writing this session, I did not anticipate that there was so much I wanted to say.

It is one of the important keys to your success in finding your dream job.

You have now only 4 sessions left before you graduate from this program. My hope for you is that you now feel more confident in what and how you do things. The thought has been to give you a set of keys to unlock different parts of the job seeking process.

My belief is that you already have most of the keys, but we have few left to give you.

The next session is called "Social Selling". It will give you an introduction to that concept, what to do on social media etc.

I write this after every session - You can always reach out and contact us if you have any additional questions.

We offer coaching both IRL and digitally.

You can read more on the webpage: www.hellstedt.org

You can also wright to us: **contact@hellstedt.org**

# SOCIAL SELLING

## A guide towards getting a job

# SUCCEEDING AT SOCIAL SELLING

Tips & Tricks on how to get your dream job!

CAREER COACH GUSTAF W. HELLSTEDT

## • SOCIAL SELLING

You should be using social media as more than a hobby. If you only use it to share fun pictures of the kids or the cat, plus a picture of your meal together combined with some fun movie clips, you don't really understand the power of the media.

In other words, you have not understood the impact, or the connection social media has on a company's sales and growth results.

Why should I care how companies use the social media? You might think, "I use social media as my private space and I love my cute cat pictures".

Well, if you are in a situation where you need a job or are looking for a change in your life, social media selling is what you need.

You need to grow and take care of your personal brand.

"Does it really matter to click around on LinkedIn or Facebook?".

The answer to that can be, "no it doesn't matter. It all depends on what you are looking for, your purpose".

If your purpose is to find a new job, it is the right social platform to use.

Social selling "A Brand called You", your personal brand, will increase your chances enormously to receive the change in your life that you are looking for.

The purpose of this chapter is to give you a basic understanding of how Social Selling works and how you can use the method to find and build relationships with potential employers, resulting in your dream job.

Enjoy reading and good luck with Social Selling!

## • WHAT IS SOCIAL SELLING

Social Selling it a fairly new term that is now widely used on sale sites. There is endless information on Google about Social Selling. It is playing an increasingly a bigger role in the evolution of change in the sales and marketing area.

Words like Content Marketing and Social Selling are hot topics. These are strongly interconnected with a flow in a common direction.

Social selling is the practice of using a brand's social media channels to connect with prospects, developing a connection with them and engaging with potential leads. The tactic can help businesses reach their sales targets. Think of social selling as modern relationship-building.

What you need is to start thinking of yourself as is a brand and a service that is for sale. You are looking for a new assignment – a job. Once you get comfortable with that thought process, you will start to see the potential of social selling.

It is the perfect tool for finding and creating relationships with potential employers.

And make no mistake, when I write "employer" I am referring to a person who might want to hire you, not the other applicant.

You can use social media to offer knowledge and above all interact with potential employers. Interacting is the key word in Social Selling. It is largely about creating dialogue and thus creating a relationship.

## • PROFITS WITH SOCIAL SELLING

The biggest benefit of using Social Selling while unemployed is your increased exposure toward the targeted companies and their key contacts. This is achieved by finding and creating relationships with potential employers through the work of Social Selling.

By actively working with Social Selling, you will find more potential employers while increasing the probability of getting an interview and ultimately a job. Your approach will not reflect the actions of the normal jobseeker, but rather someone selling services, your knowledge. What is it you can do for them? What is it you are good at? How can you prove that you have what they want? References?

At this point, a future employer can be seen as a client.

Through the Social Selling method, you will find potential employers who may even contact you. You will also be able to contact potential clients/employers yourself. This means that over time, you will be building a stable influx of new potential leads to your next job. With Social Selling, your goal is to build relationships with these potential employers and leads.

Through a deeper relationship with your leads, you increase the chance of landing a job. The chance that the potential client/employer will agree to an interview with you increases. The chance that they will choose you increases and in turn, the probability that they will recommend you to others who need your services also increases.

In business "Leading social sellers create 45% more opportunities and are 51% more likely to achieve quotas."

These numbers are based on LinkedIn statistics. If we start working on social selling in the same way when looking for a new job, we can conclude that we can greatly increase our employment chances.

## • EXAMPLES OF WHAT YOU CAN ACHIEVE WITH SOCIAL SELLING

What you can achieve varies depending on what the job market currently looks like as well as the branch of work that you are seeking. Here are some examples of important points that apply to most branches:

- Increase their knowledge of the services offered, your services
- Find and be found by potential clients/employers
- Start building a relationship with your potential leads
- Get in touch with potential leads and clients/employers
- Receive inquiries from potential clients/employers
- Book meetings with potential leads and interviews with potential clients/employers

- Maintain and be "top of mind" with your network

Example: How many times does your profile appear when potential leads and employers search your name? The more times you appear, the greater the probability is of being contacted by a potential client/employer.

## THE FOUR PILLARS OF SOCIAL SELLING

To get results through the work with Social Selling, there are a variety of activities you need to do regularly, preferably daily and at the least, several times a week.

Everything is based on four pillars. By working with these as a base, you can greatly simplify the work. You will see faster results using Social Selling if you begin with the four pillars.

The four pillars are:

- The profile
- The network
- The knowledge
- The interaction

Let's take a closer look at what this means and examine examples of activities for each pillar.

## THE PROFILE

Having a well organised and selling profile is the key to success. Your CV and your profile on LinkedIn can be seen as a modern business card.

The basic key is to have a good picture and up to date

information. If you send your CV to an employer and the information doesn't match with your LinkedIn profile, this can be seen as unprofessional. Make sure your profile is up to date.

Creating a good LinkedIn page is also a separate e-book but this step is an important part of the core basics.

The picture needs to be a clear image, not an old fuzzy picture. Calm background and with you smiling into the camera. This goes for all of your public profiles, make sure your picture is relevant.

What you post on you FB is private, at least you think it is.

A client/employer will scan your social media to find out who you are, if you fit the description.

All of your social media are platforms for you to interact with leads and potential employers.

Example: Create a profile that shows potential customers what you can help them with.

The profile should be the first step in building your reputation as a knowledgeable and credible expert in your field. Think it through so that you include relevant information that can help you create that first impression, such as previous jobs, education and special projects.

Many have posted their profile based on being found by a headhunter or recruiter. Now it's time for you to present what benefits there are for a potential client/employer to hire you.

## THE NETWORK

**"It is not about what you know, it's about who you know"**

When you develop your network, the number of contacts is not most important, it's that you develop the right contacts within your field of interest.

Who is active there, what are your target companies, places you would like to work at, potential leads, potential employers and other people active in your area?

What can you offer these people, these companies?

What is your offer statement to your potential clients?

There are several benefits to creating a large network. On several social platforms, such as LinkedIn, you get multiple benefits from having a larger network.

However, it is ultimately the quality of your network that determines the success. If you have "many contacts" who don't know who you are, you can just as easily buy a list of emails and send cold letters. This equation will always end with a bad result. Creating a large network is clearly an advantage but can never replace a quality network.

Here, too, it is important to rethink from the section about Job Seeking. The focus is on finding and then networking with potential customers of your services, remember? You are selling yourself or rather your knowledge, your services.

## THE KNOWLEDGE

Take care of your network, and your network will take care of you.

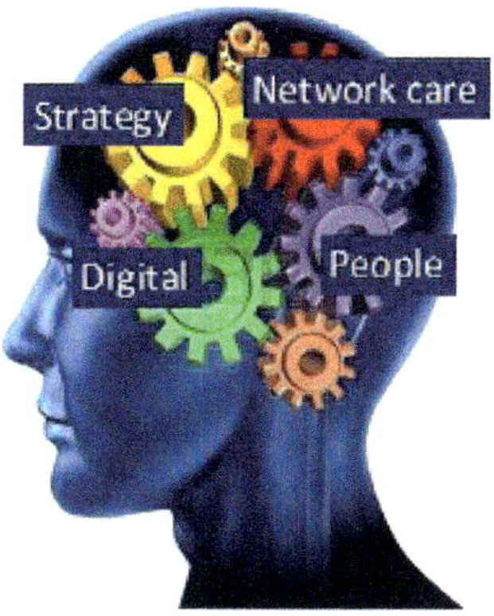


The cornerstone of knowledge is the factor many people completely miss or fail at when it comes to Social Selling. To build your status as a knowledgeable person, you need to share articles, quotes, videos and other material related to your field. It does not always have to be material that you have produced yourself. It can just as well come from leading experts that you are linked to. When sharing other people's material, always try to share your views on that specific matter.

To be successful, you need to offer content regularly. Make sure to set up a schedule so that you can create a smooth flow. Some of your social platforms are connected to each other. This means that when posting on LinkedIn you can simultaneously post on twitter. When posting on Facebook, you can simultaneously post on Instagram.

A common beginner mistake is to start sharing information about products or different offers. It does not count as knowledge and does not build relationships.

**Gustaf Willhelm Hellstedt**

Coach ◆ Speaker ◆ Leadership Advisor/Consultant ◆ Business growt...

1mo •

Don't ever doubt yourself. Harness your power and exceed your expectations.

When you feel things are not under your control, then you will have to challenge yourself to actually control the way you respond to what's happening. That will empower you more than anything else. Take responsibility, you are the cause and the solution of the matter at hand.

Some let obstacles and problems stop them. Don't let what you cannot do interfere with what you can do. Don't limit your self.

Another thing when we are on that subject. When someone (and this will happen, trust me) tells you it can't be done, it's more a reflection of their limitations, not yours.

It is not what you thinking, but what you do, that can change lives.

#change #leadership #motivation #inspiration #coaching #mindfulness #power

Example: A post that consists only of text. The post aims to arouse thoughts and gives tips to people, to inspire.

**Networking successfully is about being a person who has something to give.**

## INTERACTING

Successful sales are ultimately about relationships and interacting with others. The same goes for Social Selling.

Interacting can be anything from liking and commenting on posts, answering questions or having group discussions. There are plenty of groups to join.

That is when the relationship is created. It provides growth to your network, adds more contacts and increases qualitative networking, which improves the effect of the knowledge you share.

Interacting is what ultimately creates the meetings and business relationships that are the result of successful work with Social Selling.

If you go to a party and just sit in a dark corner, you won't have fun, correct?

You need to talk with people, dance, get into discussions... interact.

Same with Social Selling.

## • NEXT STEP

Now you have the initial basic tools in success with Social Selling. Next is training and deepening your knowledge and skills in the various areas. Social Selling is something you need to work on regularly. It is a constant learning curve.

Contact us at www.hellstedt.org, we can help you get your platforms up to date and get your foundation in place.

Your coach can deepen your knowledge and train you.

Examples of content in our educations in Social Selling:

- How to update your LinkedIn profile to attract
- How you build your personal brand
- How to build relationships with your contacts
- How to find leads and get in touch with them
- How you offer knowledge so leads contact you
- What Social Selling is, and why it works
- How to incorporate Social Selling into your everyday life

The next session is to get a bigger understanding of what "A Brand called You" stands for. Creating your own personal brand. What is that, and how is it developed? How can you grow your network through social media as well as in real life? Everything you do affects your personal brand. Every time you post a picture or a text, it all has an impact on how people perceive you as a person.

# A BRAND CALLED YOU

## A guide towards getting a job

"BRANDING IS WHAT PEOPLE SAY ABOUT YOU WHEN YOU ARE NOT IN THE ROOM."

EVERYTHING YOU ARE, SAY AND DO, REPRESENTS YOUR BRAND

## • PERSONAL BRAND

Your brand is the perception others have about you, based upon available information.

Whatever information others can come across, be it by word of mouth, articles in a paper, tags on a wall, your online profiles on social media, pictures you are tagged in, what you "like" on Facebook or Instagram, how you dress, the way you greet others, your way of speaking - whatever it might be, creates your personal brand.

It is time to start thinking about what you say and do because it leaves a trail. Take control of what creates other people's perception of you.

Everything you communicate and how you do it has an impact on how others perceive you. Your body language, dress, hairstyle, how you speak, your ringtone and your recorded message on the answering machine, all affect how you are perceived, and is part of your personal brand.

All of the above internal and external factors have an impact on the first impression you make on a prospective employer.

Remember that the image you show on social media should match how you dress and behave IRL (in real life).

It is important to invest in showing the best side of yourself instead of

trying to be someone other than yourself.

Try to improve your good sides, become your best self. Make sure everything is connected, what you say, how you say it and also how you react.

Continuity, make sure to live out your personal brand in all contexts.

1). When you meet new people

2). When writing emails

3). When talking on the phone

4). When you post on social media

5). When you go to physical meetings

6). When you attend virtual / digital meetings

7). When you record your reply message on your answering machine

8). When writing a personal letter

9). When choosing clothes in the morning

10). When making decisions

*Branding never stops.*

I hope to follow the growth of your personal brand.

Enjoy the session

## • FIRST IMPRESSION

Every day we have interactions with people we don't know.

When you are in the application and interview process of looking for a position, these first encounters are important in helping you get an offer of employment.

In this chapter, you will learn what a first impression is, why a good first impression is important, how first impressions affect you in your professional and private life.

### WHAT IS A FIRST IMPRESSION?

A first impression is the initial consideration or judgment someone makes about who you are after their first interaction with you. Several factors may influence someone's first impression of you, such as how you look, what you wear, how you speak and your overall emotional state.

When you are looking for a new position, how you represent yourself on the application, in your resume and during an interview, can all impact the recruiter and hiring manager's first impression of who you are.

I would say that this also includes how you represent yourself on social media.

**Eleven, seven, one, a millisecond? Are you wondering "How long does it take to form a first impression?"**

The answer is not totally clear, depending on which study you choose to follow, but we can agree that it doesn't take long.

A study done at the University of York suggests that a single glance of a person's face for just 33 to 100 milliseconds is enough for them to form a first impression. This study was based on 126 university students and found only slight fluctuations in their first impressions in the time between 100 and 500 milliseconds.

In conclusion, this means that in less than 100 milliseconds, the students had already made up their minds up about the person in front of them.

Another study identified a central network of brain regions involved in the decision to extend trust.

It also found that different psychological processes and brain networks are responsible for conditional and unconditional trust.

Conditional trust is contingent on the behaviour of another person, while unconditional trust is not.

Other studies have shown that gossip can help build trust which leads to how we judge people's trustworthiness based on two factors: their perceived warmth and their competence, with one taking priority over the other.

The conclusion is that people are quick to judge and because of that, you need to always act accordingly. The above studies are based on physical meetings. It works differently online.

Online we have social media, and in some cases, your personal website.

Did you know that It takes about 50 milliseconds (that is 0.05 seconds) for users to form an opinion about your website which determines whether they like your site or not, whether they'll stay or leave?

**What it all means:**

As common as it is to say, "don't judge a book by its cover," people in general are subject to an extreme level of snap judgments that immediately influence their perspectives of you.

Now you know and understand a little bit more about how quickly people make a judgment of you based on a first impression.

Let's start again with IRL (in real life) encounters.

How you look and behave matters, especially when it comes to face-to-face meetings. Teams, Zoom, Skype, e.g., are also face to face.

The fact of the matter is:

- 7 percent of an oral message consists of the actual words used.
- 38 percent consists of the tone of voice, the rhythm and the energy of the speech.
- 55 percent of the message consists of how you look and body language

This gives you an idea of how things are connected. As you know, politicians, actors, and others in the public eye, all think about theses things (or should be thinking about them). They take classes or they have coaches helping them. It affects their personal brand!

It is time for you to start thinking in the same way. If they are taking care of their career, why shouldn't you do the same? Build your personal brand and become more attractive in the job market.

In the upcoming final session, "Interview Situations", I will discuss in more detail the personal importance of both physical and digital meetings.

## • THE BASICS

You sell yourself like any other company. What's your slogan?

- Suddenly it happens (Triss – Swedish lottery business)
- Impossible is nothing (Adidas)
- What I don't know today, I can learn tomorrow (Coach GW)
- Of course I know how to do it, as soon as you teach me. (Coach GW)

It requires self-awareness to work with your brand, so it can be both tricky and sometimes fuzzy. "Personal brand" means just personal, so there is no quick fix or easy way to improve it. It's something you build up over time and it's different from person to person.

There are factors that simplify and improve the perception of who you are.

The idea here is to give you some tips and guidance for your personal brand, both on the Internet and in physical meetings.

Before we go into more detail on specific areas, I thought I'd start with some simple tips regarding how you represent yourself to the outside world.

## HOW DO YOU ANSWER THE PHONE?

Preferably you answer with your full name. Certainly not with "Hello"!

If it is an employer who calls, then it might be the first impression

"Hello".

If you don't answer, what happens? Is the phone connected to an answering service or not?

Make sure you use an answering service that gives the caller an opportunity to leave a message if you are not answering or the line is busy.

Record a personal message/greeting. Do not use the phone company's pre-recorded version. Your message should include a nice greeting, plus, who they have called and ask them to leave a message or send an SMS if urgent.

Depending on which prospective employer or recruiter you are calling, be sure to state your name, business and how to contact you if you end up talking to an answering service.

Example:

Hi, this is Johanna Smith. I'm contacting you concerning the open position as Receptionist that I have applied for. You can reach me on my mobile phone +44 123 456 789. I repeat, my name is Johanna Smith, and you can reach me on +44 123 456 789.

Talk slowly. By repeating parts of your message, it is easy for the recipient to either remember or write down the essential information.

When it comes to email, there are other points to consider. Make sure you have an email address that is serious. I have seen frightening examples that should not be used.

Example: sexyme@gmail.com

That's not the kind of email to use for contacts with recruiters and employers.

Make sure you have a professional email address. If you have a very long or complicated name, it is a good idea to shorten that when creating your email address.

Example: Gustaf-Wilhelm Hellstedt = gw@whatever.com or gwh@whatever.com, or something similar.

We have talked about this in previous sessions, but repetition is never wrong.

Think about what kind of profile picture you use in your CV, on different job pages and social media, and in the physical documents. Be sure to have a professional picture on your job application as this is also a part of your personal brand.

Use pictures where you smile and look straight into the camera, it might be your first and only chance for a first impression.

Same thing when you have a digital interview. How do you look when you attend a digital meeting? The same rules apply for a digital interview as for a physical interview.

This means that you should show respect for the person you meet by dressing properly.

This all may sound trivial, but it's not. It's about respect, whether you're looking for a job in the warehouse or as a mechanic, a salesman or CEO. No matter what job you are looking for, you should always show respect for a prospective employer.

You want the person you're interacting with to get a good impression and feel that you are a match that can work for them.

We are talking about your personal brand, a topic that will be repeated throughout this session. Everything you communicate with the outside world is part of this. Everything you say and do, everything you write, all of the pictures you show, is a representation of you, or at least how people can interpret it as you.

Imagine that you are an artist. You have a blank canvas in front of you, a brush, and paint to use. You will now start on this painting and in your head, you have an idea of what it is you want to convey to the viewer. You create your painting, and it will be interpreted by the viewers. Maybe they'll discuss it with other people, this piece of art of yours.

That's how your personal brand works.

## WILL YOU NEED YOUR OWN WEBSITE?

If you are a recent graduate or work in the service sector, then a website may not be necessary.

You should have your own website if you:

1). You are a photographer or graphic designer with a portfolio to show.

Samples that can be displayed and are difficult to include in a CV are well suited for a website. It will be an excellent place to market yourself. An employer can easily see what your work which increases your chances of being headhunted. If your work is in a visual format, then you can create a good website with substance.

2). You run your own business or are a freelancer.

As a freelancer, it becomes essential to showcase what you can do for your clients. A website is a great way to describe which services you offer and how a client can contact you. If you have samples of your work, you can easily display it on your website.

3). It is expected of you.

In some cases, you are expected to have a website. If everyone you compete with has one, you'll probably be overlooked by employers if you don't have one. My advice is to find out how it works in your particular industry and how others with similar products do it.

How to build a website is a completely different type of session. We are not going to get into that. However, I would like to say that today it is easier than you think to build a website, with tools that are available online and easy to use.

I can recommend some quick tips:

1). Make sure you have your contact details on your webpage. Today, more people go into websites via mobile than via computers, so make sure that the webpage is accessible via mobiles. It's about a first impression. It is considered to be unprofessional if the page is not mobile-friendly.

2). Stylish. You don't want a page that looks like it was made by a first grader in school.

Today's schoolchildren probably know better than us what a webpage should look like, but you understand what I mean. Your page should feel modern and easy to navigate without taking hours to load.

3). Fits your brand. You need to think about your personal brand. What shape and style fits? Again, it becomes unprofessional if the message stands out too much from what you're trying to convey about your personal brand. Look at similar pages and get inspiration.

4). Use templates. There are lots of templates online. In addition, through the various tools in which websites are currently built, you are offered a lot of templates, e.g., in WordPress or Wix.

5). If you are uncomfortable in creating your own page, ask for help. It will save you a lot of grief.

## YOUR EMAIL SIGNATURES.

It is something you need to have both on your computer and your phone. Make sure your signature is professional and reflects your personal brand. If you are skilled, you can include a short video greeting. That will make you stand out more from the rest of the job hunters. Make sure the video file is not too big!

Best regards

John Smith
+44 123 456 789
john.smith@mailaddress.com
www.linkedin.com/in/johnsmith/

Who is John Smith – short video message

## • ONLINE – LINKEDIN

**The importance of a good first digital impression**

First impressions are important because human nature compels us to hold on to our initial impression and we find it difficult to change this impression even when the other person presents us with evidence contrary to the initial belief.

This makes it very important for us to understand how we portray ourselves, not only physically, but especially online.

As a job seeker, there are four important points to consider for your branding.

We have in previous sessions covered most of points and now we tie it together in this session. It all becomes your job seeking brand, your personal brand.

Yes, you become a package that is introduced to recruiters and future employers.

Your pitch is one of the ingredients in this mix of material. It needs to match the rest and you need to be able to deliver it both verbally and in writing.

This includes your cover letter and CV. If you choose to have a picture on the letter, pick one that is professional.

If you choose to have your picture on your CV, pick a professional one, but not the same one as on the cover letter.

I do recommend using pictures if they are good quality. If I am recruiting and going over a lot of applications, the one that catches my attention, I look at first. This means that the first part of the CV ticks most of the boxes, plus, a good picture is attached to the application.

I have received feedback from some of my coaching clients saying that "it's artificial, the recruiter should pick the one they want based only on knowledge and experience."

I agree, in the best of worlds it should be that way. However, with today's competitive work market and so many applications for every job, why take the chance not to be seen?

It is up to you! How badly do you want a job?

Online you have your social media channels where you interact with the world. Let us start with the most important site for job hunters, LinkedIn.

I have given lectures about how to create LinkedIn pages but here we will just review the basics. If you need more in-depth tips, you must book a separate coaching session with me.

Let us take a look.:

**What do you think is the *first* thing anyone sees when they click on your profile?**

Yes, that is correct, it's your profile picture. That's the first thing to be noticed. Remember, LinkedIn is different from Facebook. It is a platform for highlighting your professional self. For this reason, the image also needs to reflect that. Don't use the same picture here as on your other social media platforms.

After all, it is easier than ever to quickly take a picture. I suggest asking someone to take the picture for you. Remember, that it should be an image that reflects your professional self.

Even the background image on LinkedIn should reflect who you are in your professional life. If you can't find something that fits, choose another suitable image, such as a nice landscape.

The main point is that you don't forget that this picture also represents who you are and what you stand for.

A lot of people don't understand that it is possible to adjust the background. Having a good picture makes you stand out from the crowd. It is way to highlight who you are, to brand yourself.

**The *second* most important point is to have a well-written presentation.** After your picture, an employer and recruiter focus on the written content.

Your presentation will be a more complete version of your pitch where you will describe your skills and qualities.

Feel free to bring up something that you are passionate about. If you can, sum up your personal brand in a couple of sentences.

Everything varies depending on who you are and what type of job you are looking for. You must adapt your page accordingly.

A LinkedIn page works very much like a digital CV, so show off your experiences and skills. This CV is open to the public. You need to treat it as a CV and not like Facebook.

List your previous work experience, preferably with company name (and logo) as well as your position. It is important to add a description of the company, what you did there, and what you accomplished in your position at each company. If the previous employer has a profile on LinkedIn, you can link your CV to them or the business.

Don't forget to use all of the options that the site provides. For example, "Skills and Endorsements". Here you can list your different skills, and even better, both former colleagues and employers can verify them via "Endorsements".

**The *third* most important point is "Recommendations".** You can both obtain and make recommendations. If you have performed well in a previous position, then do not hesitate to ask your old manager or colleague to recommend you. That, if anything, strengthens your personal brand. Wise as you are, you realize that by writing recommendations for others, it becomes easier to receive some for yourself. Good for your networking, something you can benefit from in the future.

**The *fourth* most important point and definitely not the least, be active!**

Don't forget that LinkedIn is a social-media platform. Thus, you do not have a static page.

You can connect with many potential employers on LinkedIn, include them in your personal network.

Write status updates, comment on other people's posts, share relevant articles. Show your professional side here, not your private.

Nurture your personal brand.

1). Use the big top background, both with a picture and text. Use a background picture that pertains your work experience or sends a vital thought provoking message to the receiver. If you can't find anything that represents you as a package, then use a nice nature picture. Don't waste the space.

2). Use a profile picture that fits your work profile. Look professional.

Face the camera and smile. Make sure that the background in the picture doesn't distract by taking the focus off of you.

3). In the profile, you can see that I have highlighted some words by repeating them in more than one place.

Coach, Advisor, Business – Growth Specialist plus Development Expert. You will also find the word Speaker, leadership and international.

All of these words are picked up by LinkedIn algorithm, as well as by search engines like Google.

4). Use words that you can show that you are available to work and with what.

5). There is plenty of information provided on the top part of this LinkedIn page.

6). A business name and your last place of employment. In this case, one of my own companies.

7). Show which school/University you went to.

8). There is a box where you can write what services you provide.

As you can see, there are many ways to show who you are in this top space of your LinkedIn. When done right, it will also trigger search engines and different algorithms. This means that when someone is Googling or searching LinkedIn for a coach or business development expert, e.g., my page will show up. How do you utilize this space today?

You can make it interesting and easy for employers and recruiters to see what you can do for them. It triggers them to read more.

When one Googles or searches LinkedIn for someone in your field of work, the odds increase that you show up more than you think. This is also a part of your personal brand.

LinkedIn consists of so much more. We can only scrape the surface here. For more information, you need to book a special coaching session with me.

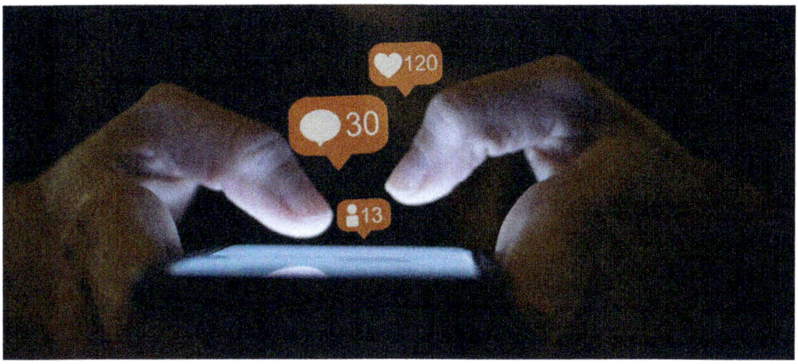

# • ONLINE – FACEBOOK AND MORE

## FACEBOOK

Among the first things an employer will find when they Google your name, is your Facebook Page. Are you ready for them to read it?

It might be the first impression of you for a recruiter or employer. What is it you are conveying? How does your Facebook page depict you?

Keep your Facebook profile clean and tidy.

A lot of people have the opinion that it's their private page, to some extent that's true. You can keep it completely private by never making your posts public. But that's not what we're talking about here.

There is a benefit of allowing an employer to see who you are, you can make some posts public for that reason.

Make sure your profile looks good and conveys a suitable image of you. This also applies to a website, because your Facebook is basically your website, a stylish page with a good profile picture and cover photo that matches your personal brand.

Of course, it doesn't have to be overly professional, it is after all, as we stated earlier, your private side. It needs to be presentable. Remember, it is a part of your personal brand.

## DETACH INAPPROPRIATE IMAGES.

What you don't want is for a potential employer to see old sloppy party pictures from a few years back. Maybe it was fun then, but today, they become part of your personal brand. Do you want that?

They make a bad first impression! Review your profile and remove tags on photos, but also posts that aren't appropriate. The images are still there, of course, but not visible to an employer who is searching for your name.

## BE CAREFUL WITH YOUR OPINIONS.

As an example, I can mention that I recently routinely liked a training video posted by a well-known public figure that got caught buying sex. I didn't think about it and hade continued to follow him as we share some interests, which include cooking and physical training.

I read what he writes, but never comment on what he posts. Of course, even that can be perceived as a double standard, but I never comment or like his postings.

Some time ago, I accidently did klick 'like' on his post. It resulted in both personal messages and a lot of sour comments from both loved ones and other more distant contacts. This means that these contacts also follow him. The bottom line is that it wasn't good for my personal brand, which resulted in me going back into the post and remove my "like".

It's important to think about what opinions you support as you post on Facebook. Some posts can, of course, be completely harmless while other posts can be good for your brand. If you want to be someone who cares about certain things, Facebook is an excellent media to show it. Just carefully choose what it is you are supporting. What you want to avoid, above all, are radical political opinions, religion and things that can be perceived as purely offensive. By the way, Swedes are considered among the most easily offended people on Earth (me being from Sweden).

In any case, it can be perceived as a deterrent for an employer. Again, it all depends on how you want to promote yourself.

## A SHORT ON TWITTER.

One way to get attention is to find a context that is right for you and for your personal brand and then twitter about it.

Who are important key people in your niche or industry? Follow them and what they write about. What hashtags are trending right now? Don't hesitate to retweet if you find interesting tweets from the ones you follow.

Tweet frequently and regularly. It's an artform to get people to follow you on this platform. You need to follow relevant discussions, retweet, write your own interesting tweets, share interesting links to articles, and more.

Make sure everything you do corresponds with your personal brand.

Always be professional since everything you write will remain. Think about it, can you stand your ground and defend your opinion? Does it sync with your image, your personal brand.

Even if you can delete what you wrote, someone may have seen it if it was something that you wrote in a discussion that perhaps got a little out of hand. Can what you are writing damage your personal brand?

We have seen quite a few bad examples over the years.

Tweeting right can get a lot of attention and make people in your industry notice you.

## INSTAGRAM AND ALL THE REST

All the above, the same concerns for LinkedIn, Facebook and Twitter also apply for Instagram and all of your social media platforms.

What does your profile picture look like? What kind of content do you post? When you go through your posts over time, what kind of image are you creating for yourself? How are you branding yourself?

Think before you post and make sure to have a strategy for all of your social media outlets.

What do you want people to think and feel when they hear or see your name? When you have decided on that, it is up to you to implement it into the minds of others.

Your brand identity tells people who you are, what you do, why you do it, and how you do it.

**A picture says more than a 1000 words**
Profile pictures

## • NEXT STEP

Wow, that was a long session.

A few more session and you are done. How is your work going with using what you have been provided with so far? It's one thing to read and listen through what is included in the TBS – Three Block System, but the real value is in the implementation of what I have been teaching you.

Go back and repeat what you learned in the first session. Start to implement the gained knowledge, step by step, if you haven't already started.

**You need to become a "Transformational thinker" vs. "Transactional".**

The transactional thinker always thinks about the HOW, while transformational thinker is thinking of the WHY.

It's not "How do I get a job". The better question is "Why should they employ me"?

Everybody talks about HOW. From now on, if you begin by asking yourself WHY, it means that you have become a strategic "Transformational" thinker rather than a tactical "Transactional" thinker.

Please, reach out If you have questions, don't hesitate to contact us.

# INTERVIEW SITUATIONS

## A guide towards getting a job

STOP BELIEVING IN LUCK, AND START BELIEVING IN YOURSELF

TALENT WILL GET YOU IN THE DOOR, BUT CHARACTER WILL KEEP YOU IN THE ROOM

## • INTERVIEW SITUATIONS

Finally, we have arrived at the end, only one short session left after this one.

Our journey has taken us from starting with a SWOT assessment in session one, which focused on 'yourself', to preparing for job interviews. I believe that you now are ready to take on any challenge in your quest to find a job.

My goal is to build you up, step by step, with knowledge and hands-on advice about how to do things in such a way that you become attractive in the job market. That you stand out from the competition for the open positions.

You have worked on finding out your characteristics in session two, traits that come in handy during interview situations, as does your pitch from session three.

Your CV from session four took you all the way to the interview situation, with the help of the cover letter from session eight.

The downside is that without setting goals and being SMART, as you learnt about in session five, you might not have analysed the job advertisement you worked on in session six that instructed you to write the application.

Practising on cold calls from session seven was helpful to get the interview. Knowing how to connect with the right people is never wrong, as you learned in session nine.

Implementing the TWC system from session ten was also helpful. Now you are booking interviews, being confident and relying on your very own personal brand, which you have created thanks to knowledge gained from session twelve.

Step by step, you have built yourself up to be ready to tackle interviews.

A job interview is not a test of your knowledge, but your ability to use it at the right time. And a job interview is like a first date.

- Good impression count.
- Awkwardness can occur.

- Outcome is unpredictable.

Enjoy the session

Gustaf-Wilhelm Hellstedt

www.hellstedt.org

Let us start with some ground rules for how you as a job seeker can best prepare yourself for an interview.

**Number one rule when you meet a person for the first time.**

Start on a positive!

Whatever events happened on the way to the interview, start on a positive.

I don't care if you crashed the car on the way, if you got robbed or your spouse wants a divorce. If you start on a negative, you will forever be remembered as a negative person.

◈What beautiful weather we have today...

◈I love the entrance to your office building...

◈Congratulations, I read a tweet that you just won the tender for...

Going for an interview can be a real stress booster, if you are not properly prepared. Let me give you some introductions, some things you can do to get ready for a tête-à-tête with a prospective employer.

## WHY IS IT IMPORTANT TO PREPARE?

Interviewing is a skill, making practice essential in becoming a better interviewee. Practicing involves learning how to answer questions related to your role and studying them.

I have coached numerous clients, but if you don't have a coach, you can also hook up with a friend and allow them to ask you a series of questions.

Doing this assesses how well you answer each question in the moment and how well you approach questions that are unfamiliar to you.

During a 30-minute meeting with another person, we send out approximately 800 non-verbal signals. Something to always remember, be aware of your body language!

## PRACTICING IS A TIME TO:

- Gain constructive feedback
- Improve your comfort
- Increase your confidence
- Understand your body language

Preparing for an interview at home, better prepares you for the real interview.

By practicing the interview processes, it will help clarify your responses to certain questions.

The coach or mock interviewer you choose to hook up with can identify your strengths and outline your weaknesses.

For example, a coach interviewer will notice and advise you on areas such as:

- Speaking clearly
- Shortening answers
- Smiling more often
- Sitting up straight

When you know many of the questions they might ask and understand how to answer them, it relieves stress and increases your comfort level. When you're comfortable at an interview, you answer each question clearly and more adeptly.

Your confidence rises. Knowing how to answer questions feels empowering. Confidence within an interview increases the chances of remembering the skills and experiences you earned in previous positions.

Your interview coach can also help you improve your professional etiquette. This includes how you greet your interviewer and how you leave the interview.

In the sessions 9 and 12, Networking and A Brand Called You, there are tips and advice that will help guide you.

There are different stages of preparation. There is research and training as well as some simple mental steps to remember.

Sleep well the night before the interview.

Ensure you gain proper amounts of rest before your interview. Doing so ensures that you are more aware and more alert when answering questions.

When you are alert, you pick up on subtle cues from the interviewer such as their body language or their tone. Understanding their mindset helps you adapt to the interview by imitating their physical posture or other movements.

Prepare your clothes the day before, gives you peace of mind. Adapt your attire to the company you are meeting with. It is better to dress up a little than the other way around. It signals that you take the interview seriously. Most important is that you feel comfortable in the clothes.

Consider eating a healthy meal several hours before your interview. Consider foods rich in protein, healthy fats and fibers.

## • RESEARCH

Before going into the interview, you need to research the company along with its history, values and mission. Check their official website first, then move onto other sources. If there are any client, customer or employee reviews, study them and identify any recurring themes that might alter your decision to work with them.

It also prepares you to answer any questions relating to the company, proving to your interviewer that you familiarised yourself with who the company is.

Knowing their history can give you a better understanding of the company culture.

Always read about a company's values, very good information about a workplace. Do I really want to work at this company? Good or bad values can be the tipping point.

Knowing and understanding their values is vitally important for your interaction with them. It is that gained knowledge that you can use during the interview.

To read about the vision they have and goals for the years to come, gives you an idea of what the prospects are within the organisation.

If the information is not easily found on the website, try having a look at their financial reports. That is normally in the public records. The managing director regularly updates the company report which gives you a very good idea of how they are developing as a business.

In general, the financial reports are good to study to see how the business has been doing for the last few years. Have there been a lot of cutdowns? Have they increased and then decreased the workforce?

Are sales going up or down? Salary levels will also tell a story; do they pay well or are they cheap?

Don't forget to research your interviewer.

Along with researching the company, identify whom within the organisation might interview you and research them as well.

Identify their professional social media profiles and scan through their interests. It often helps to find common ground with your interviewer and bring it up during the interview.

For example, if you mention that you both enjoy sailing, you immediately stand out to the interviewer, ensuring they take additional consideration toward you after the interview is completed.

By looking at the LinkedIn profiles (you can, if you like, do this anonymously).

Here you can follow the work history and how long they have been with the company. Knowing more about the person you are going to meet, also seeing pictures of the person, is to your benefit. You will feel more relaxed, like when meeting someone you already know just a little.

Use the company's social media accounts for your research. There might be interviews with employees, testimonials from employees or company employee reviews.

**Press Releases are another good source of information and can teach you a lot about a company you might want to work for.**

The press section of a company's website can tell you about the company's most recent news events, like new products, new hires, new partnerships, etc.

Knowing this information can give you a feel for how the company is strategically positioning itself within its industry. An interviewer will be assuming you know the industry and will probably want to hear your thoughts on the firm's activity. Your ability to provide feedback shows, even if you would not be directly connected to a new product or strategy, that you are paying attention.

The interviewer has methodically chosen questions to reveal more about you and your real interest for the company.

They need to understand if you are a match. What is in it for them?

Researching brings to light if the company has won awards or reached financial milestones which have been highlighted in a press release; it allows you to ask questions that show you are interested in the company as a whole and not just preoccupied with your own potential advancement. Even if you want the job, the interview is not just about you.

## KNOW THE INDUSTRY

I take it that we are in agreement that you won't go to a job interview without doing your research first? Showing that you have an understanding of a potential employers importance within their line of industry is to your advantage.

Some extra homework pre-meeting won't hurt you. It will be expected from you to be well educated in and having a vast understanding of the industry.

This applies to job seekers with previous job experience. If it is the first time you are applying for a job, it will not be expected in the same way. Nevertheless, do the extra homework about the industry you are interested in. The more knowledge you can show that you have, the better chance you will have of getting the job.

Industry news bulletins, e.g., recent acquisitions, can allow a job seeker to pose questions to interviewers about their impact on the business.

It's a good way of showing that you're paying attention. It shows that you are putting the business first by trying to understand how the larger picture impacts the organisation, not just the position you are applying for.

**Another way to find information about the company you are about to be interviewed by, is to look at the** company websites. It provides, in most cases, a section that displays the organisations leadership.

It's a good idea to look these people up on sites like LinkedIn and see where they've been and what they've done. Along the way, you'll stumble upon other employees; and through social media, you can learn more about what's going on within the company.

Looking at Twitter, Facebook, hashtags or searching for a company's name within the feeds to see what their employees are talking about, can be advantageous.

Connecting with an employee and opening a dialogue can also lead to a better understanding of what it's like to work there. Try to understand what type of personality excels in that business and what type of personality will struggle.

## • THE DIGITAL INTERVIEW

**A lot applies for a physical interview situation**

What is so different about interviewing virtually? It is less than you might think. Digital interviewing technology has advanced to the point where it's nearly the same as meeting in person.

The last year has had a big impact in virtual meetings. In this everything-virtual world we're in right now, most of us have had experience with connecting online. Still, there are a few differences to note.

I am going to give you sixteen hands-on tips on how to prepare and conduct your digital job interview.

1). When it comes to doing a digital interview, you need to treat it as if it were face-to-face...because it is.

2). You prepare the same way as if it were a physical meeting. Everything is the same when it comes down to preparations. You need to make sure that your equipment works and that your Internet is stable.

3). If you are using a PC, make sure that the computer and software are updated. I have seen a few PC's freeze up in the middle of presentations and interviews. The main reason being that they had not updated in a few days.

4). If you are working via Mac, then you can relax a little bit. However, make sure that your software is functioning properly.

5). Test your AVL – Audio, Visual and Lighting.

6). If you are using your phone, consider propping it up so you don't have to hold it throughout the entire interview. For one, your arm could get tired if you're holding it up. For another, no one wants to see your "three chins", or your nose hairs, if you're looking down at the screen.

7). Make sure that whichever device you are using, that it is powered up a 100% before the interview starts.

8). It's also important to make sure your device is able to host whatever digital app the interviewer is using, whether it's FaceTime, Teams, Zoom or Google. Download the necessary app days before the interview, not 20 minutes beforehand.

9). Next thing to remember is your backdrop.

Yes, there is the option to use a digital backdrop, but that is never a good idea. If you make a quick movement or lean too much in one direction, you might end up going out of frame.

I have conducted almost a thousand coaching calls during the last twelve months, so trust me when I say I have seen more ways of misusing backdrops and cameras online than I have ever wanted...

10). Make sure that you have a neutral clean backdrop; that is all you need. You don't want the kids, dogs, cats or mother-in-law walking in on you when in an interview situation. So, make sure you are not disturbed by anyone.

11). You dress as if it was a physical meeting. Preferably, if possible, stand up when you do the interview. It gives you more confidence and your voice will sound better. If you sit slouched into your sofa, you will compress your lungs and your voice will sound strained.

12). Make sure that you don't look down into your computer. The person on the other side will feel like you are looking down on him; and that is the wrong signal. We don't want the camera to close to you either.

13). Half chest picture is the best, so make sure to stand correctly to optimise this.

14). Put the camera on the same level as your face so you can look straight into it.

When doing the interview, make sure you look straight into the camera on your PC/Mac. We tend to look at the computer screen, on the image of the person we are talking with. But you will come across as distant if you don't try to look straight into the camera eye most of the time. In that way, the feeling will be that you are very present in the conversation.

15). Practise your body language in front of your computer camera, especially facial expressions and hand movements. If you don't have a coach, use a friend that can help you with this.

16). After your call, send an email thanking them for the interview, plus confirm if you have agreed or decided on something.

If you follow the above hands-on advice, things will go smoothly.

The advice that never can be repeated enough is:

Practice – Practice – Practice

## • INTERVIEW QUESTIONS

There are several types of interview questions that requires different ways of answering.

Some say there are two different types of questions, and some say fifteen; I have found over twenty. I have picked out a total of twenty-four as an introduction for you. Interviewing is not a pure science. Nor is it an art. Part of it is based on science, and part is art and part is ethereal.

I would say that it is simply an imperfect form of communication. It is designed to increase the predictive validity of a potential employer and employee relationships. Still imperfect though.

Let me explain the different types.

**1. Credential verification questions**

This type of question includes "What is your GPA (Grade Point

Average)?"; "How long were you at X company?", and "What courses did you attend at University?"

This is also known as resume verification questions. The purpose is to objectively verify the credentials presented in your background.

**2. Experience verification questions**

In an experience verification interview, the interviewee answers questions about his or her actions in a past employment situation or other past experiences.

The interviewee demonstrates his or her skills and abilities by describing past achievements or experiences.

These types of questions include, "What were your responsibilities in that position?" and "What did you learn in that class?". The purpose is to subjectively evaluate the experiences in your background.

**3. Opinion questions**

This type of question includes "What would you do in this situation?" and "What is your greatest weakness?". The purpose is to subjectively analyse how you would respond in a series of different scenarios. The questions seek to measure where you stand on issues in the workplace, or in your industry (even privately in some cases).

These questions require a measured response that exhibits industry insight. A question like, "Where do you see our industry headed over the next 10 years?" requires an answer that demonstrates your awareness and knowledge of current business-related trends and events. A common interviewer approach might present "What would you do?" questions to get a sense of how you would behave in a given scenario.

**4. Behavioral questions**

From an employer's perspective, behavioural questions are a goldmine of information that is utterly unavailable from traditional resumes and cover letters.

This type of question includes "Can you give me a specific example" of how you did that?" and "What were the steps you followed to deliver that result?" The purpose is to objectively measure past behaviors as a potential predictor of future results.

Behavioural questions are an excellent window into a candidate's problem-solving abilities, experience demonstrating initiative, and more.

The questions begin "tell me about a time when..."

There is no way to "prepare" for these questions other than having thought seriously about the work that you have done, the situations that you have worked in, the problems you have solved, and the goals you have achieved.

It is also a time to reflect on the times when things didn't go as planned. What did you learn? How do you incorporate that knowledge into the work that you do today?

**5. Competency questions**

This type of question includes "Explain a way in which you sought a creative solution to a recent problem you needed to solve." or "Can you give me a specific example of your leadership skills?" A potential employer will ask you competency interview questions to find out whether:

- You have relevant experience for the job you're applying for.

- You are reflective of your past work experience and aware of instances where you've developed professionally.
- You are aware of what they need.
- You can cope with pressure.
- Your personality would fit with their existing employees.

Competency-based questions let you talk; they are open and invite a response that tells the employer about a real-life challenge that you have faced.

The purpose is to align your past behaviours with specific competencies which are required for the position.

**6. Brainteaser questions**

In the final rounds for some types of roles, like very analytical or technical positions, you will likely encounter the brain teaser questions. They are used to test several of your specific skills, including logic, math, critical thinking, creativity, and the ability to perform under pressure. Many times, your answers are actually irrelevant. It is all about how you reached your answers that matters.

This type of question includes "If I roll two dice, what is the probability the sum of the amount is nine?"; "What is 1000 divided by 73?" to "How many ping pong balls could fit in a Volkswagen? The purpose is to evaluate not only your mental math calculation skills, but also your creative ability in formulating the mathematical formula for providing an answer (or estimate, as can often be the case).

**7. Case questions**

This type of question includes problem-solving questions ranging from: "Volvo claims it is the safest car in the world because fewer people die in a Volvo than in a car made by any other manufacturer in the world. What's wrong with this conclusion? "to "Your client is a ski resort. Global warming has made it such that natural snowfall has been reduced by 50%. The client is concerned. What should they do and why?"

The purpose is to evaluate your problem-solving abilities and how you would analyze and work through potential case situations.

**8. Nonsense questions**

This type of question includes "What kind of animal would you like to be?" and "What color best describes you?" The purpose is to get past your pre-programmed answers to find out if you are capable of an original thought. There is not necessarily a right or wrong answer, since it is used primarily to test your ability to think on your feet.

**Some thoughts**

It is interesting to note that the first three types of interview questions listed have a predictive validity for on the job success of just 10 percent. 10 percent predictive validity is the same level that is generated from a simple resume review.

Brainteaser questions test intelligence, commonly a key competency for most positions. They increase the predictive validity to 15 percent.

Case questions raise the predictive validity to 25 percent (and slightly higher for consulting positions).

Behavioral and competency interviewing yield a predictive validity of 55 percent. Still far from perfect, yet much more reliable for most interviewers.

That was just eight types of questions. As I indicated in the beginning there are plenty more. I will introduce you to sixteen more.

**9. Situational interview questions**

A situational interview is similar to a behavioral interview where candidates are asked specific questions about what may happen in the workplace. The questions typically involve problem-solving issues that arise in the workplace.

**10. Communication skills interview questions**

Good communication skills are essential for workplace success. When you interview for a job, the hiring manager will ask about communication skills, including how you handle issues, how you handle difficult situations, what you expect as far as communications from management, and other questions related to your ability to communicate.

**11. Interpersonal skills interview questions**

Regardless of the level and type of job you are interviewing for, your interpersonal skills matter. Hiring managers want to be assured that you have the interpersonal skills necessary to get along with colleagues, co-workers, supervisors, managers, clients, vendors, and/or customers.

**12. IT Interview questions**

When you are interviewing for an Information Technology (IT) job, you will be asked more focused and specific questions about your education, skills, certifications, languages and other IT areas of expertise.

**13. Leadership interview questions**

When you are being interviewed for a job pertaining to a leadership role, the hiring manager will want to know about past experience that qualifies you to lead. This includes your leadership style, accomplishments and your expectations for the future.

### 14. Management interview questions

When you are being interviewed for a management position, the interviewer will want to know about your experience, your management style, what you have accomplished in the past, and what your expectations are for the future.

### 15. Sales interview questions

When you are interviewing for a sales position, your goal is to sell yourself to the hiring manager. A sales job interview is among the most challenging of interviews, because candidates need to do more than just respond to questions.

### 16. Company culture interview questions

Company culture is the personality of a company. From an employee's perspective, it defines what it's like to work for that company. Interview questions about company culture are designed to determine whether you will be a good fit for the organization.

### 17. Interview questions about leaving your job

When you're interviewing, you will be asked why you left or are going to leave your job. Here are interview questions, along with sample answers, related to leaving your job, getting fired, and what you have been doing if you are currently unemployed.

### 18. Interview questions about salary

Interview questions about salary can be tricky. When you answer questions about compensation at your previous job(s), you need to be honest; your salary can be verified by a prospective employer. Questions regarding your salary expectations can be difficult to answer in a way that ensures you receive a fair salary based on your work experience.

**19. Interview questions about yourself**

When an interviewer asks questions about you, they are trying to determine how good of a fit you are for the company. Is your personality a match for the company culture? Are your goals and job expectations a match for the position the company is considering hiring you for? How will you fit in with the current team?

**20. Motivational interview questions**

Interviewers commonly ask about motivation during a job interview. When you're asked about motivation during an interview, the hiring manager is trying to understand what drives your need to succeed. They want to determine if what motivates you is in line with the job responsibilities.

**21. Personal interview questions**

Personal interview questions are questions about you personally: your personality, your work style and work ethic, how you handle stress, what you expect from an employer, and how you handle certain situations. Before you head out to a job interview, review these personal interview questions and sample answers to get an idea of what you'll be asked and the best way to respond.

**22. Teamwork interview questions**

When asked about teamwork during a job interview, it's important to show enthusiasm for working on a team vs. independently, if the position requires teamwork. Give specific examples of successful teamwork results.

**23. Time management interview questions**

Employers are always concerned about productivity. When they interview candidates for employment, they want to know how productive they can expect the person to be and how well the applicant manages their time.

**24. Qualifications interview questions**

One of the most important parts of successful interviewing is to relate your qualifications to the job you are interviewing for. It's critical to show the hiring manager that you have the required qualifications.

As you can see, there are plenty of different types of questions you can be asked. Go through them all and practice, practice, practice. Get comfortable with who you are and how to answer the different types of questions.

## • YOUR QUESTIONS TO THE INTERVIEWER

When the recruiter or employer is satisfied and you have performed really well with the interview, you feel confident. This is good, but there is one step more you need to be able to do well on.

That is when they ask: "Any questions for us?"

If you sit there and have nothing to ask, what impression are you giving them?

The key is that having smart questions ready in advance reflects your drive; that you've done your homework, and that you're invested in learning more.

It can also show what kind of thinker you are revealing your true personality. This gives you an extra boost as the candidate who thinks critically and successfully digs for information.

Don't forget, the answers you receive will help confirm whether or not you are making the right choice concerning the company that is interviewing you.

After all, it's not all about impressing the hiring company, the company should impress you, too. That's the difference between a good job and a dream job; making sure that not only does it look good on paper, but that it's the right fit for you.

The very process of asking questions completely changes the dynamic of the interview as well as the hiring manager's perception of you. Asking questions also gives you the opportunity to reveal unknown details.

You should have at least four questions ready to discuss in the event the interviewer has already answered one or two on your list.

**1. Who do you think would be the ideal candidate for this position and how do I compare?**

This question is a quick way to figure out whether your skills align with what the company is currently looking for. If they don't match up, then you know to walk away instead of wasting time pursuing the wrong position.

**2. What do the career paths of those who have previously held this position look like?**

This question lets you know whether this job is a dead end or a good career move.

**3. Beyond the hard skills required to successfully perform this job, what soft skills would serve the company and position best?**

Knowing what skills the company thinks are important will give you more insight into its culture and management values; this will allow you to evaluate whether or not you fit in.

**4. How would you describe the company's culture?**

This question gives you a broad view of the corporate philosophy of a company and how it focuses on employee satisfaction. You should already have an idea of the company culture from your initial research, let's see if it matches with the given answer?

**5. What do you like most about working for this company?**

This question allows you to "create a sense of camaraderie" with the interviewer, because interviewers usually like to talk about themselves, especially things they know well.

This question will give you a chance to hear the benefits of working for the company, but from an insider's perspective. The question can throw the interviewer off guard, which makes the answer even more interesting.

**6. What are the challenges of this position?**

If the interviewer says, "There aren't any", then take that as a warning sign. You should be wary of the position's personal growth possibilities.

**7. If you were to hire me, what might I expect in a typical day?**

This shows your eagerness for the position. It gives you a better idea of what the job will be like on a daily basis. This will help you decide whether or not you want to pursue it.

A frank conversation about job expectations and responsibilities will ensure not only that this is a job you want, but also one where you have the learned skills to succeed.

**8. What have past employees done to succeed in this position?**

The main point of this question is to get your interviewer to reveal how the company measures success.

**9. What type of employee tends to succeed here? Which qualities are most important for doing well and advancing at the firm?**

This question shows the interviewer that you care about your future at the company, allowing you to decide if you're a good fit for the position.

When the interviewer tells you what she's looking for in a candidate, you will know if it fits your profile.

**10. Can you share more about how the company supports its employees with professional development opportunities?**

While many candidates may want to know the potential for growth before taking a job, asking about promotions suggests to recruiters that you think the current position is beneath you. A question structured like this circumvents the taboo of asking about promotions.

You don't want to imply that you're looking for a higher position before you've been hired, trained or even given the chance to prove your abilities.

Instead, ask more open-ended questions; or ask anecdotes of past employee success stories for a more roundabout way to find out how the position can help you grow.

**11. Is there anything we haven't covered that you think is important to know about working here?**

This is a good wrap-up question that gives you a break from doing all the talking. You may also get answers to questions you didn't even know to ask yet are still important.

These questions can and should of course be customised based on the job you're applying for, the company's focus, and what you want or need to know. Now you're prepared with a solid list to help make sure you know what you're signing up for in your potential new job and that your potential new employers also know what they're signing up for with you.

## ● NEXT STEP

Congratulation, you have now concluded your last session in the TBS - Three Block System. Well, almost – there is still one to go. Shorter and just a follow up on this one.

My sincere belief is that you are now very well prepared to achieve your goal of getting a job, your dream job.

As stated before, the key to your success is speed of implementation. To implement the knowledge from the 14 different sessions you have completed in this course.

Don't postpone things you need to do to get a job, that won't work. Tomorrow never comes, of course tomorrow will always be tomorrow. So, if you want something done, make tomorrow today.

I think you are far too smart to be the only thing standing in your way.

I have given you the tools; the rest is up to you.

You always have the possibility to reach out to me. I would be happy to personally coach you.

You can read more on the webpage: **www.hellstedt.org**

You can also wright to us: **contact@hellstedt.org**

**All the best of success**

**Gustaf-Wilhelm Hellstedt**

# TOP 10 THINGS NOT TO SAY AT AN INTERVIEW

## A guide towards getting a job

DID YOU REALLY SAY THAT?

## • 10 TOP THINGS NEVER TO SAY AT A JOB INTERVIEW

At a job interview you feel the pressure. You want this job really badly and need to make a good impression. You want to be the perfect candidate that really fits in with everybody at the company.

And it is so easy to slip up, to say something really stupid just because you want them to like you and be impressed by you.

What you say and how you say it is imperative to helping the interviewer determine whether you are a strong candidate and a good fit for their company and culture.

Think carefully about the things you don't want to say and the things you want to make sure are covered.

Slipping up at this stage can make all the difference.

But have no fear, I will give you some examples of things not to say.

**1). In five years' time I will have your job.**

**I see myself sitting in your chair.**

If they ask you the question "-Where do you see yourself in five years' time?"....do not give this answer.

Displaying confidence is a good thing, however by saying things like this you come across as cut-throat and ruthless. The hiring manager or recruiter are there to assess if you will fit in well with the team.

You need to come across as likeable and pleasant. So the above sample was not a good way of achieving that. Remember that first impression lasts...

**2). How quickly will I be promoted?**

**How much does this job pay?**

**When do I get vacation?**

Asking these questions before you even got a job offer will make it easy for the employer to rule you out.

You focus in getting time off and what they should pay you. Don't start the interview with "-What is in it for me?" questions. That is called self-serving and is not appreciated.

Your job at the interview is to show what you can do for them and not the other way around.

You come across as someone that will slap-off at first given opportunity. The issues are important and will be discussed but you need to demonstrate your value first and fore most.

**3). I don't like my job.**

**I don't like my current boss.**

**My co-workers are toxic.**

The interviewer may ask you questions like "Why are you looking for a new job?" or "What didn't you like about your previous positions?" Answering these types of questions in a manner that avoids saying anything negative about your previous employer or the job can show your ability to remain professional and positive regardless of the situation.

One of the fastest routes out of getting a job is by badmouthing your current employer or previous manager. That will only reflect very poorly on yourself. Shows lack of emotional intelligence and that you have a victim mentality. Shows that you have a bad attitude and difficult to work with. Remain positive and you will be remembered as positive. You want to come across as a team player and not a complainer.

**4). What does you company do?**

**Could you give me an overview of the company and the products?**

**What job am I being interviewed for?**

You cannot turn up at an interview not knowing the basics. Not knowing anything of the company or the position. If you turn up totally clueless it shows disrespect.

Show interest, show that you want this job. Do not come across as a lacy person that cannot even go online and read about the company.

Try to have a clear understanding of the company's mission and vision statement and what they do to achieve them before your interview. Doing this will allow you to ask more detailed questions about the company.

Best way to make a good impression is to be positive and coming well prepared to the interview.

**5). It's on my resume.**

When they ask you a question, you answer them in a polite manor. Yes, it is on your resume, your CV, but they want to hear it from you and not read about it. By this type of answer, you only come across as very arrogant.

Try to answer the questions by using specific examples that prove your experience or skills or explaining how your qualifications are relevant to the position.

They ask questions to get to know you and maybe expand on the question around that specific point on your resume. Your primarily goal is to show the hiring manager that you are their top candidate.

**6). I don't know!**

Any answer is better than "I don't know". If you don't have the answer, do not make something up. Buy yourself some time by asking the interviewer to clarify or repeat the question. Gives you time enough to think. And if you still don't have the answer, you can surround the question with what you do know. You can steer the conversation to something you know. This is what you see on TV all the time when they interview politicians. Just make sure that it is relevant to the question.

**7). I don't see myself working here for more than a year.**

**I am planning to start my own business as soon as possible.**

What you are showing is that this job is just a stepping-stone for your next career move. Saying this is like pointing a gun at your forehead and pulling the trigger.

As an employer one is looking for a long-term commitment. You will in most cases cost money in the beginning. It takes a bit of time before an employee actually pays off. If you just want the job for a very short period of time, why should I as an employer take you on. I want someone that wants to stay on, build a career in the company. Show commitment, long term commitment, at the interview.

**8). I am not sure I am a good fit for this job.**

**I don't have all the experience you need.**

It is not you job to make that evaluation. Let the interviewer make their own decisions.

If you are applying for the job, why should you at an interview tell the interviewer that they shouldn't hirer you? Keep your self-doubts to yourself. This is not the place to express them.

Don't plant seeds of doubts with the interviewer. Don't focus on your potential shortcomings, focus on selling values that you will bring to the position, to the company.

Focus on what you can do and not on what you cannot.

When answering questions about relevant experience, make sure you mention transferable skills that will be beneficial to the role, such as strong communication, organization, problem-solving and time-management skills.

**9). I don't have any questions.**

Remember that an interview is a two-way street. Prepare questions for the interviewer about the company and the position. Not having any questions shows little interest in the job and the business. When asking questions, you display that you have both knowledge about and interest in the company. It is an opportunity, don't miss out on that. The number of questions you should prepared depends a bit on what level you are on. For higher positions, more questions than the average 3-4.

**10). I really need this job.**

**I need this job or I won't be able to pay my rent.**

Desperation is not the key to success, trust me! Don't beg the interviewer, convince them by showing strength and knowledge. Come prepared, not desperate. You can't force them to like you, but you can make yourself attractive. It is like going on a date. If it is the right employer, they will recognize your talent and your skills. Keep your dignity.

Don't answer questions with a Yes or No, tell a story instead. The interviewer is trying to extract as much information as possible about you, your job is to accommodate that.

Always bring along copies of your resume/CV, two for the interviewer and one for you. Be prepared that the interviewer might want you to go through the resume with them.

If they ask for your resume and you don't have and you refer them to one of your emails, that indicates that you are ill prepared and unorganised.

After the interview you send a thank you email and reiterating your interest for the position.

This will bring you one step closer to get your dream job.

Before interviews you always make your preparation. Just like in sports, you don't turn up unprepared and out of practice. So, practice on job situations. Show your passion and be persistence in you job hunting.

Your smile is your logo!

Body language is very important.

- 7 percent of an oral message consists of the actual words used.

- 38 percent consists of the tone of voice, the rhythm and the energy of the speech.
- 55 percent of the message consists of how you look and body language.

I hope this was helpful.

Go to the webpage www.hellstedt.org for more tips and guidelines for your job hunting.

# TESTEMONIALS

I wholeheartedly recommend Gustaf-Wilhelm as a coach/ advisor.
I contacted GW to help me close a business deal. I knew I needed someone experienced to help me get more insight and someone with more negotiating skills to close the deal in a good way.
Thanks to GW and his great communication skills and vast knowledge I managed to come out very much on top. I am forever grateful.

**Ben Freedman**

I recommend Gustaf-Wilhelm Hellstedt to any business person who wants to sharpen their game.
By embracing Gustaf-Wilhelm's unique business coaching techniques I gained great insight about myself, my inner conflicts and strengths. I was able to apply this greater self-knowledge to solve my business challenges and even more importantly to life changing decisions.
A super experience.

**Thomas Smith**

Gustaf-Wilhelm is extremely knowledgeable and professional. He has the best resume and cover letter tactics and information, and he can ensure you have a professional and polished product moving forward. Not only that, he also up-dated my LinkedIn profile into something I really needed. Before meeting Gustaf I had no idea how important your LinkedIn was and what it could look like. He made me understand more about my social media profile and boosted my personal brand so that I now feel I have a strong brand. Very grateful!

**Steven Underwood**

I felt so down after all the rejections on my job application. Then I met Gustaf! Firstly, he boosted my self-esteem, something well needed. He showed me the way forward from average to outstanding. To quote GW "The key for you is change. If you keep repeating what you always have done you will always end up at the same place".
We changed everything from my resume, cover letter to my social media. But mostly my mindset, thanks to Gustaf I now see thing differently. Forever grateful, I immediately got interviews lined up thanks to my super curriculum and other application documents. I highly recommend Gustaf-Wilhelm Hellstedt, both as a job coach but also as a life coach.

**Karin Alm**

Gustaf is among the most positive-oriented people I have had the pleasure to meet. I have had the privilege of attending a series of inspirational lectures held by Gustaf and give him my highest recommendations. Gustaf is not only a natural and gifted speaker but insightful and imminently practical for today's business leaders and professionals. Through his hands-on approach, I got the tools to communicate effectively in challenging situations.

**Charlotte Al Khalili**

A storyteller with a perfect mix of knowledge, experience, and humor.

I have been a client of Gustaf for 3 months. During this period, the sessions have been performed via Teams due to Covid-19.

He has the ability to lecture with humor and engage the group.

Gustaf is straightforward and clear, always sees the positive in a situation, and always welcomes a discussion. For me, Gustaf has been a great advisor, good support, and a brilliant coach who does his job with empathy and joy.

**Caisa Littorin**

# BIO

*"-It goes hand in hand if individuals know where we are going then we can walk on that path together to achieve our goals. The goals become mutual, something only possible through communication. A way to reach out and change the world to become an even better place."*

Gustaf-Wilhelm Hellstedt

Making people grow is something Gustaf-Wilhelm is good at and also passionate about. To lead and work with people. The biggest asset of a company is the human capital, the actual working capital. What creates revenue? It is people - management, staff and clients working together, nothing more and nothing less. A common culture that binds all together.

But his knowledge is not limited only to this after a career as an officer in the special forces, entrepreneur and business owner, marketing strategist and much more.

*What I don't know today I can learn tomorrow.*

A main theme through Gustaf-Wilhelm's life has been working with strategies, people and growth. To help organisations, and people, to reach their best potential, is what he wants.

"-It goes hand in hand if individuals know where we are going then we can walk on that path together to achieve our goals.

The goals become mutual, something only possible through communication. A way to reach out and change the world to become an even better place."

If I don't know where I am going, how can I know when I am there? And  if you don't know where you are going, the risk is that you end up somewhere else...Make sure to set your goals, both for yourself and for your business. Communicate your

vision and your goals so everybody involved understands.

Gustaf-Wilhelm also has a passion for art and antiques as a former international art and antique dealer. His range of expertise also includes IT, civil security and many more subjects as philanthropic advocacy, business advisory. His coaching ranges from leaders as Ministers, CEO's, entrepreneurs to just people that wants to grow.

A fun fact is that he also has occurred in almost 70 different roles on screen, in movies, tv series and commercials. Even staring, back in the days, in a tv documentary about himself.

However, born and raced in Sweden he is considered un-Swedish in his manners, in very a positive way. A world traveller with the manners of a true gentleman, a renaissance man of his time.

As a known alchemist of connections Gustaf-Wilhelm is always keen in interacting with his audience.

https://www.linkedin.com/in/gwhellstedt/

Printed in Great Britain
by Amazon

71507977R00136